Managing Criminal Justice

A collection of papers

Edited by David Moxon
Home Office Research and Planning Unit

LONDON: HER MAJESTY'S STATIONERY OFFICE

P

Dr P.A.J. Waddington

First published 1985

ISBN 0 11 340811 0

Home Office Research and Planning Unit Publications

Many of the studies collected together in this book were first published in the *Home Office Research Studies* series: titles in this series are listed at the end of the book, together with titles in the earlier series, *Studies in the Causes of Delinquency* and the *Treatment of Offenders*. Other studies included first appeared as *Research and Planning Unit Papers* which contain material of a rather more specialised nature. All Research and Planning Unit publications result from research undertaken within the Home Office to assist in the exercise of its administrative functions, and for the information of the judicature, the services for which the Home Secretary has responsibility (direct or indirect) and the general public.

Contents

Foreword

An awareness of the interdependence of the agencies of the criminal justice system underlies much recent Home Office research and policy. It is no longer sufficient to think of the various parts of the criminal justice process in isolation. A much deeper and more practical understanding flows from a consideration of interactions between the various stages of the process.

Much of the research which has fuelled this new understanding of interdependence issues has emanated from the Home Office Research and Planning Unit and been published in separate journal articles or papers. It seemed useful to bring this work together so as to assess its cumulative impact. The resultant collection of papers makes a strong case for the usefulness of the interdependence concept. The Research and Planning Unit will be well pleased if the joint publication of this set of articles leads to further public debate of these important issues and to yet more improvements in the workings of the system.

MARY TUCK

Head of the Research and Planning Unit

Editor's note

The papers collected together in this book were in the main written by researchers working within the Home Office Research and Planning Unit. However, some chapters were written by academics from outside the Home Office who were invited to contribute either because they had conducted research in relevant areas on its behalf or because their particular expertise enabled them to fill gaps in Home Office funded research.

Floyd Feeney, author of Chapters 2 and 9, undertook research on advance disclosure and interdependence for the Home Office whilst he was Director of the London office of the Vera Institute of Justice. He is Professor of Law at the University of California. Mr Pullinger, author of Chapter 3, formerly worked in the Home Office Research and Planning Unit but now works for the Export Credit Guarantees Department. Ken Lidstone, author of Chapter 5, is a lecturer at the Centre for Criminological and Socio-Legal Studies at the University of Sheffield. Andrew Sanders, author of Chapter 7, is a lecturer at the Institute of Judicial Administration in Birmingham. Peter Jones, formerly of the Home Office Research and Planning Unit and author or co-author of Chapters 8, 10 and 14, is an Assistant Professor in the Criminal Justice Department of Temple University, Philadelphia.

The views expressed are those of the authors and do not necessarily reflect the views of the Home Office.

Some of the chapters in this book draw on data provided by the Home Office Statistical Department and we are grateful for their assistance.

1 Introduction

DAVID MOXON

The way that the criminal justice system is managed affects us all. It affects us both as potential – and sometimes actual – victims of crime, and because the system makes substantial demands on the nation's resources. The aims of the system were summed up in the 1984 Home Office Working Paper on Criminal Justice which stated:

> 'The central objective [of criminal justice strategy] is to sustain the rule of law:
>
> a by preventing crime wherever possible;
> b when crimes are committed, by detecting the culprit;
> c by convicting the guilty and acquitting the innocent;
> d by dealing adequately and appropriately with those who are guilty and by giving proper effect to the sentences or orders which are imposed.'

Much of the research undertaken or sponsored by the Home Office has related in some way to these aims. The emphasis of the papers which follow is on the working of the criminal justice system as a whole and on the interdependence of the different agencies which comprise the system. Although it is only in recent years that the phrase 'criminal justice system' has come into general use much of the recent research of the Home Office Research and Planning Unit in the area of criminal justice process has been driven by the systems concept. Researchers have increasingly looked at issues not solely in their own terms, but with a view to their system effects. Yet since much of this research has been published in isolated journal articles or pamphlets, its full impact has perhaps not yet been fully absorbed.

The 1984 statement of the aims of the criminal justice system used the phrase 'adequately and appropriately' in describing the disposal of offenders. This phrase embodies a principle central to the management of criminal justice and at the heart of much research. For justice to be 'adequate and appropriate' it must treat offenders in a way seen by the public to strike a proper balance; neither over-processing the trivial nor neglecting to mark severe disapproval of the serious. Hence research has been aimed not only at defining and elucidating the system, but also at an assessment of its efficiency in achieving 'adequate and appropriate' justice. Concern that matters should be dealt with at an appropriate level is reflected in the growing interest in alternatives to criminal sanctions – non-prosecution in trivial cases; reparation; and the extension of fixed penalties to include minor motoring offences. If disproportionate resources are devoted to minor matters this is not only wasteful in itself but may draw resources away from other activities, in particular the processing of serious cases. Several studies in this book draw attention to the problems caused by delay. The growth in custodial remands, which burden the prison system, and the effects on trials of the fading of memories of events are examples of such problems. These studies bring out the very real sense in which 'justice delayed is justice denied'. Decisions on minor cases have wider repercussions, on the system as a whole.

Since the cost of the criminal justice system falls on society, it is always in competition for funds with other public services. The actual or likely costs or benefits which flow, or may be expected to flow, from particular policies are important considerations in the formulation of priorities. It is for researchers to identify problems – to show where policies are failing to realise their objectives; to monitor the effects of new measures; to identify good practices which deserve to be more widely applied; and simply to describe how things are working. The aim is to provide a solid basis for policy decisions in relation both to the resources that should be devoted to the criminal justice system and the best way of allocating resources to different elements within it.

The Home Office has substantial responsibilities in relation to the financial and manpower resources used by agencies in the system and has a duty to ensure that such resources are efficiently used. At the same time, a careful balance has to be struck between central and local control. A measure of local independence is important for two main reasons. First, there are very real differences in local circumstances which may call for different responses – practices which are appropriate in large cities may be much less suited to rural areas. Second, there is no monopoly of wisdom at the centre and many useful developments spring from local initiatives. However, local autonomy does mean that a variety of practices evolve in relation to a whole range of activities – cautioning, sentencing, fine enforcement, remand and so on – and some practices will inevitably be more efficient or more appropriate than others. It is part of the function of research to find out which practices are particularly successful, or to draw attention to variations which lead to uneven justice so that greater consistency can be encouraged. Examples which are discussed in the book include fine enforcement, sentencing and cautioning practice, all of which have been found to vary widely across the country and where lessons learned from studying a range of local practices can usefully be disseminated.

Overview of the system

Something should be said as to the structure of the book. It forms a whole greater than its parts. The first three articles explore the main theme of interdependence from different viewpoints. In the first chapter of Part I, Floyd Feeney both discusses the theoretic concept of interdependence and gives practical examples of its usefulness. Through a detailed examination of the way that various agencies work together in one police force area he shows how they currently achieve cooperation and resolve conflicts, identifies some of the potential barriers to success, and develops ideas for promoting fuller cooperation and integration.

Hugh Pullinger approaches the subject of interdependence from the perspective of the operational researcher. In Chapter 3 he points out that the major parts of the criminal justice system are to a large extent controlled independently of each other and seek to realise objectives which derive mainly from their particular operational needs. Problems arise because the parts interact to such an extent that disparities between objectives can result in severe strains within the system. Prison overcrowding and unacceptable court delays are symptoms of such strains. The author draws on concepts from systems theory as an aid to understanding the nature of the criminal justice system, its work and its problems.

In Chapter 4 Patricia Morgan describes a computer model, developed by the Home Office Research and Planning Unit, which simulates the passage of defendants through the criminal justice system of England and Wales. Its prime function is to show how changes – for example in policy, crime patterns or the way cases are processed – will affect each part of the system. The way the model can be used is illustrated with examples which show the likely impact of specific changes.

After these opening general articles, the subsequent sections of the book (Parts II and III) present a series of specific studies of particular aspects of the criminal process. In order to clarify as far as possible the constant interaction of the system, the material has been arranged in a pattern which follows an individual's progress from arrest through to final disposal. Inevitably not all stages in the process have been studied and researched with equal intensity, but we believe the articles taken as a whole make a powerful case for the usefulness of the interdependence concept. Studies which deal primarily with the police have not (except in relation to cautioning) been included, as many of these studies have been brought together in another recent Research and Planning Unit volume, *Policing Today* (Heal, Tarling and Burrows, 1985). However, the role of the police at key stages in the criminal process forms a part of a number of the studies which have been included – the importance of their role as gate-keepers to the system as a whole cannot be overstressed.

The pre-trial process

In Chapter 5 Ken Lidstone of Sheffield University examines the way in which magistrates exercise their powers in relation to summonses and warrants. The relationship between magistrates and the police has a major bearing on the way these duties are performed, and on the efficacy of these safeguards against the undue exercise of police powers. The author concludes that this is one area where cooperation has been achieved at the expense of that independence which is essential if magistrates are to make effective use of their powers in the pre-trial process.

Many cases where the evidence against a suspect would be sufficient to sustain a prosecution never come to court because they are filtered out by the police, being dealt with by way of a formal police caution. The way the police exercise their discretion in relation to the cautioning of offenders has major implications for the courts, the probation service and for the police themselves. The policy and practice of police forces in relation to cautioning is examined by Gloria Laycock and Roger Tarling in Chapter 6. The authors found big differences in cautioning rates between forces and whilst some of this variation could be attributed to the kinds of offender dealt with, there was found to be wide variation in the policies of different forces. Since this research was completed the Home Office has issued detailed guidance to the police with the aim of promoting greater consistency in cautioning policy[1].

The system of prosecution has attracted much attention in recent years, and an independent prosecution service is in the process of being created. In Chapter 7 Andrew Sanders provides an overview of the prosecution system of England and Wales, drawing on research on prosecution decisions and the guidelines used by the Attorney-General. Not all will share the author's pessimism that the objectives of the new Crown Prosecution Service will be undermined by entrenched practices and attitudes. He warns us that it could be a mistake to expect too much of the new service too quickly. Structural changes will not of themselves ensure improved practices.

In Chapter 8 Peter Jones, Roger Tarling and Julie Vennard examine the operation of committal proceedings. These were originally conceived as a constitutional safeguard against the citizen being brought to trial on insubstantial evidence. Yet the great majority of committal proceedings are now 'paper' committals, whereby a defendant is committed to the Crown Court for trial by an examining justice without consideration of the evidence. The number of acquittals ordered on the direction of the judge has cast doubt on the effectiveness of committal proceedings in filtering out weak cases. The findings show that committal proceedings do in fact filter out a considerable proportion of weak cases and, perhaps surprisingly, finds no evidence that the full committal operates as a more effective filter than the paper committal.

In 1975 the James Committee argued that the interests of both fairness and efficiency required the introduction of disclosure procedures for the magistrates' courts. It was felt that existing procedures encouraged elections for jury trial because that was one way the defence could obtain disclosure in cases triable either way.

On the other hand, the police were concerned about the effect that disclosure would have on the way they prepared summaries or obtained witness statements, and the costs that might be incurred. Chapter 9 describes a study which was undertaken by the Vera Institute of Justice which examined the effects of

1. Home Office Circular 14/1985.

different systems of advance disclosure both on the courts – in terms of changes in the proportion of guilty pleas and elections for jury trial – and on the police in preparing statements or summaries. In demonstrating that advance disclosure could have a useful impact on guilty pleas and elections for Crown Court trial, at moderate cost, the study was helpful in shaping the statutory system which was introduced in May 1985.

One cause of the increase in the prison population in recent years has been the sharp rise in the remand population. Such growth could result from a change in the offence mix of those remanded in custody; more defendants being remanded in custody overall; or those who were remanded being held in custody for longer periods. It has long been recognised that there is wide variation in the extent to which defendants are remanded in custody in different areas. This highlights the fact that the size of the remand population depends also on the policies and attitudes of the courts. In Chapter 10 Peter Jones seeks to explain the reasons for differences in the use of bail by different courts. The most important reasons for these differences were found to be the police remand decision, the offence type and court policy.

There is general agreement that delays in dealing with defendants works against the ideals of justice. Memories of events fade; defendants are liable to be remanded in custody for longer periods; and adjournments incur substantial financial costs. Changes in police and court procedures provide one approach to reducing delays. It has been argued that the imposition of limits on the time taken to deal with cases could act as a spur to such changes and a provision in the Prosecution of Offences Act 1985 will permit statutory time limits to be introduced at a future date if current experiments suggest that this would be worthwhile. In Chapter 11 Roger Tarling looks at the reasons for delays and suggests how procedures might be changed to reduce them; and Julie Vennard looks at the impact of statutory time limits in the United States, where there is evidence that the potential impact of time limits has been weakened because the rules can too easily be bent. The author concludes that safeguards against abuse, allied to a firm commitment to enforce reasonable deadlines, are crucial to the success of such a system.

The trial and after

The decision to have a case heard in a magistrates' court or the Crown Court is one which has a substantial impact on the resources which the case will absorb and for pre-trial waiting times. It has often been claimed that magistrates are more likely than juries to accept doubtful prosecution – and especially police – evidence, and that summary procedures do not provide as fair a hearing for the defendant who pleads not guilty. In Chapter 12 Julie Vennard provides the first empirical evaluation of the outcome of contested charges in both magistrates' courts and the Crown Court in terms of the evidence adduced in the course of the trial. Her findings support the view that the chances of acquittal are significantly higher in the Crown Court, and suggest that juries are markedly less inclined than magistrates to accept the evidence of prosecution witnesses as sufficient to sustain a conviction. There have been claims that juries' readiness to acquit increased as a consequence of the removal of the property qualification from jurors in 1972. Some have argued for a more selective approach on the grounds of the increased complexity of some types of case and the risk of intimidation or subversion of a jury which includes a convicted person. In Chapter 13 Sid Butler examines acquittal rates in relation to the available statistical and research evidence, but finds no firm evidence that the changes in eligibility for jury service increased juries' propensity to acquit. However, there was some suggestion that longer waiting times and changes in the not guilty plea rate were associated with higher acquittal rates.

The need for the criminal justice system to respond to crime in a way which is both adequate and appropriate, having regard to all the factors in a case, is of special relevance to the sentencing of offenders. Perhaps to an even greater extent than for other decisions in the criminal process, views as to what is adequate and appropriate are likely to differ widely, and this has major implications for the way in which offenders are treated by different courts. The main focus of Chapter 14, by Roger Tarling, David Moxon and Peter Jones, is on the sentencing practices of individual adult and juvenile courts, and the research shows that there is wide variation in the practice of different courts. The study of juveniles takes the analysis one stage further by applying the concept of a tariff to the overall pattern of juvenile sentences. It shows how the juvenile offender progresses up the tariff according to the type of offence committed and as the number of previous convictions rises.

Fines are by far the most common penalty applied by the courts and effective enforcement of fines is therefore essential to the credibility of the criminal justice system. The subject has understandably attracted a number of research studies over the years. Growing unemployment has posed particular difficulties for fine enforcement, and this is reflected in the increase in the number of defaulters imprisoned over the past decade – though the growing realisation that default is strongly associated with unemployment, and the need to set fines at realistic levels, may have made some contribution to a recent fall in the number of defaulters imprisoned. Enforcement can be a complex task, involving police, prisons and the probation service as well as the courts. In Chapter 15 David Moxon draws together the threads from the various complementary studies that have been undertaken by the Research and Planning Unit over the years. These show the importance of swift and persistent action in the event of default, and suggest that the threat of imprisonment is less persuasive in securing payment than is often supposed.

The theme of interdependence is particularly well illustrated in the final chapter. George Mair records how, in a demonstration project in Hampshire organised and monitored by the RPU, it was shown that co-operation between judges, magistrates, justices' clerks, probation officers and others could promote maximum use of various alternatives to custody without in any way circumscribing the independence of the courts or their ability to impose serious custodial sentences for serious crime. However, the problem of securing lasting change was highlighted by the fact that old habits soon returned once the project ended.

This last project is of interest not only in itself but also in that it perhaps points the way towards further studies in the Interdependence area. More experimental or demonstration projects are needed which will test out various methods of improving the efficiency and effectiveness of the system. The current work in the Bristol courts discussed briefly in Chapter 2 is another example of this type of approach as also is the work on advance disclosure recorded in Chapter 9. The Home Office is developing studies which will involve monitoring and studying specific initiatives at a local or demonstration level. Meanwhile we hope that this book will act as a stimulus both to further research and to policy thinking on interdependence issues.

2 Interdependence as a working concept

FLOYD FEENEY

There may well have been a time when criminal justice was viewed as a series of separate processes connected neither with each other nor anything else. These times have long since passed, however, and today there is widespread agreement that the work of the various criminal justice agencies is closely related and that together these agencies form some kind of 'system'. There is much less agreement, however, about the nature of this system and the implications of such related concepts as interdependence of the criminal justice system.

The general idea of a system dates back at least to the ancient Greeks, who saw systems as some kind of organised whole. By the eighteenth century the system concept had already assumed great importance in branches of theoretical physics such as mechanics where it appeared in full mathematical garb. In the nineteenth century the term began to be applied to biology, and has since been extended to a wide variety of fields including engineering, physiology, international affairs, political affairs and even language. In the late 1950s and early 1960s the concept was further refined and systems analysis appeared as an 'in' method for analysing complex problems. It became common at this time to think of systems in almost every field of human and scientific endeavour. While some earlier criminal justice studies had taken something of a systems-type approach, it was not until this era that the term 'criminal justice system' first began to be used.

The application of systems concepts to criminal justice which followed these developments bore almost immediate fruit, leading to a much better understanding of the linkages among the various parts of the system and the way that the work of each agency affected the work of the other agencies involved. This knowledge proved to be very useful in thinking about criminal justice problems and 'criminal justice system' rapidly became a standard part of the criminal justice vocabulary.

The explicit application of systems concepts to criminal justice produced a number of other results as well. It exposed a great deal of divergence in the way that agencies approached particular problems and showed that the policies followed by one agency often undermined or were at cross-purposes with those followed by other agencies. It also demonstrated just how complex and interdependent the various parts of the system actually are.

Public drunkenness was an early example used to illustrate the kind of divergencies that systems analysis could expose. Enforcement efforts for this crime at this time typically involved a large number of police arrests followed in America by short jail sentences and in England by fines. In both countries the offenders were rapidly back on the street, and the whole process started over again. Calculating the enormous waste of police and court effort in this revolving-door situation, systems analysts sought to devise treatment approaches that would make more productive use of the resources expended. They argued explicitly that there were benefits to be gained in overall system accomplishment by transferring resources from the police and the courts to the treatment end of the system. Experiments with detoxification programmes for street alcoholics were one result of their efforts.

Some of those who first sought to apply systems concepts to criminal justice were less impressed with the linkages among criminal justice agencies, however, than with their fragmentation. They argued that criminal justice was in reality not a system but a 'non-system'. Judged strictly by the formal definitions developed by theorists these analysts made a persuasive case.

A very broad definition, used by some general systems theorists, for example, views a system as a set of entities whose relations are specified so that deductions may be made from some relations to others or from the relations among the entities to the behaviour or history of the system. A more detailed formulation requires that (1) the system under investigation be explicitly distinguished from its environment, (2) the internal elements of the system explicitly stated, (3) the relationships between the elements of the system and between the system and its environment explicitly stated, (4) the use of canons of logical or mathematical reasoning in deductions relating to these relationships, and (5) the confirmation of assertions about these relationships through scientific methods.

Even the strongest proponents of the systems approach would be hard-pressed to claim that their efforts meet the precision required by these standards. Despite this, however, most of those involved in criminal justice have come to think of it as a system. There is also considerable agreement that the system includes: (1) the police and the prosecution; (2) the defence; (3) the courts; and (4) corrections, including probation and the prisons. The medical, mental health, welfare, education and private security systems are all seen as closely related systems but not as part of the criminal justice system As the criminal justice system receives not only clients but also political guidance, financial support, information and personnel from the larger society, it obviously is part of the general political, economic and social systems of the larger society.

One of the central features of all systems is the interdependence of the various system parts. The concept of interdependence is therefore a natural part of the systems idea. In recent years, however, interdependence has taken on special meaning in the criminal justice system, particularly in Great Britain. As this special meaning has a considerable overlap with the more general systems approach, it cannot be defined in ways that sharply distinguish the two concepts. It is perhaps best understood, however, as meaning that what one criminal justice agency does is likely to affect and be affected by other agencies and that a detailed knowledge of the kinds of interactions that are likely to take place is essential for undertaking system improvements. The idea is thus explicitly concerned with the development of improved performance in functions that cross agency lines.

In the criminal justice system interdependence occurs at many different levels – national and local; agency head and working officer; strategic, tactical and mechanical. Strategic level choices include large questions of system design or structure, and in Great Britain are generally made at the national level. Included in such choices would be issues such as whether there should be an independent prosecution service, whether probation resources should be increased in order to provide more sentencing alternatives to prison, and whether the police should receive a much larger share of the system's resources than the courts. Questions such as how the defence function is to be organised and financed and whether greater efforts should be expended on prevention as opposed to apprehension and punishment also involve strategic issues likely to be decided at the national level.

Tactical level choices generally concern use of the resources available to particular criminal justice agencies. Whilst these choices can be made at many different levels wtihin a given organisation, they are generally made locally rather than nationally. Decisions of this kind include such things as the deployment of police forces, the hours of service provided by the courts, and how the duty solicitor rota is to function.

Perhaps the most fundamental sense in which criminal justice agencies are linked together at the tactical level lies in the process of discretionary decision-making by which cases are adjudicated and transferred from one agency to another. Cases typically begin with the discovery of a crime and the apprehension of a suspected offender by the police. After deciding whether to prosecute, the police pass the case on to the courts for adjudication. The courts in turn often secure the services of the probation service to assist in the sentencing decision, and in this decision may pass the case on either to probation or the prison service. This process is rather like an assembly line in which each agency's workload is essentially controlled by the actions of the previous agency. In most instances the decision of the transmitting agency is largely discretionary, but the receiving agency generally has little or no say in the decisions made. Probably the most important of these discretionary decisions are the decisions to arrest, to prosecute and to sentence. Obviously policies such as cautioning and non-charging by the prosecution are of major importance in this system of discretionary decision-making.

In addition to these aspects of criminal justice that derive from deliberate strategic and tactical choices about the way that criminal justice agencies should go about the business of fighting crime and processing suspects there are also aspects that relate to more administrative or mechanical functions. Issues relating to these aspects of the system are largely efficiency issues. What is the simplest and most efficient way to carry out the policy choices that have been made? Both police and the prisons, for example, transport prisoners to and from court, whilst the police, the magistrates' courts, probation and the prisons may all at one time or another become involved in collecting fines or sharing information.

A 1984 study of police, magistrates' courts, probation and prisons in Avon and Somerset by the Vera Institute of Justice identified over 80 major areas of interagency operation that responsible officials considered in need of improvement. These suggested improvements involved all three kinds of interdependence: strategic, tactical and mechanical. The majority of the issues identified were of the mechanical type. Field study and analysis of some of the more important topics produced a number of major findings concerning interdependence:

- *Scheduling of magistrates' courts.* Hearings in some areas are heavily concentrated on certain days of the week, creating uneven workloads for other agencies, particularly prosecuting solicitors, the police and probation.

- *Utilisation of police, probation and prison personnel at magistrates' courts.* Virtually all police time spent as witnesses and much of the time of police assigned to court duty is attributable to not guilty listings. Last minute changes of plea cause much of this time to be wasted. Pretrial reviews offer some hope of reducing this wastage but have thus far proved erratic and have not yet been carefully tested. Social inquiry reports occupy much probation time and present listing difficulties. Police and prisons both transport prisoners, with duplication sometimes resulting because of the inflexibility of present rules.

- *Witness issues.* Most of the time spent in court by civilian witnesses is also attributable to not guilty listings, and much is also wasted by last-minute changes of plea.

- *Bail practices and remands in custody.* Remands in custody that are committed to the Crown Court differ greatly from those disposed of in the magistrates' court. Such remands are usually held because of the seriousness of their offence, are rarely bailed prior to disposal, rarely receive non-custodial sentences and frequently use the remand in absence procedure. Remands in custody disposed of in the magistrates' courts, on the other hand, are often held because of the need for a cooling off period, are often bailed prior to disposal, frequently receive non-custodial sentences and rarely use the remand in absence procedure.

- *Fine enforcement.* There is considerable uncertainty as to the percentage of fines that is actually collected, raising questions about the effectiveness of present procedures. Present procedures appear to be fragmented among agencies and costly. There is a growing doubt as to whether fine warrants should be enforced by the police or the magistrates' court.

– *Summonses and warrants.* Large amounts of police and court time are consumed in attempting to enforce summonses against the 20 per cent of offenders who repeatedly fail to appear. Present rules impose no penalties on these offenders and place all the responsibility for dealing with such cases on the system. Present methods for issuing summonses which require lengthy internal police reviews and personal consideration by the magistrates or the clerk to the justices involve delay, duplication of work, cost and a lack of accountability.

– *Sharing of information and statistics and computer development.* Probation, prisons and some magistrates' courts have problems obtaining previous conviction information quickly and efficiently and there is some duplication of effort in the collection of case results. As computerisation is proceeding rapidly but separately in all agencies, there is a need for more interagency planning to assist in the sharing of information and to ensure coverage of interagency operations.

The fact that interaction takes place on so many different levels complicates the execution of tasks that cross agency lines. Tasks that are important in one agency and dealt with at a high level are often peripheral in another and dealt with at a very low level. Whilst this kind of variation is not always a problem, it can inhibit communication and lead to difficulties.

A single agency. One possible implication of the close linkages involving the police, the magistrates' courts, the Crown Court, probation and the prisons is that these agencies (and others such as the soon-to-be-created independent prosecution service and the defence solicitors which are arguably part of the criminal justice system) should be merged into a single organisation. Such an entity would undoubtedly have a clearer policy focus than the present array of separate agencies, would probably be easier to manage and would almost surely be more efficient.

Efficiency is not the only goal of criminal justice, however, and it has long been clear that fairness is better served if the process of judging guilt and imposing sentences is kept separate from that of discovering crimes and punishing offenders. More primitive and more totalitarian societies may combine these functions, but those that care about the liberties of the citizenry do not. It is one thing to urge the police to go all out to discover and apprehend wrongdoers when some other agency has been given the independence necessary to rigorously assess the evidence assembled by the prosecution and quite another when a single entity serves as both prosecutor and judge. Even those who argue for a crime control rather than a due process model of criminal justice, generally are not seeking a single all-powerful agency. Ensuring the independence of each separate decision-maker as to policy matters, necessarily requires a grant of some independence concerning efficiency matters as well. In this context the creation of an independent prosecution service will no doubt increase the integrity of the decisions made but in all likelihood at the price of adding some further inefficiency.

About improved interagency coordination. One possible reaction to the conclusion that it is neither feasible nor desirable to attempt to integrate all criminal justice agency functions into a single entity is that efforts for improvement should be focused wholly on the internal workings of the various agencies involved. Such a strategy has the attraction of concentrating improvement efforts on familiar terrain and avoiding expectations about interagency functioning that may prove to be unrealistic. It also seems almost a truism that interagency functions are unlikely to be better managed than internal agency functions and that improvements in internal agency management are likely to have a significant spillover effect into interagency areas.

It would seem wrong, however, to abandon the attempt to improve the way that agencies work together. Functions and relationships involving more than one agency are at least as important as those within the individual agencies and are clearly crucial to the efficiency and effectiveness of the criminal justice system. The interagency decision-making process is at the very heart of the system, whilst the more mechanical functions are also very important. These functions and relationships are not self-managing, however, and like functions and relationships within individual agencies and within other systems they require management and direction. Present methods for providing this work are adequate in some respects but leave much to be desired in others. There is a need therefore to attempt to improve these methods, however difficult that may prove to be.

Consultation and liaison. A third possible strategy for improving the way that agencies work together is to emphasise consultation and liaison, particularly at the local level. Of course, many methods of consultation and liaison, both formal and informal, already exist throughout the criminal justice system. Magistrates sit on police authorities, probation committees and prison boards of visitors. Magistrates' court user groups include representatives of most agencies, and many agencies have specific individuals designated as liaison officers to other agencies with whom they have important relationships. Many informal methods of consultation and liaison also exist.

In the Avon and Somerset study the agencies involved all reported that their relationships with other agencies were good, and relatively few gaps were found in the methods of consultation and liaison in use. The study nonetheless found that the channels of communication were not as open and clear as might be desirable. Whilst immediate operational problems were generally worked out amicably and quickly, longer-term and more complex issues appeared harder to identify and were handled more erratically. Among other things, agencies often made major changes of policy affecting other agencies without either notification or consultation. In the absence of specific operational issues, there also appeared to be little incentive to review long-standing arrangements which arguably had ceased to be efficient or effective for either of the agencies involved.

Whilst it seems clear that improved consultation and liaison would assist in addressing these problems, achieving such improvement will not be easy. The need for independent decision-making, which makes a single agency for criminal justice inadvisable, places practical limits on the results that can be accomplished by consultation and liaison as well. In addition to these jealously guarded decision-making prerogatives, the agencies have different internal organisations, administrative styles, recruitment and promotion patterns, academic disciplinary preferences and funding sources and formulas.

One recent hopeful development is the creation of magistrates' court user groups. These are still in their infancy but are likely to prove quite useful as they become better established. As they are court centred, they do not always include representation from agencies such as the prisons and do not provide an ideal forum for discussing problems that do not involve the magistrates' courts. It is doubtful at this point, however, that additional committees, at either high or low levels, would be productive. Better institutional underpinnings for interagency cooperation, such as more interagency training, would undoubtedly be very helpful as would more systematic designation of liaison officers. Unconventional methods of consultation and liaison might also be worth considering, but run the risk of adding work without helping the problem. Such methods might include development of a standard documentary method for notifying other agencies of actions that could have a major impact on them (a 'probation impact report') or periodic reviews by agency heads of some standard list of questions related to interagency performance.

Incentives. Significant improvement in interagency functioning at the local level is likely to be generated, if at all, only with much stronger incentives for cooperation than those that are now present. These may be very difficult to attain.

One approach to the creation of such incentives has been attempted in the United States, where large sums of national monies were made available for local criminal justice purposes on condition that the local agencies involved developed system-wide plans for improvement. The planning process thus created was largely successful in bringing local agency heads together to discuss criminal justice matters in ways that had not often been done before. Overall system improvement is generally believed to have been modest, however. The planning process rarely sought to deal with tough issues and often was little more than a method for carving up the available monies.

Any new methods for creating incentives for cooperation and integration could be expected to encounter some of the same problems. Nonetheless it may be useful to consider what possibilities there are. Two possible ways for creating new incentives without using large sums of money might be (1) to encourage more explicit bargaining among criminal justice agencies as to functions and services; or (2) to create a small incentive fund to encourage cost-cutting experiments that run across agency lines.

(1) *Interdependence as bargaining.* Agencies involved in the criminal justice system have many different kinds of contact with each other. When one agency wants something from another, it normally requests what it wants. If the other agency can do what is requested, it will generally do so without attempting to extract any price. If the matter requested is difficult or expensive, however, the other agency may refuse or indicate that it can assist only if it is provided with the resources needed to undertake the task. The requesting agency will then either drop its request, provide the resources or seek to find some third party, such as the local authority, to do so. If the requesting agency attempts to provide resources itself, it may provide money or offer to trade a service that it believes the other agency might like. Whilst trades of services of this kind have not been investigated, it is likely that they increase efficiency and effectiveness.

One possible method of creating greater incentives for interagency cooperation might be to promote and facilitate trades of this kind. Whilst it might be assumed that agencies that are already in close touch with each other have already identified all trades of this kind that they might choose to make, it is not clear that this is so. Trades are indeed often made, but as they are not the normal way of dealing with requests from sister agencies, they almost surely have not been developed as fully as they might be. There are risks as well as potential gains in this idea, however. If it proved possible to get such a process started, it might destroy other forms of cooperation. Agencies might cease to provide cooperation in situations in which there was no *quid pro quo*. Moreover, hard as it might be to initiate such a process on any sizeable scale, it might be even harder to stop.

(2) *An incentive fund.* An alternative idea might be to create a small incentive fund for financing interagency projects with cost-cutting possibilities. If operated under appropriate guidelines, such a fund could help to focus attention on the need for better management of interagency problems and could probably be made to produce savings that were demonstrably greater than any funds utilised. Guidelines for such a fund might specify that it would finance only those projects that truly went across agency lines, whose aim was to cut costs, that could become self-financing in a short time (one year or less) and that if successful could document the savings produced. Consideration might even be given to attempting to develop ways of recouping part or all of the cost of grants from savings generated. Such a fund would have greatest impact if operated locally but with periodic national review of its fidelity to the

guidelines. This concept could be used either as a broad-based measure to encourage initiative in many areas or as a demonstration project in a particular area designed to produce ideas that might be applied elsewhere.

A much bolder step would be to try to use the price mechanism directly to affect interagency functions. Members of the prison service have, for example, from time to time argued that the courts should be charged for transportation of prisoners to and from court. If the courts were given the responsibility and the funding for this function, they would have a much clearer incentive to minimise the use of transport and to seek the most efficient means of carrying out that which was necessary.

Whilst determining which agency should be responsible for specific functions would involve a considerable amount of arbitrariness, it probably would be possible to divide up many of the functions in ways that would permit the price mechanism to be used in their management. Establishing such a system would be a major undertaking, however, would carry no assured benefits, would pose many risks and would be highly disruptive.

Other steps. Other structural steps which might be useful in improving inter-agency functioning are to equalise the present cost-sharing formulae or to create some general administrative authority to transfer functions or budgets.

(1) *Equalise the present cost-sharing formulae.* Some of the present tensions in the criminal justice system derive from the fact that local authorities contribute differing amounts to the various services. It is not surprising that some local authorities seek to shift functions away from the police for whom they provide 50 per cent of the funding toward the magistrates' courts for whom they provide only 20 per cent or probation or prisons where there is no local contribution. Tensions of this kind might be lessened and the value of local authority review procedures increased if the contribution formulae for the various agencies were equalised. The gains from such a change are difficult to assess, however, and may not be worth the disruption that they would entail.

(2) *Administrative authority to transfer functions or budgets.* In any complex system of organisation there are likely to be problems where one entity stops and another begins. Boundary definitions are necessarily vague and leave much to be worked out on the ground. Shifts in agency priorities present special difficulties because they often affect other agencies. Whilst many of these boundary problems are best worked out locally by those closest to the situation, some important issues such as those involving fine enforcement may not be solvable in this way. As these issues are probably not numerous, it is feasible and possibly preferable to deal with each as a separate matter as it arises. It would also be possible, however, to create a more general framework for resolving issues by giving the Home Secretary

specific statutory authority to realign functions or make transfers between budgets.

Conclusion

The idea that what one agency does is likely to affect or be affected by other agencies is now widely accepted throughout the criminal justice system. This idea has proved to be quite useful in understanding the full dimensions of issues and in helping to solve particular problems that arise. Systematic reviews of contacts and processes involving more than one agency, can also be useful in identifying problems and critical points for intervention. The idea of interdependence also seems to hold some promise for improving the overall management and direction of the criminal justice system. Realising that promise is no easy task, however, and the full potential of the concept remains to be established.

3 The criminal justice system viewed *as a system*

HUGH PULLINGER

Introduction

The main concerns of both policy and research have often been to study a particular part of the criminal justice system and to consider courses of action which might enable it to meet specific objectives. Professor Feeney has described, in Chapter 2, something of the way in which the nature of the criminal justice system *as a system* – its *systemic* nature – has gained more prominence in recent years. This chapter takes a closer look at the theoretical concepts underlying the systems approach. It discusses the relevance of these concepts to the criminal justice system as an interacting network of agencies which displays certain formal properties common to all systems. Examples of these properties include interdependence, control and communication. These can fruitfully be studied to provide insights into the performance of the criminal justice system and to point to possible improvements.

Interdependence is a key concept in 'systems thinking', and Floyd Feeney's examples underline the current concern about interdependence in the criminal justice system. More generally, the systems view of the criminal justice system has started to permeate the thoughts of many involved in criminal justice activities. The Home Secretary, giving evidence to the House of Commons Home Affairs Select Committee in 1984 said, in reference to his strategy for the Home Office, that:

> 'Our principal preoccupation is, and I believe ought to be, the Criminal Justice System which, incidentally, I wish to see treated in all that we do as a system.'

The emphasis on interdependence which is now given to the work of the Home Office Research and Planning Unit is reflected in the 1984/85 Home Office Research and Planning Unit Programme, which stated that: 'In order to study the criminal justice system at any point it is necessary to be aware of the interdependence of its component parts. Changes at any point have repercussions elsewhere: it is impossible to affect output at any one point without considering inputs elsewhere' (Home Office, 1984a). The project on interdependence by the Vera Institute of Justice and the Research and Planning Unit's criminal justice system model, described in Chapter 4, are the most obvious examples of a growing awareness of the need to do more than study the system's separate parts in isolation. The model employs operational research methodology in perhaps the first major attempt at a practical application of the systems view of the criminal justice system.

The current surge of interest appears to be in part a response to the challenge of meeting ever-expanding demands within tight financial constraints. Delays in magistrates' courts and prison overcrowding could of course be alleviated by substantial increases in public expenditure – some increase in prison building is indeed in progress – but the main emphasis has to be upon making the best use of available resources. To meet this aim the parts must cooperate in making the complete system run as smoothly as possible.

Systems

So what exactly is a *system*? The word 'system' may be used in many ways but the common core of the definitions includes the ideas of organisation, interconnectedness and complexity. A system may be defined as 'an organised or connected group of objects' or 'a set or assemblage of things connected, associated or interdependent, so as to form a complex unity'. This concept is the focus for a wealth of theoretical and practical material which can be used as a framework for systems studies of the criminal justice system.

The systems age[1]

Pioneering work on modern systems theories began in the 1930s and 1940s. Since then interest has increased steadily, resulting in several varying approaches which have been applied to practical problems. They all rely (conceptually) on modelling the system being studied. Computers are often used to manipulate these models to consider the consequences of change.

'Systems Engineering', developed in the 1950s, was described as 'the science of designing complex systems in their totality to ensure that the component subsystems making up the system are designed, fitted together and operated in the most efficient way' (Jenkins, 1969). 'Systems Analysis' was extensively used by the RAND Corporation in the USA to appraise the costs and other implications of alternative means of reaching a goal in a wide variety of settings. 'Systems Dynamics' has been applied by Forrester (1961, 1962 and 1971) and others since the 1960s to study large complex organisations, and forms the underpinning for many systems models in use today.

Beer (1972 and 1979) has used the tools provided by *cybernetics* (defined by Wiener (1948) as 'the science of control and communication in the animal and the machine') to improve '. . . the design, control and performance of systems geared to the achievement of pre-determined ends'.

1. Ackoff (1974): 'Although eras do not have precise beginnings or ends, the 1940s can be said to have contained the beginning of the end of the Machine Age and the beginning of the "*Systems Age*". This new age is a product of a new intellectual framework in which the doctrines of reductionism and mechanism and the analytical mode of thought are being supplemented (not replaced) by the doctrines of *expansionism* and *teleology* and a new *synthetic* or *systems* mode of thought.'

More recently Ackoff (1974) and Checkland (1981) have developed methodologies which explicitly take account of the disparities between the goals of the various participants or groups of participants in the system. Jackson and Keys (1984) explain that 'According to Ackoff (1974), problem solvers are increasingly faced, in the systems-age, not with separable problems, but with "messes" – systems of interdependent problems' and that the focus for these problem-solvers should be on planning for and design of systems. 'Moreover, organisations are *purposeful* systems which contain purposeful parts and which are themselves parts of larger purposeful systems. Hence organisations have responsibilities to their own purposes, to the purposes of their parts and to the purposes of the larger systems of which they are parts. These responsibilities may often seem to conflict. The principal task of the manager and management scientist is to learn how to remove any conflict between these levels of purpose.' Ackoff proposes 'interactive planning' as the way to deal with problems in this context. This is planning which is participated in as widely as possible, is continuous, to cope with change, and which involves, simultaneously and interdependently, as many parts and levels of the system as possible.

Systems concepts

Certain central concepts can be gleaned from these varying approaches which may usefully be applied to the criminal justice system. Some of these ideas will be familiar and some are of a more specialised or technical nature.

A system will possess channels of *communication* and *control.* In a human organisation, communication of the state of the system to the control centres will often trigger a response which will be communicated to the appropriate parts to attempt to change that state (*feedback*). The effectiveness of this process will depend on the system's monitoring capacity, the efficiency of its *information* channels and the degree of control which can be exercised. Beer analyses the problems of organisations in terms of their *viability*, that is their capability of responding to environmental changes, even if they were not foreseen at the time the system was designed. For a system to adapt in this way it must be flexible enough to take on a *variety* of states to match the states of its environment (it must achieve '*requisite variety*').

When a system is observed as a whole it exhibits properties which its parts do not possess (eg a human being may have a sense of purpose, which cannot be said of the parts of the body). These properties are known as *emergent* properties and arise as one observes higher levels of a *hierarchy* of subsystems. This concept is important to Emery (1981), who answers the question 'what constitutes systems thinking?' by saying: 'There have in fact been two arguments for a systems approach to the analysis of living phenomena[2].

2. This includes social phenomena. Emery concentrates on this strand of systems thinking, which is more appropriate to our needs, rather than on mechanical and electronic systems (although these still have many features in common).

First has been the argument that only such an approach will reveal the "Gestalten" properties that characterise the higher levels of organisation which we call "living systems". Second has been the argument that many of these Gestalten properties are common to the different levels of organisation of living matter (from bacteria to human societies) and hence provide a valid and powerful form of generalisation.'

A system may be characterised as either *closed* (where interaction with its environment is minimal) or *open* (as is the case with social systems, where the environment has very important connections with the system). Emery (1981) believes that 'it has been shown that living systems, whether individuals or populations, have to be analysed as "open systems", ie as open to exchanges with an environment. Human organisations are living systems and should be analysed accordingly. The fact that it faces us with the task of analysing forbiddingly complex environmental interactions gives us no more excuse to isolate organisations conceptually than the proverbial drunk had when searching for his lost watch under the street lamp "because there was plenty of light" when he knew he had lost it in the dark alley.'

The idea of a *purposeful system* is a further useful concept which is explicit in Ackoff's work and which brings in the consideration of *objectives*, *goals* and *aims*. The objectives of the parts of the system and the individuals involved will almost inevitably conflict to a certain extent. So part of a systems study will be concerned with the reconciliation of these objectives. This is also a major concern of Checkland who builds up *'rich-pictures'* of the problem situations which contain the varying perceptions of the people involved.

Summary

Systems theories and methodologies can provide a structured approach to analysing the activities of organisations such as the criminal justice system. System modelling of the criminal justice system can lead to an understanding of its purpose and can illuminate the informational and organisational requirements for managing its operations. Using the ideas outlined above, we may hope to get to grips with some of the problems of coordination and interaction in the criminal justice system.

The criminal justice system

Defining the system

Where does one draw the boundaries of the criminal justice *system*? For example, should Parliament, as the source of criminal law, be included? The choice of definition will depend on the purpose that it is intended to serve. However, the criminal justice system is commonly considered to be the combination of sub-systems concerning the police, magistrates' courts, Crown Court and higher courts, the legal profession, the prison service and the probation and after-care service (see Figure 3:1). The diagram shows the hierarchical nature of the criminal justice system, where a hierarchy may be defined to consist of 'entities which may be meaningfully regarded as *wholes*, which are built up of smaller entities which are themselves wholes . . . and so on' (Checkland, 1981). It deliberately avoids the use of precise, rectangular boxes for the sub-systems in an attempt to convey the rather inexact nature of the sub-system boundaries. The prison sub-system will, in addition to the prison service itself, contain such organisations as the Home Office Prison Department, the Parole Board, the Howard League for Penal Reform, National Association for the Care and Resettlement of Offenders, Preservation of Rights of Prisoners and the Prison Officers' Association. Similarly the other sub-systems variously include the Police Complaints Authority, Association of Chief Police Officers, the Police Federation, the Criminal Injuries Compensation Board, the Justices' Clerks Society etc. The overall system contains the Lord Chancellor and his department, the Attorney-General, Solicitor-General and Director of Public Prosecutions (and their staffs).

The Home Office Research and Planning Unit computer model of the criminal justice system adopts a somewhat narrower definition. It only explicitly specifies the parts of the system which the Home Office or Lord Chancellor's Department can exert influence over and which significantly affect the passage of defendants through the system. All other elements of the criminal justice system are considered to be extraneous. It is clear that neat boundaries between sub-systems are impossible and also that there is no fixed delineation between the criminal justice system and its environment. We can see the 'open' nature of the criminal justice system in Figure 3:2. It is very strongly affected by outside influences – its input, in terms of offenders/defendants, is affected by social and environmental factors (so the requirement for criminal justice system resources is largely determined from outside – it is largely demand-led); the laws which it has to uphold are imposed by Parliament; and there is a strong influence on the system's operational policies emanating from the Government and the public.

A further problem in attempting to describe the criminal justice system *as a system* is one of terminology. How does one refer to the people dealt with by the system? The names used at present include suspect, defendant, offender, inmate etc. These are all dependent on the stage of the criminal process at which the person finds himself – there is no general term for a 'person in the criminal process'.

This has both advantages and disadvantages. It is right that the people are not all tarred with the same brush. On the other hand, the use of the names 'defendant', 'suspect' etc will immediately put one's mind into 'courtthink', or 'policethink' and will militate against considering that 'defendant' or 'suspect' as someone to be dealt with by the whole system. This is a small but important indicator that the advantages of systems thinking about the criminal justice

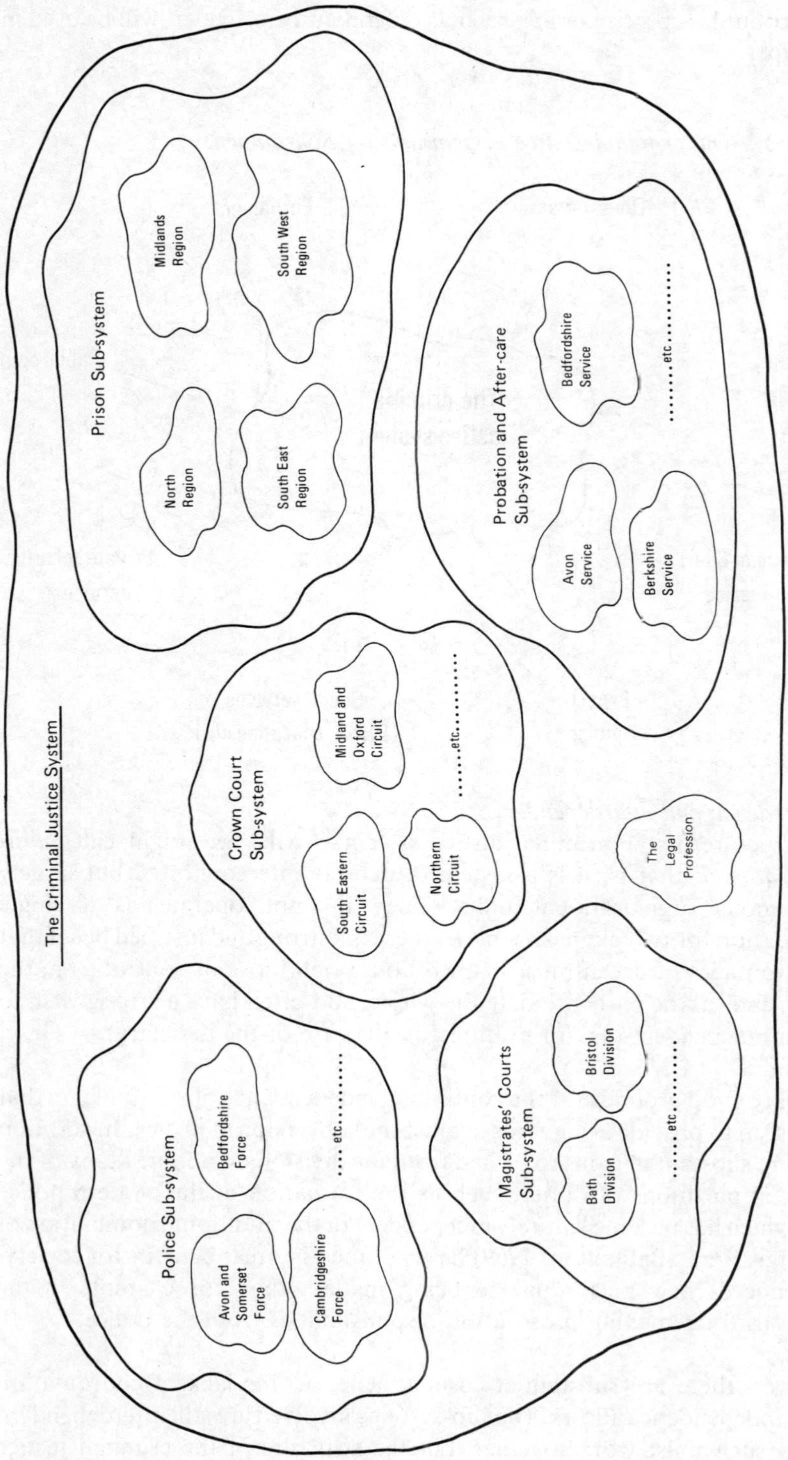

Figure 3:1 *The criminal justice system – a hierarchy of systems*

system will not be easily won. In the absence of any more general term, the familiar but less precise terms, such as defendant or offender, will be used in this paper.

Figure 3:2 *The criminal justice system and its environment*

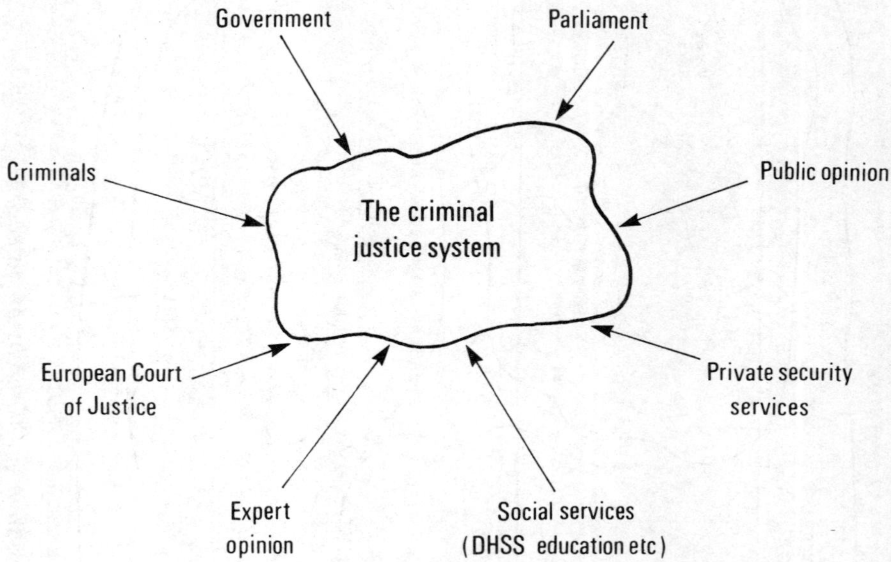

Independence and interdependence

The structure of the criminal justice system is what we might call *multi-organisational*, that is, it is a system of densely interconnected but largely autonomous organisational units. They do not operate as a single organisation for two main reasons: (i) there is a strong and justified belief that the advantages of decentralised control outweigh those of control from the centre; and (ii) the parts pre-date the whole, and often have a strong wish to remain independent (as, for example, in the case of the judiciary).

There are good grounds for the continuing independence of sub-units, in that this is seen to provide safeguards against the subversion of justice. In addition there are substantial gains to be had from the division of labour. Many of the historical partitions of duties, such as the formation of the modern police force which has become 'entirely independent of the traditional domination of the magistracy' (Babington, 1969) have resulted in great benefits for society. And indeed, new partitions are being made today, for example in the proposals for removing prosecution responsibilities from the police.

However, there are substantial costs attached to the lack of coordination which independence allows. The sub-systems involved are still interdependent and as such must work together, but the structure of the criminal justice system at present will mean that the efficiency of operations will tend to be low.

So what are the problems involved in coordinating the various criminal justice system sub-systems whilst simultaneously maintaining the necessary levels of independence? At a general level we can start by considering the possibility of conflicting objectives.

A plausible overall objective might be 'to contain and respond to crime in a just manner'. The major objectives of the various sub-systems of the criminal justice system are subsumed within this overall goal and do not appear to be contradictory. The police aim to 'maintain peace and order in society without constraining freedom to act within the law'; the courts wish to 'dispense justice (ie to fairly sentence the guilty and acquit the innocent)'; and the post-sentence agencies attempt to 'implement the judgments of the courts'. These objectives stem from the prevailing political philosophy and, assuming this has a coherent form, we should not expect contradictions. So a move towards a sub-system goal should result in progress towards the system-wide objective. However, when resources are taken into account we have a different story. For example, consider the attempts of the police to clear up reported crime; the courts to deal with cases speedily; and the prisons to provide humane conditions for inmates. All of these are practical manifestations of the sub-system goals but we can see that with limited resources these objectives will conflict. In practice some divergence in aims will, in any case, be introduced by differences in the personal views of those involved in the system.

Within a sub-system there can be further tension between the goals of individuals or of organisational units. The Director-General of the Prison Service will have objectives which differ from those of the Prison Governors; the Lord Chancellor's aims will not be the same as those of his court officials. Systems studies can help in identifying how the lower level goals contribute to overall goals. One such study has been carried out at a youth custody centre where the Home Office Research and Planning Unit sponsored research by the staff of the Systems Department of Lancaster University. Checkland's (1981) methodology was used to look at the goals of the prison as defined by the Governor, and to produce models including the activities necessary to achieve the goals, and the information required to support these activities. These idealised models were then compared with reality with the aim of identifying information deficiencies and designing a more comprehensive information system.

The objectives of the police have also been looked at in some detail. Work was carried out by the Police Effectiveness Evaluation Panel and reported on by the Home Office Scientific Research and Development Branch (1984). Through extensive consultation with police and researchers and through observation of activities, the panel arrived at a hierarchy of agreed policing objectives. These ranged from the broadest ('to maintain peace and order in society') to the specific (eg 'to investigate traffic accidents').

A policing experiment was set up in a particular West Midlands sub-division and changes in the effectiveness of the police were assessed. This was done by systematic consideration of the objectives and the monitoring of progress towards them. The study concludes that the methodology employed holds promise for further applications in the police area. It may also be adaptable for use in other parts of the criminal justice system.

It was noticeable from this study that there was no reference to working within the wider objectives of the criminal justice system. Nor was there mention of operational links with the other criminal justice system agencies. This is also the case with other sets of policing objectives such as those proposed by the 1962 Royal Commission on the Police. It is clear that the interactions with other sub-systems are not seen as being of high priority. However, these interactions are extremely important. Probably the most important interaction arises from the decision of whether or not to refer a defendant to a further sub-system. Examples include the police decision to prosecute, the decision to commit a defendant for trial at the Crown Court, and sentencing decisions. It is only by studying the system as a whole that the effects of these interactions can be properly investigated. It will also only be possible to coordinate the criminal justice system if the individual parts are made aware of their responsibilities with respect to the aims of the wider system.

Information and communication

The criminal justice system can only work effectively if it has sufficient communication between its sub-systems. Beer's work in applied cybernetics (1972 and 1979) stresses the importance of properly designing the information channels which link the different functions of an organisation and the organisation with its environment. Control is dependent on information, and the complexity and size of the criminal justice system means that, if its actions are to be directed, this information has to be managed properly. The structure of information flows, the methods of information handling, and the techniques of reducing the information to manageable levels are all of prime importance. This section proposes ways in which the criminal justice system can address these issues.

One major requirement is for management information concerning the performance of the system, this should be disseminated and used to trigger corrective or coordinating actions as and when necessary. Performance information should show how the processes and activities of the system relate to its goals, and can then be used to achieve control and coordination of the system's operations. The Government's financial management initiative stresses the need for such monitoring, and many government departments are currently investigating performance measurement schemes. The Home Office is no exception, for example Goldman (1984) has suggested an approach to prison performance measurement, based on setting objectives and targets, which expresses performance in terms of the effectiveness, efficiency and economy of the various activities undertaken. This would be based on information related to goals and provide a better idea of performance than does the commonly used reconviction rate.

Decision-making may be assisted by comparison of parts of the system and through analysis of past performance. One example might be in the magistrates' courts, where the consistency of sentencing could be improved by comparing a court's present sentencing practice with its own past record and with other courts. Another example where standardisation could be encouraged is in police forces' use of cautioning. In each of these examples the system can benefit from the improved use of information.

The advent of information technology provides many opportunities for increasing the quality and timeliness of information available to those in the criminal justice system. This should increase the efficiency of operations and help to coordinate agencies involved in, for example, the scheduling of cases for court hearings. Here there are often a large number of people representing varying interests to be organised, including magistrates or judges, court clerks, defendants, witnesses, juries, lawyers, police and prison officers. Rapid changes of circumstances occur and the new schedules need to be quickly and accurately drawn up and conveyed to the parties involved.

Generally, the use of information in the criminal justice system can be made more effective through the application of computers both in the day to day work of the system and in strategic planning. Firstly this could be done by incorporating information into the *knowledge-bases* of computerised *decision support systems*. These would help the decision-maker by analysing often very large quantities of data on relevant factors, and thus extend his capacity for dealing with complexity. Operational management decisions such as prison inmate security classification could be aided in this way. Secondly, models of the criminal justice system can help in planning resource requirements. They can examine possible future scenarios with a view to feeding information into plans for staffing levels, building programmes etc.

The use, abuse or non-use of information can make or break organisations. In the criminal justice system effective communication is essential as it can lead to control within sub-systems and coordination between them. So it is very important that the criminal justice system has properly designed information flows and channels of communication.

Conclusions

The problems of the criminal justice system which relate to its systemic nature are not easy to alleviate. Serious thought needs to be given to inter-agency information flows and to performance measurement. There is also a delicate balance to be struck between independence and control in attempting to achieve the objectives of criminal justice. In addition it is necessary to work within the tight rein of the expectations of the Government, Parliament and the public. The important first step towards achieving a balanced and effective system is to encourage participants in the system to consider it *as a system*.

Systems studies can help to identify areas where the criminal justice system could work more efficiently and effectively. The purpose of the criminal justice system can be pinned down more precisely; the uses of information can be improved; and radical but practical re-designs of the system could be proposed. In addition, systems concepts should be employed to structure a general debate about the nature of a criminal justice system which will reconcile the aims of the system itself, its sub-systems and the wider society of which it is a part.

4 Modelling the criminal justice system

PATRICIA M MORGAN

Introduction

The criminal justice system model illustrates perhaps more clearly than any other project yet, the central importance now attached to the concept of interdependence. Whereas most studies necessarily focus on a particular part of the system, the model is explicitly concerned with the system as a whole.

Defendants are dealt with by the agencies that form part of the criminal justice system in a clearly defined order. The police system usually comes first, the exceptions being those cases where a prosecution is brought by an agency such as the local authority or the Post Office. The output from the police operations, in terms of the number of persons prosecuted, largely determines the workloads of the other parts of the system.

The magistrates' courts are normally the next to deal with defendants after they have been charged or summonsed by the police. Changes in policy which determine the type of court that can try certain offences, or changes in the practice of defendants in electing a jury trial where there is a choice, affect the balance of workload between the magistrates' courts and Crown Court. More appeals against conviction or sentence in the magistrates' court will cause extra work for the Crown Court. If more fines are imposed by the Crown Court, extra work arises for the magistrates' courts in collecting and enforcing payment.

Between the workloads of the courts and the prison and probation systems, the most obvious link is sentencing practice; there are, however, less obvious interactions which arise from court delays. Increased delays in hearing cases cause increases in the population remanded in custody, and hence in the prison population as a whole. Increased delays in the courts will also necessitate more court appearances for those remanded in custody, and will increase the workload of prison and police officers in escorting prisoners to and from the courts. If courts hold extra hearings to cater for the demands, more prison staff are needed to staff the Crown Court and more police officers for the magistrates' courts. Further, more cases being heard will increase the demand for reports from the probation service.

Changes in the prison system, in factors such as remission or parole, are likely to affect the probation system in that they will vary the numbers of persons requiring after-care, whether mandatory or voluntary. There can be effects on the earlier parts of the CJS too. If earlier release from custody results in an offender re-offending sooner, he may re-enter the system more quickly, and thus cause an increase in the number of persons prosecuted in subsequent time periods. Another interaction between the prison and probation service is the pre-release supervision which is given to those in custody; this forms a substantial part of the probation officer workload.

The growing interest in the criminal justice system as a system brought an increasing awareness that the types of interactions described needed to be taken into account in forward planning. The model was developed in response to this concern.

Choosing the type of model

It was first necessary to decide on the questions that a model would need to address. These fell into two groups. The first group consisted of questions about the effects that specific types of changes would have on the workloads of the individual agencies that make up the system. An obvious change would be an increase in the recorded crime rate; other changes would normally arise as matters of policy, for example in the criminal law, or as gradual variations in the practice of the police, the judiciary, the magistrates, or the defendants themselves. The second type of question was concerned with the effects of constraints on resources. The model needed to be able to assess the deterioration – or improvement – in performance (necessarily measured in some fairly simple way) that would arise from resources being constrained while workloads increased, stayed constant, or decreased.

The second type of question raised the problem of defining measures of the performance of different parts of the system. For the courts, the 'waiting time', ie the time that a defendant must wait before his case is dealt with, was felt to be an important measure for a number of reasons. First, undue delay is felt to be unfair to the defendant. Second, delays for those remanded in custody can cause increases in the prison population. Third, as Sid Butler points out in Chapter 13, there is some statistical evidence to suggest that the longer the delay before a Crown Court hearing, the more likely the defendant is to be acquitted. In order to take account of these delays, the model had to be capable of representing the courts as bottlenecks, at which backlogs of cases will form when defendants cannot be dealt with sufficiently quickly.

For the prison system, overcrowding is perhaps the most important problem in that it causes stress to both prisoners and staff. The model had therefore to be capable of showing how the level of overcrowding might be increased or reduced as a result of changes that are made. This meant that the prison population had to be represented to a reasonable degree of accuracy, and had to be compared with the available accommodation to show where overcrowding was likely to occur.

The model required

The idea of a model of the criminal justice system is not new. Of the previous work done in the United States, perhaps the best-known model is known by the acronym JUSSIM (Blumstein and Larson, 1969). Some trial use of JUSSIM II helped in clarifying the features that would be needed in the model for England and Wales.

The model needed to be able to show the effects of constraints on resources on the waiting times of cases in both the magistrates' courts and the Crown Court. If the cases that are ready for hearing at a particular court in a month, say, cannot be dealt with in that month, a backlog of cases will build up. (In a model, such a backlog is usually called a 'queue'. These terms will be used synonymously in this chapter.) Ideally, the model would have included a straightforward relationship between the number of cases ready for hearing each month, the time taken to hear the cases, the resources available, and the length of the queue. The situation is, however, complicated by the many types of cases that require different average lengths of hearing time in court, and also by the priority that is given to certain cases, for example to those remanded in custody. An alternative approach in such situations is to use the technique of simulation.

Simulation uses the power of a computer to reproduce the flows of work through the system over a given period of time. Individual or groups of cases are generated, and are made to take different paths through a simplified system in proportions that reflect actual practice. Resource constraints in the courts (ie courtrooms, magistrates, judges, recorders and court staff) can be represented, and have the effect of limiting the number of cases that can be processed – and hence passed on to the next stage – in a given time period. Delays which result from these bottlenecks in the system can be recorded, as also can various other statistics about the passage of the cases. Further, the prison population can be built up over a period of time, and account taken of changes in the rules regarding the time spent in custody on remand, remission, and parole. When a simulation has been developed which represents the historical situation sufficiently accurately, changes can be made to the simulated system – such as making different assumptions about the resources available – and the simulation repeated to observe the effects

Flows of defendants

It was clear from the outset that the planned model would be fairly complex. There would, therefore, be practical advantages in subdividing it into a number of sections, which could be developed separately and later linked together. The obvious division was into sections corresponding to the main parts of the criminal justice system, ie the police, the magistrates' courts, the Crown Court, the probation and the prison systems; each part has distinct sets of resources, and each is concerned in a different way with the handling of defendants. These sections are called the sub-models.

A further section was needed to provide the link between the main parts of the system. It was decided that this section – called the *flow model* – would record the details of all the defendants in the system, and would represent their passage between the police, the courts, prison and probation sections. Factors to be recorded would include age, sex, and offence, together with the stage that the defendants had reached in their contact with the system, and the time that they had waited at that stage. The shaded sections of Figure 4:1 show the parts handled by the *flow model*.

The advantage of this approach was that all the parts of the model that required detailed data on defendant characteristics were grouped together in the flow model. The main data source for information on defendants was the Home Office court statistics database, which is compiled by the Home Office Statistical Department from data supplied by the police, and is used to produce the published volumes of Criminal Statistics.

A simulation works in cycles. A time period is chosen and a certain sequence of events is assumed to take place within this period. When the calculations for one period are complete, the calendar is assumed to be put forward by a month, the next period starts, and the model cycles back to the first event again. As the model cycles through a series of time periods, records are kept of important measures such as the queue lengths for courts, the prison population and the number under supervision. In the model that was developed, a time period of four weeks was chosen: hence a run of 65 time periods would correspond to five years of real time. In using the model, such a period would usually correspond partly to the past and partly to a projection into the future. During each time period, the model would then go through the following series of steps that are illustrated in Figure 4:1.

Events in a cycle

At the beginning of a cycle, the police sub-model estimates the number of defendants that are prosecuted in the period on the basis of assumptions about the crime rate and other factors which will be described later.

During the cycle, defendants are grouped at four points according to the stage they have reached in their involvement with the system (shown by circles in Figure 4:1). On first entering the system after prosecution by the police, defendants are added to those that entered the system in previous cycles and are waiting (at stage I) for hearings in magistrates' courts. As the cycle progresses, they might be moved between stages or might stay at the same stage until a later time period.

Next, the magistrates' courts sub-model decides how many defendants can be dealt with during the four week period, and an assumed pattern of sentences is applied to the proportion found guilty in these court hearings. Some of those dealt with will be committed for trial at the Crown Court; others are tried summarily and committed to the Crown Court for sentence, or appeal to the

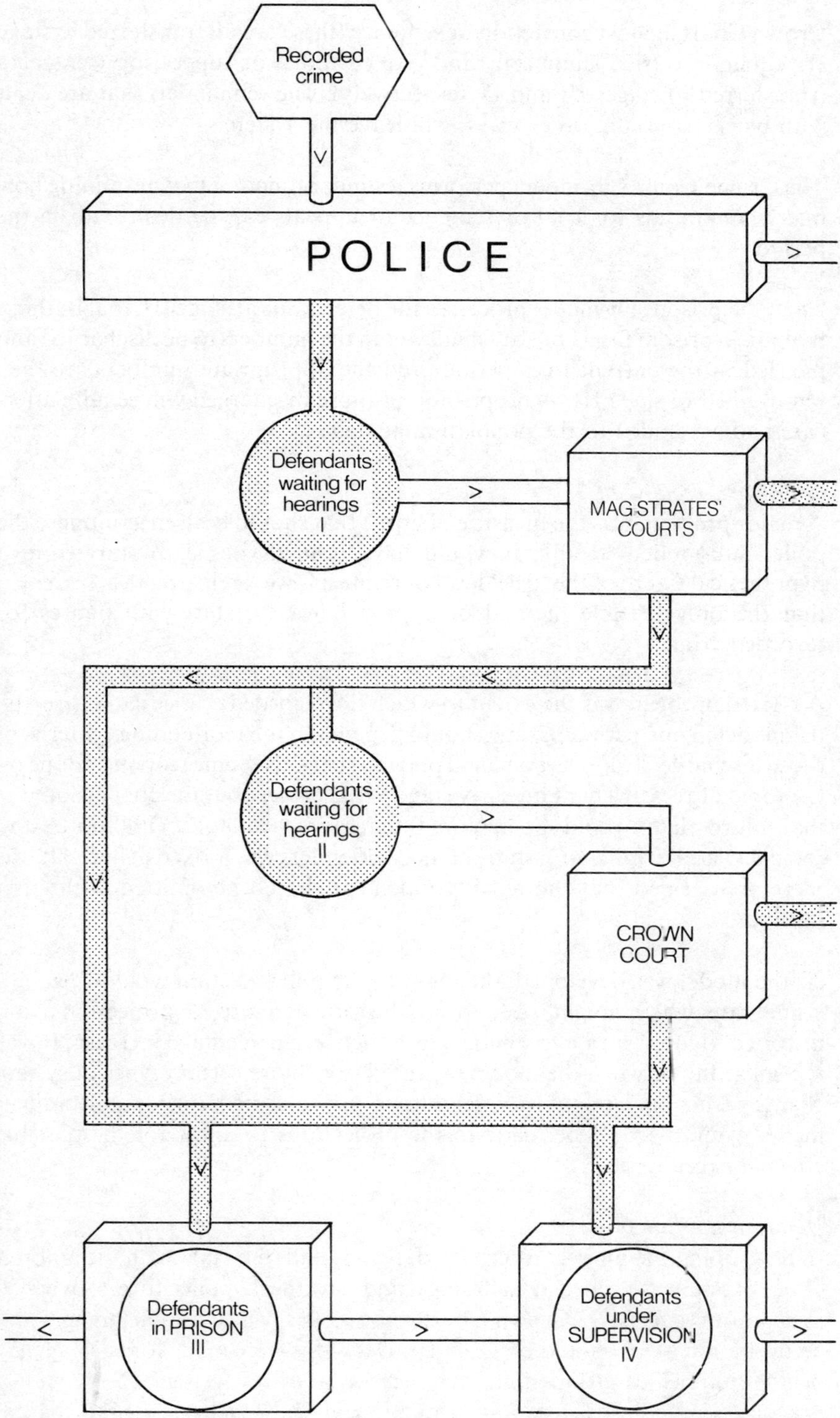

Figure 4:1 *Structure of the model*

Crown Court against conviction or sentence (these are all transferred to stage II); others are tried summarily and give custodial or supervisory sentences (transferred to stages III and IV respectively). The remainder, that are dealt with by the courts in other ways, will leave the system.

The Crown Court sub-model performs a similar function in determining how many committals for trial or sentence or appeals can be dealt with in the period.

Next, the prison sub-model processes the defendants at stage III, that is, those that are in prison. Decisions are made about the numbers to be discharged and paroled in the current time period, and the appropriate numbers are then removed from stage III. A proportion of those discharged will require after-care and are added to the population at stage IV.

Crime and recidivism

A major problem was the measure of crime that should be used as input to the police sub-model. Ideally, it would have been desirable to start from a hypothetical figure of the 'true' level of crime. However, in practice, it seemed that the only feasible method of approach was to start with figures for recorded crime.

A related problem was the extent to which the recorded crime figures used by the model in one period of time should depend on the reoffending patterns of those discharged from the system in previous periods. Some work was done on the topic of recidivism at an early stage in the project but the conclusion was that more data would be required than was available. (Phillpotts and Lancucki's 1979 follow-up study of 5,000 offenders was looked at here.) It was therefore decided that the recidivist element should be omitted in the first instance.

As the model was developed, the input to the police section would then be a crime rate which might be either a historical figure, a projection from historical figures, or a hypothetical rate such as a percentage increase. It was recognised that, when the model was used to explore certain types of system changes (such as reductions in lengths of prison sentences), suitable adjustments would need to be made to the projections to allow for the possible effects of recidivism.

Detail in the flows

In developing the model, important decisions had to be taken on the amount of detail that was needed at each stage, and how the 43 police forces, over 600 magistrates' courts, 92 Crown Court centres, 140 prison establishments and 56 probation areas should be grouped. Decisions were made for each agency on the number of groups that were necessary to reflect real differences of practice. For police forces and probation areas, which are county based, divisions between metropolitan counties and non-metropolitan counties were judged to be necessary. For the Crown Court and the prison system, which are organised on a geographical basis into six circuits and four regions, it seemed appropriate to retain these divisions. For the magistrates' courts, the obvious differences of practice seemed to be related more to size of the court than to any geographical factors. Hence large urban courts had much in common, as did small rural courts.

A consequence of the different groupings made for each system is that the flows of defendants have to be regrouped at several different stages during a model cycle. Hence defendants divided by police force group when prosecuted by the police, must be regrouped into five magistrates' courts groups before stage I (of Figure 4:1). Similarly, they are regrouped into six Crown Court circuits before stage II.

Use of resources – the sub-models

In the overall plan for the model, the appropriate sub-models were to record the resources of the police, courts, prison and probation systems. These were also to model the relationships between the resources used and the defendants processed.

The police sub-model

The main function of the police sub-model was to decide the number of defendants that were to be prosecuted in each four weekly time period. Account had to be taken of the recorded crime rate, the level of police resources available (in terms of manpower and possible overtime) and also the various policy options that were relevant. One important policy factor concerns the proportion of effort devoted to different tasks, for example, criminal investigation, traffic policing and uniformed patrolling; a second concerns policy on the choice of whether to prosecute or caution, or, in the case of motoring offences, between prosecution, written warnings or other possible deterrent action.

An actual or hypothetical total police budget needs to be supplied as input to the police sub-model for each year of the run. In each simulated year this total budget is divided between the different types of police manpower, overtime, and goods and services, and gives rise to the total man hours available for each of the main functions: ie CID, traffic, uniform branch, and administration.

Obtaining the necessary relationships between the police manpower devoted to crime detection and the number of persons prosecuted caused some problems. After initial attempts at an approach based on the difficulty of detection of crimes (using work by Crust, 1975, and Steer, 1980) a fairly simple approach was adopted, based on research by Burrows and Tarling (1982). In this, the 'clear-up' rate for each offence group depends on the current workload of the CID or uniform branches (in terms of the crimes per officer), the crime mix, and the police strength per head of population. For summary and motoring offences, relationships were derived between the numbers of offences reported and the police strength in the uniformed and traffic branches (Reeson and Vicary, 1982). More detail about the police section of the model is given by Barton (1984).

Magistrates' courts sub-model

The magistrates' courts' section was designed to carry out two main functions: to determine the number of cases that can be dealt with in each time period when fixed court resources are assumed; and to estimate the extra staff and courtrooms that would be needed if the workload increased. For either function, current or improved standards of efficiency in the use of resources were to be assumed.

To carry out the first of these functions, the model estimates, from the assumed resources, the court sitting time that is likely to be available to hear cases; the resources consist of the numbers of magistrates, court clerks, other court staff and courtrooms. The sitting time is divided between adult, juvenile and domestic hearings, and a proportion of the adult and juvenile time is allocated to contested cases.

The next task is to estimate the court time that would be needed to hear the cases that are waiting. Assumptions are made (on the basis of research studies that were carried out) about the number of times that defendants are remanded before the final hearing, and about the length of time required in court to hear cases of different types.

In calculating which defendants can be dealt with in the current period, account must be taken of the relative priorities accorded to different types of cases. A proportion of these are assumed to be dealt with on first appearance, and some priority is given to these: otherwise priority is allocated on the basis of the length of time the case has waited, whether the defendant is in custody, and the category of offence (indictable/triable-either-way, summary/non-motoring and motoring). The handling of priorities caused some difficulty in developing the sub-model; no simple priority rules proved to be adequate in representing current practice. A solution was found whereby a set of priorities was applied to a percentage of the waiting cases, then applied again to a further percentage, and so on. In this way no one category of case is always accorded the lowest priority.

To estimate the increases in court staff that would be required to cope with an increasing workload, statistical relationships were derived which relate the staff in individual courts to the workloads of the three categories of offence. To estimate the extra courtrooms needed, the hearing time required to hear the waiting cases (for each court group) is divided between the individual courts in the group in proportion to the annual workload, and compared with the number of courtrooms available. If more than 1,000 hours per courtroom per year would be needed for any court, a new courtroom is judged to be required. Improvements in efficiency can be included by increasing the length of the court sitting day, or by decreasing the hearing times of cases in the smaller courts to nearer those of the larger courts.

The magistrates' courts sub-model probably suffered the most from shortage of data. Some parameters had to be estimated, so these were based on the judgement of those involved with the system, or on practice in a small sample of courts. One approach which was adopted in dealing with such gaps was to vary the estimates when running the model to see the effect that small increases or decreases would have. More detail of the sub-model is given in Rice (1984).

Crown Court sub-model

The Crown Court sub-model performs a similar function to the magistrates' court sub-model; it does however work in terms of 'cases' rather than defendants, which means that appropriate conversions of the flows have to be made when entering and leaving it. The sub-model estimates the number of cases that can be dealt with in each time period when there are fixed, and therefore limited, resources. The resources include high court and circuit judges, recorders and members of the administrative staff, and also the numbers of courtrooms available.

Again, an important feature of the sub-model was found to be the scheduling of cases and the priority given to those remanded in custody. A simple priority system was devised in which the highest priority was assigned to those in custody, and the next highest to the length of time that the case had waited. This meant that a case involving a defendant remanded in custody would be heard before a case involving a bailed defendant, regardless of the relative time each had waited. However, when the model was run with this scheduling system, more priority seemed to be given to defendants in custody than was the case in recent years. Because of this, an alternative priority scheme was included as an option, whereby the highest priority is given to the length of time the case has waited, and whether the defendant is in custody or on bail is considered next. These two alternatives give extremes within which the real situation lies.

A related area of some uncertainty was the minimum waiting time that a case must wait before it could be heard in the Crown Court. If the model was to be able to show the effects of changes in resource levels, it had to be capable of handling the situation in which there were more than adequate resources, and so the waiting time for hearings is sharply reduced. In such a situation, allowance must be made for the preparation time that cases will need before the Crown Court hearing. This was particularly difficult to assess when waiting times were fairly long, and when there was, as a result, little pressure to prepare cases quickly. Hence, rather arbitrary values were initially assumed which were based on waiting times in different circuits. Runs of the model have shown, however, that the minimum waiting time is important when absolute priority is given to custody cases. When the second method of scheduling is used, ie when the length of time waiting is the main criterion for priority, the preparation time is only important when increased Crown Court resources are assumed.

Prison sub-model

The task of the prison sub-model was to reproduce the numbers in custody, either on remand or sentence, in each time period. The prison population obtained in this way was then to be compared with the number of prison places assumed to be available so that measures of overcrowding could be obtained.

The population remanded in custody (the 'remand population') in each time period is taken directly from the numbers waiting for hearings in either type of court, in custody. The population of sentenced defendants in custody is built up from the numbers given custodial sentences, by both magistrates' courts and the Crown Court, the expected distribution of the lengths of sentences, and such factors as the percentage given parole and the level of remission assumed. Account is also taken of the time defendants have spent in custody on remand.

The sentenced population is later divided into groups which correspond to the four security categories in each of the four prison department regions; and each group is compared with the number of prison places of the same category in the same region. Each training prison is regarded as having a maximum level of overcrowding depending on its design, whereas local prisons have no such limit. Local prisons are assumed to house those in each group for whom there are no places in training prisons in addition to those with short sentences and those remanded in custody. Where possible, overcrowding is levelled out between training prisons in a region and the local prisons, when account is taken of the maximum levels mentioned above. In this way measures of overcrowding are obtained in each region.

Users of the model may assume that one or more new prisons will be built in a specific year of the run; these must be given security categories and sizes. The effect of the extra capacity on the overcrowding in the region can then be shown.

Running the model

The model will normally be used to reproduce the working of the system over a number of *past* years, and then to project forward into the future. Assumptions must be made on how certain elements of the data used in the run are likely to change in future years. Changes are likely in the amount of work coming into the system; the resources available to it; the percentage of defendants electing jury trial; the percentage of defendants remanded on bail rather than custody; and the percentage of defendants given specific sentences.

One approach is to use projections based on recent trends in these factors; this requires the data to be kept up to date. Alternatively, arbitrary assumptions can be made about factors that will or will not change in future years. This second approach should be useful in exploring the relative magnitudes of the effects of specific types of change on the workloads, and hence the resource needs, of other parts of the system. In this way the model is used as a tool for exploring the interdependence between the different sections of the system rather than as a direct predictor of future events.

Types of change

Three broad types of changes can be considered. The first concerns changes in the volume of work entering the system; the second, changes in the type of work that arises or in the way that this is handled; and the third, changes in the resources available in any or all of the constituent parts of the system.

The volume of work entering the system can be changed in a number of ways. The volume of serious crime for each year of a run is one input to the model and so can be changed directly. Changes in the number of summary and motoring offences dealt with are assumed to arise from changes in police manpower strength. Also, changes in policy can be made in the police sub-model which can cause more or less use to be made of prosecution as compared with cautions or written warnings, which will in turn affect the volume of business entering the courts. Hypothetical changes in the volume of non-police prosecutions can be made as required. Alternatively, the police sub-model can be bypassed and assumptions made about changes in the volume of defendants prosecuted for the three main categories of offence each year. This determines the workload of the magistrates' courts directly. The examples of model runs shown later in the paper are of this last type.

The second type of change relates to the offender, the type of offence, and the way in which the offender is dealt with. Changes might be made relating to any combination of these categories. For example, the proportion of offences committed by specific age or sex groups might be assumed to change; the volume of recorded crime might remain the same but the mix between different categories of offence might change. Decriminalisation can be considered by selecting the relevant specific offences and causing no proceedings to be taken on these. Other possible changes lie in the rights of the defendant to elect for Crown Court trial for specific categories of offence; the practice of courts in remanding cases in custody or giving bail; and in the practice of defendants in pleading guilty or not guilty. The effects of changes of practice by the courts in the listing of cases can also be studied. An obvious example would involve giving more or less priority to custody cases to assess the likely change in the remand population.

The model can also be used to look at some of the effects of changes in sentencing practice. In relation to custodial sentences, changes in the lengths of sentences can be explored, as can changes in the practice of imprisonment of fine defaulters or civil prisoners, and in the remission or parole factors. Consequent changes in the prison population would usually be calculated. A slightly different approach would be to use the model to look at the changes in sentence length that would be needed to reduce the prison population by a given amount.

The third type of change concerns the resources available in the system and the efficiency with which these are used. In the courts area, insufficient magistrates or judges, court clerks or courtrooms will cause queues to increase, unless courts are assumed to become more efficient by sitting longer hours or increasing the throughput of cases. In the prison section, shortages of places will cause the model to show increased overcrowding, to some extent in the training prisons, but mainly in the local prisons. If sufficient staff are not available for new prison establishments, these will not be opened. In the police area, the model assumes that increases in manpower will cause marginal increases in the clear-up rate for serious crime and will cause more traffic and summary offences to be processed (on the basis of the statistical relationships described earlier).

Examples of model runs

In this section, a number of runs of the model will be described as illustrations of how it might be used. Some results from these are shown in Figures 4:2, 4:3 and 4:4. The runs assume that a number of arbitrary changes are made to the system. These changes are based on the situation in 1980, and are assumed to take place in the five year period following this; when only one change is made, for example a decrease in motoring cases, this is assumed to be made in the first year after 1980 and to remain the same for the following four years. It must be emphasised that these changes are *not forecasts*, but are hypothetical changes which are made for the purpose of studying the extent to which increasing workloads can be partially offset by other changes in the system. Three types of change are considered: changes in workload, changes in resources available, and changes in the rules regarding committal to the Crown Court. It is assumed that there are no increases in efficiency in the courts; that is, the lengths of the sitting day and the rates of throughput of cases are assumed to be the same as in 1980.

The changes made in the runs are as follows.

Run A – an increase in the persons prosecuted for indictable/triable-either-way offences each year of 10 per cent of the previous year's level;

Run B – run A increase with a decrease in the persons proceeded against for motoring offences to 80 per cent of the 1980 figures for all the following years;

Run C – run B changes plus an increase in magistrates' courts' resources by 2 per cent per year after 1980;

Figure 4:2 *Magistrates' courts backlog*

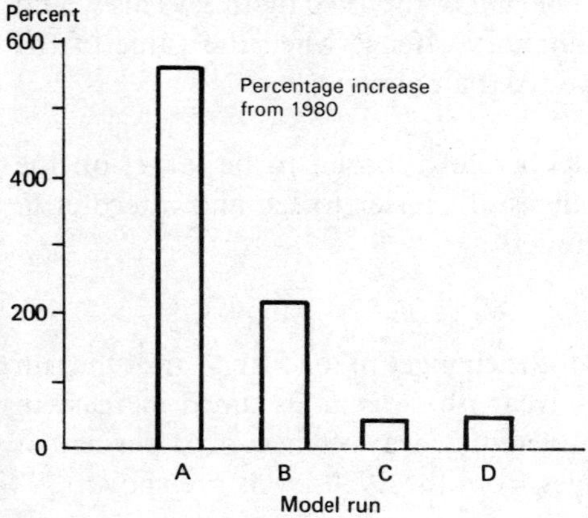

Figure 4:3 *Crown Court backlog*

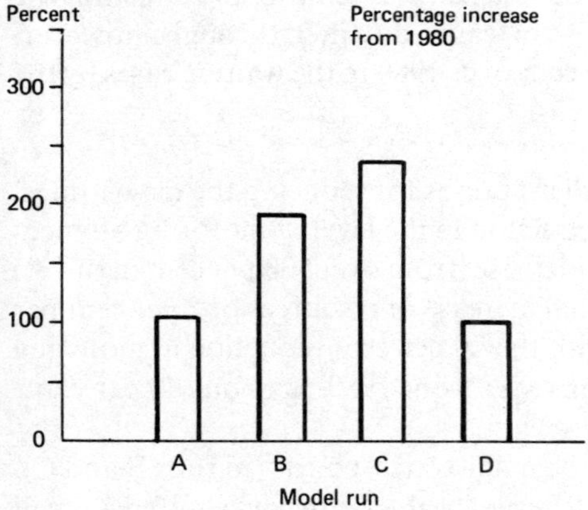

Figure 4:4 *Remand population*

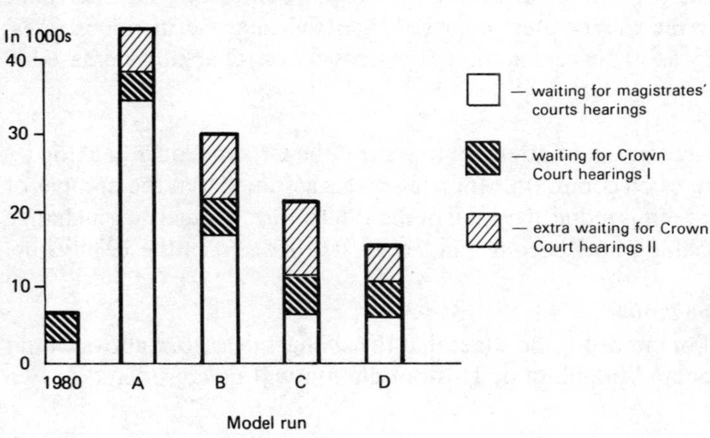

Run D – run C changes with a reduction in committals to the Crown Court for trial for offences of theft to 50 per cent of the 1980 figures. (This would be achieved by making theft a summary offence when the value of the property stolen was less than some fixed amount.)

Most of these changes have been deliberately chosen to be large, on the grounds that the effects of such changes are easier to see and interpret in learning about the best use of the model.

The effects of change

Figures 4:2 and 4:3 show the effects of the changes in the fifth year of the run on the queues for the courts. In this year, there is an assumed increase in persons prosecuted for indictable/triable-either-way offences of 61 per cent of the 1980 level. The percentage changes from the 1980 levels are shown.

In run A, the number of defendants waiting for hearings in the magistrates' courts has increased by over 500 per cent over the 1980 figure. Because there is such a build-up of waiting cases at the magistrates' courts, the effect on the Crown Court is much less. Some extra cases do filter through, however, causing an increase of about 100 per cent over 1980 in the waiting cases by the fifth year.

Runs B and C show the effects of other options for reducing the magistrates' courts' queues. First, a 20 per cent reduction in the level of motoring offences is assumed: this reduces the backlog increase (from over 500 per cent in run A) to about 200 per cent. Then, an annual increase of resources of 2 per cent per year is assumed (run C), together with the 20 per cent reduction in motoring offences; this reduces the backlog increase from 1980 to about 40 per cent.

As the queue of cases is reduced in the magistrates' courts (in runs B and C), more defendants charged with indictable/triable-either-way offences will have their cases heard. As a result, there will be more committals for trial, and the backlog of the Crown Court will start to rise. Figure 4:3 shows the increases in the Crown Court backlog which result from the increased throughput in the magistrates' courts. When the increase in magistrates' courts' queues was 40 per cent in run C, the Crown Court backlog increased to 240 per cent.

Run D shows the results of attempts to reduce the Crown Court backlog by changing the rules on committals for trial. If it is assumed that the number of committals for theft is reduced by half of the 1980 figure, a much larger change is seen. The backlog now becomes just over 100 per cent of the 1980 value.

The remand population

The next point of interest is the effect that the changes described above would have on the remand population. This population will be considered in two parts: those waiting for hearings at magistrates' courts, and those waiting for hearings at the Crown Court.

For the first group, the results of the runs are fairly straightforward: the population in the fifth year is shown in Figure 4:4 (unshaded). From a starting value in 1980 of about 2,700, the population increases sharply in run A to the height of 34,400; this corresponds to the 500 per cent increase in the magistrates' court backlog in Figure 4:2. The population is reduced to 18,000, and 6,600 in runs B and C, and remains at the same level in run D. It does, therefore, follow the same pattern as the queues for the magistrates' courts' hearings, but the increases over 1980 are about twice as high. This is probably because custody cases are not given the highest priority in the magistrates' courts in the model. Cases that are dealt with on first appearance are given some priority, and so are bail cases with long waiting times.

The second part of the remand population, consisting of those awaiting a Crown Court hearing, varies with the assumptions made about priorities in the Crown Court and the minimum preparation time for cases (as mentioned earlier). The results of two alternative sets of hypotheses are shown in Figure 4:4: namely, that custody cases are given absolute priority over bail cases; and the second, that priority is given to cases that have waited the longest.

In the first case (I), the populations produced by the model are shown in Figure 4:4. From a figure of 3,800 in 1980, there is a rise to 4,500, 4,600 and 4,800 in runs A to C, and then a small decrease to 4,600 again in run D. This means that, while the number of outstanding cases in the Crown Court rises by 240 per cent in run C, the part of this backlog in custody only rises by a small amount (about 25 per cent). It seems in fact, that with these priority assumptions, the level of the population is determined largely by the minimum preparation time. It would then need an extraordinarily high increase in workload to raise the population far above this level.

If the alternative option is assumed (II), ie that priority is given to those that have waited the longest (custody cases only being given priority over those cases that have waited the same time) a very different pattern emerges. The extra population is shown in Figure 4:4. The population in custody waiting for Crown Court hearings rises from 4,400 in 1980 (slightly higher than the actual level) to 11,000 in run A, and further to 13,400, and 15,300 in runs B and C. With the committal change in run D, the population increased to the lower figure of 9,600. The pattern of increases here follows the increases in the Crown Court queues, and is marginally higher for most runs; this is what might be expected from the assumption made about priorities. The minimum preparation time here does not appear to be important.

These runs indicate some of the effects of reducing workloads, reducing committals, and increasing resources on the size of the remand population. The priority given to custody cases in scheduling court hearings is seen to be important. The work done suggests that for both magistrates' courts and Crown Court, there is scope for giving higher priority to custody cases in this respect. The minimum time required to prepare cases will then operate as a restraint on reducing the remand population. Future research could therefore be directed towards identifying factors which affect this preparation time.

Summary

A model of the criminal justice system has been developed and is operational except for the probation section. It can be used to look at some of the effects of changes of policy in one part of the system on the workloads and needs for resources in the other parts.

It represents the passage of defendants through the police, magistrates' courts, Crown Court and prison systems by simulating their progress through a series of stages over a number of years. The resources needed to deal with the defendants are estimated at each stage. When resources are insufficient in the courts to handle the waiting cases, backlogs or queues build up. Defendants in these queues who are in custody form the remand population.

The model was constructed using data from 1979 and 1980 and reproduces, broadly, the behaviour of the system in these years. Updating the detail of the data beyond 1980 has not yet been attempted. Projecting the running of the system forward to other years is achieved by using projected crime rates, or by postulating specific changes in crime rates or in the volume of cases to be prosecuted in the courts.

Some examples are shown which illustrate the use of the model. A high increase in workload is first postulated, and then other changes are made to offset its effects on the delays in the courts and on the remand population. Application has shown also how the remand population varies with the assumptions made about listing priorities in the courts and the minimum preparation time for cases; it suggests that there is scope for giving more priority to custody cases.

5 Magistrates in the pre-trial criminal process

KEN LIDSTONE

Introduction

Interdependence suggests independent components working together, each relying to some extent on the other but each independent of the other. However, when the efficient operation of the criminal justice system depends upon the interaction between and the interdependence upon the component parts of that system; and its effectiveness as a system of justice depends upon the independence of some of those parts from other parts; there is a danger that too great an interdependence can lead to a loss of independence. This is the particular danger affecting the role of magistrates in the pre-trial process. They are in theory a safeguard against the abuse of the process of prosecution or the arbitrary exercise of police powers. Thus the public depend upon magistrates to protect them against such abuse and the police rely upon magistrates both to ensure that cases deserving of prosecution are in fact prosecuted and to ensure that police powers can be exercised in proper cases. Magistrates must also, in the present system, rely upon the police to ensure that their workload is kept within reasonable bounds. As is suggested in the previous chapter it is in fact the police who make the prosecutorial decisions which affect the workloads of the courts. However, in theory it is the magistrates who are the masters of their workload for it is they who are the 'gatekeepers' to the criminal justice system, deciding which cases will or will not be prosecuted, examining informations laid by the police and other prosecutors and deciding whether or not a summons will issue ordering a person to appear before them to answer the accusation. They are therefore, in theory, a safeguard against the citizens being dragged before a court on insubstantial evidence but in fact a study of the actual operation of the summons procedure (Lidstone, 1983) reveals that it is a purely administrative process, not the judicial act which it may once have been. In fact it is the police upon whom the magistrates' courts must depend to keep their workload within reasonable bounds. Further, the safeguard represented by the requirement that the police obtain the authority of a magistrate's warrant or order before taking certain actions has been undermined by a lack of independence; by too great a dependence upon the police and by the growth of common law powers shortly to be replaced and extended by statute, which enable the police to act on their own authority.

This chapter looks at the role of the magistrate in the issue of process, the issue of warrants to search premises and the issue of fingerprint orders, and considers the changes in their role and the interdependency of the magistrates, the police and the prosecutor in the light of the Prosecution of Offenders Bill and the Police and Criminal Evidence Act 1984.

The issue of process

The laying before a magistrate of an information alleging an offence and the issue by magistrates of a summons requiring the alleged offender to attend at a court to answer the accusation was described by Donaldson L.J. in *R v Gateshead Justices ex parte Tesco Stores Ltd* [1981][1] as 'a constitutional safeguard of fundamental importance' even though it was recognised that the majority of prosecutions are brought by experienced and responsible prosecuting authorities. The Royal Commission on Criminal Procedure (1981) had earlier described the consideration of an information by magistrates as a 'virtual dead letter in practice' and proposed its removal. Observation of the process in three magistrates' courts showed that the procedure was entirely administrative with no consideration of the substantive offence alleged and no refusal of an application for a summons from the police or other authorised prosecutor. Ninety-seven per cent of magistrates interviewed had never refused an application for a summons and the 3 per cent of refusals were all in respect of prosecutions by private individuals. Magistrates fell into four broad categories. Those who trusted the clerk to check the information and who signed without more ado; those who signed in the belief that they had no discretion to refuse to do so; those who recognised that even if a discretion existed, which they doubted, there was insufficient information upon which to act; and those who trusted the police not to bring frivolous prosecutions and therefore signed everything.

The 'judicial act' represented by this process is clearly a myth and is accepted as such by all within the system. In those courts which had been computerised the human element had been reduced to a minimum, even the signature of the clerk, acting as a justice of the peace, may be applied mechanically; while in the non-computerised courts stipendiary and lay magistrates laboriously signed batches of summonses giving no consideration to the offence alleged and whether it should be prosecuted. The only occasion on which such consideration was given was the application by private individuals for a summons, usually alleging common assault[2]. In this respect the magistrates were playing the role assigned to them in the nineteenth century before the modern police forces were created. Then they were the 'professionals' checking the excesses of the lay prosecutors; today the roles are reversed, lay justices are, in theory, expected to check the excesses of a professional prosecutor. Whether in committal proceedings or in the issue of a summons, it is asking a lot of lay justices that they review the decisions of the professional police officer or solicitor. Add to this a huge volume of applications for summonses for offences which often admit of no defence, which contain only the barest factual information about the offence and therefore raise no evidential issues and provide little scope for the exercise of any discretion to

---

1. 1 All ER 1027.
2. The Prosecution of Offences Bill places no check on the initiation of prosecutions by persons other than the police. While the Crown Prosecutor may take over such a prosecution and drop it, the initial check will continue to be the magistrate.

refuse to issue a summons[3] and one sees the 'constitutional safeguard' of the judicial scrutiny of informations for what it is: a historical excrescence which is of no value to the present system.

The creation of a Crown Prosecution Service by the Prosecution of Offences Bill, which is before Parliament at the time of writing, creates a new area of interdependence but fails to deal with the means of initiating proceedings and may not provide an effective filter for cases coming into the magistrates' court. It is clear that the means of initiating proceedings must be separate from the means of filtering out certain cases. The Royal Commission on Criminal Procedure, having recognised that the judicial scrutiny of informations laid by the police was an ineffective check on their discretion to prosecute proposed that it should be replaced with a single procedure incorporating both the summons procedure and the arrest and charge procedure[4]. No action has been taken on this recommendation but it is implicit in the Prosecution of Offences Bill that the procedure for initiating prosecutions is separate and distinct from any check on prosecutorial discretion. The 'responsibility for the propriety of taking so serious a step as to require the attendance of a citizen before a criminal court'[5] which is under the present procedure a judicial responsibility, is to be shared by the police, who will continue to initiate proceedings, as in practice they do now, and to decide whether to caution or take no further action. If they decide to initiate a prosecution the case will be handed over to a Crown Prosecutor who may decide to discontinue the prosecution in appropriate cases. The relationship between police and prosecuting solicitor was identified as crucial to the efficient running of the criminal justice system by research conducted for the Royal Commission (Weatheritt, 1981). The relationship between the Crown Prosecutor and the magistrates' court will be no less crucial. Magistrates and their clerks have never been able to control the input into their courts, yet given limited resources some control over that input is vital to the efficient running of those courts and to the effective administration of justice in this country. The Prosecution of Offences Bill gives the Crown Prosecutor the power to discontinue any proceedings in a magistrates' court without the consent of the court. This is an important and necessary power but it is likely to be exercised rarely given the inevitable bias in favour of continuing a case once started, and then only in respect of those cases which the Crown Prosecutor believes should have been dealt with by way of a caution or no prosecution. This will operate as an additional filter, keeping out of the courts the minor cases which can be dealt with otherwise than by a prosecution. There are, however, many offences in respect of which a caution or no prosecution will not be appropriate and which are deserving of a monetary penalty. In such cases the Crown Prosecutor has no alternative; he

3. There are some rather weak authorities which suggest that magistrates do have a discretion to refuse to issue a summons, and thereby act as a check on the abuse of the prosecutorial power, but it is now probably confined to refusal on those occasions when the application is considered vexatious or trivial.
4. 1981 Cmnd. 8092 paras. 8.2 to 8.5.
5. *R v Gateshead Justices* at 1029.

must prosecute. But in failing to provide for some alternative to prosecution the Prosecution of Offences Bill fails to appreciate the future dependency of the magistrates' courts upon the Crown Prosecutor as a means of controlling the input into the criminal justice system and misses a golden opportunity to provide for a radical alternative to prosecution. In many continental jurisdictions minor offences may be dealt with under some form of 'penal order' scheme under which a prosecutor is empowered to fix a monetary penalty to be paid as an alternative to prosecution. The order, if accepted or not responded to within a specified period, is treated as a fine imposed by a court and, where necessary, recorded as a conviction[6]. In Scotland the Stewart Committee (1983) has recommended that the Procurator Fiscal be empowered to offer such 'fines' as an alternative to prosecution. As in continental jurisdictions the alleged offender can choose instead to have the case heard before a court. Powers to offer mitigated penalties as an alternative to prosecution already exist in respect of certain revenue offences[7]. Powers to compound criminal proceedings applies only to offences under the Customs and Excise legislation, and under the VAT code, and does not extend to offences in relation to VAT at common law or under the Theft Acts 1968 and 1978. However, the 1985 Finance Bill will extend the powers of the Customs and Excise by giving them the power to impose financial penalties without reference to the courts in respect of all but the more serious offences in respect of VAT. Penalties will be up to 100 per cent of the amount of tax involved in the case of the more serious offences and up to 30 per cent in respect of the less serious breaches. The Bill will provide for a defence on the grounds that the taxpayer exercised 'all due diligence and had a reasonable excuse for failing to comply with the VAT law' which will mean that many alleged offenders will still appear before the courts but a significant number of cases will, nevertheless, be removed from the trial process. Such powers may readily be extended to include other revenue gathering offences, for example, failure to obtain a television licence[8] and other minor offences, conviction for which

6. See for example the Petty Infraction Code in West Germany summarised at Appendix 1 of the Royal Commission on Criminal Procedure's Research Report No. 10, Prosecutions by Private Individuals and Non-Police Agencies (1980).

7. The Customs and Excise Management Act 1979, s.152 gives the Inland Revenue the power to offer a mitigated penalty and the Vehicle (Excise) Act 1971 gives the Minister of Transport a similar power in respect of vehicle excise duty.

8. For a study of the sentencing of TV licence evaders and a discussion of some of the issues involved in a mitigated penalty scheme for such offences, see Softley, TV Licence Evasion, Home Office Research and Planning Unit Bulletin No. 18 (1984). Future research may indicate to what extent increases in taxation and licence fees lead to greater evasion and thereby to an increase in the workload of the courts.

would only justify a monetary penalty[9]. This could remove from magistrates' courts up to 50 per cent of the present workload of cases, all of which raise no justiciable issue and which contribute significantly to the reputation of the courts as impersonal 'conveyor belts' dispensing fines rather than justice. The removal of such cases would free the court of what is often in truth an administrative chore and leave them with more time to deal with those cases which contain justiciable issues and are worthy of their attention.

Magisterial authorisation of police actions

English law has always had high regard for the sanctity of the person and his property. In the pre-trial process this is reflected in the requirement that the police obtain judicial authority for certain actions when the citizen does not, or may not, consent: in particular the issue of an order permitting fingerprints to be taken or a warrant authorising entry to and search of premises, by force if necessary. In theory the 'warrant safeguard' demonstrates the interdependence of the magistracy and the police and the dependence of the public upon the independent judicial officer balancing the needs of the possibly over-zealous police officer against the privacy of the individual and doing justice to both and to society by permitting the police to act in those cases in which there are good grounds while denying them the power to do so when there are not. Unfortunately the reality is different. The role of magistrates has been undermined by police practices, by developments in the law, by the professionalism of the police and by the virtual surrender of their independence by magistrates who passively accept their ineffectiveness as a safeguard.

The issue of fingerprint orders

Section 40 of the Magistrates' Courts Act 1980 permits a magistrates' court to order the fingerprint of a person appearing before the court charged with an offence, or answering a summons alleging an imprisonable offence to be taken by a constable using such reasonable force as is necessary. The section suggests a court acting in its traditional role as a buffer between the individual and the state represented by the police; giving impartial consideration to the reasons for requiring fingerprints and thus protecting the citizen. However, research revealed that no applications were made in three courts over a three month period of observation and 83 per cent of magistrates questioned had not been asked to issue a fingerprint order in the past twelve months[10], yet a

9. The fining of motorists in breach of road safety requirements to maintain their vehicles may be counter-productive if the reason for the lack of maintenance is lack of money. The exercise of a discretion not to prosecute by some police forces, conditional upon the motorist effecting the repair within a stated period, may be more effective as a road safety measure. If police have such a power why not give a Crown Prosecutor a similar power to offer repair as an alternative to prosecution?

10. The study involved only adult courts. The 17 per cent of magistrates who had issued fingerprint orders in the preceding 12 months included a number of those on the juvenile panel. Applications in respect of juveniles are more numerous given the protection afforded them on arrest which makes it harder to bluff them into consenting.

study of police charge sheets and arrest records for the same periods showed that all persons arrested and charged, or summonsed for an offence punishable with imprisonment, were in fact fingerprinted and photographed.

The reasons for the lack of magisterial involvement in this area were not hard to find. The police as a body did not see the taking of fingerprints as an infringement of liberty, rather they saw it as a routine police operation to be carried out in respect of recordable offences, that is all those offences for which the Central Record Office record fingerprints. Systematic observation of the procedure in police stations was not possible but brief observation and considerable discussion with those responsible for the procedure, served to emphasise the routine nature of the procedure which appeared to be accepted as such by persons arrested who generally acquiesced in the process. Those who did not were generally persuaded to do so, not least by the fact that fingerprinting and photographing was usually the last stage in the procedure before being released on bail. On the rare occasion in which an application to magistrates appeared to be necessary, an application was prepared but was seldom made, the person usually being persuaded of the inevitability of the application being granted and therefore 'consenting'.

Here one sees the police acquiring independence from the magistracy by their practice, aided and abetted by the ignorance of the average suspect. If statutory safeguards are to be effective then one must be aware that a system of statutory interdependence can quickly be subverted by such practices. So far as the taking of fingerprints is concerned the Police and Criminal Evidence Act 1984 gives the police statutory independence from the magistracy by making a superintendent the authorising officer. Section 61 of the Act, while stating the general rule that a person's fingerprints may not be taken without the appropriate consent, permits a superintendent to authorise the taking of them without consent if the person is detained at a police station and charged with, or informed that he may be prosecuted for, a recordable offence, if, but only if, there are reasonable grounds for suspecting the person's involvement in a criminal offence, and for believing that his fingerprints will confirm or disprove his involvement. Those are in fact fairly restrictive conditions given that fingerprints will only rarely prove or disprove the person's involvement in crime[11]. The police will, however, continue to require fingerprints as a matter of routine for record purposes and the fact that s.61(2) requires that consent to the taking of a person's fingerprints must be in writing will not prove to be a significant hurdle nor will it ensure that the 'consent' is an informed consent. The signature is likely to be as routine as the taking of the fingerprints.

---

11. See Baldwin and McConville: *Courts, Prosecutions and Convictions*, Oxford 1981, p.108, where it is suggested that fingerprints play little part in the investigative process.

The issue of search warrants

The requirement that an independent judicial officer should satisfy himself that it is in all the circumstances right to issue a warrant authorising the entry to, and search of, premises and the seizure of any articles found which are the proceeds or evidence of crime, is the most visible, and for many the most important, of the magistrates' safeguarding roles. But this role has also been undermined by police practices, by developments in the law and by magistrates themselves who instead of emphasising their independence of the police by adopting an inquisitorial approach to police application, passively accept almost all that they are told, thus reducing a judicial hurdle to an administrative stepping stone. Observation of the issue of search warrants in three courts over a period of three months, together with a study of all search warrant applications over a six month period, showed that the police supplied very little information justifying their suspicion or belief that prohibited goods would be found on the particular premises and that magistrates seldom asked any questions aimed at establishing the reasonableness of such suspicion or belief. The mystique surrounding the informant system, coupled with the lay magistrates' acceptance that the professional police officer knows best how to do his job and may be trusted to do it, has led to a standard form of information being used which states that 'information has been received from a reliable source' but which seldom provides any facts pointing to the reliability of the information or its source. The fact that no application was refused during the observation period and that 97 per cent of magistrates interviewed could not recall refusing an application for a search warrant to the police, is evidence not that warrants were being issued on insubstantial evidence, but that magistrates failed to establish that there was substantial evidence and thereby surrendered their independence and in doing so upset the balance of interdependence which is at the root of an effective safeguard.

Other factors tilted the balance in favour of the police. These are (a) the growth of common law powers to enter and search premises, and (b) the ability of the police to gain access to premises for the purpose of search with consent (whether explicit or otherwise) of the suspect or occupier. Seventy-four per cent of searches in three provincial police force areas were conducted under common law powers or with consent, while only 17 per cent of such searches were backed by a magistrates' warrant. That 44 per cent of searches were justified under common law powers to search without a warrant after an arrest demonstrates the law's trust and confidence in the police and the lessening of their dependence on the magistracy for the authority to search. The fact that 30 per cent of searches were conducted with 'consent' further increases their independence from the magistracy. This, if true consent, would be no bad thing for it would indicate a public trust and confidence in the police and render the need for a judicial safeguard unnecessary. However, it appears that it is seldom a true consent but relies upon ignorance of police powers and a fear of the consequences of non-cooperation[12].

The Police and Criminal Evidence Act 1984 increases the independence of the police from the magistracy in relation to search of premises, while increasing their dependency upon them in relation to the detention of suspects. Section 15 of the 1984 Act contains a number of provisions which seek to ensure that the warrant requirement is the safeguard it was intended to be. If there is also a change of attitude among the magistracy, and there are indications that greater prominence will be given to this aspect of their duties during training, then the procedure can be an effective safeguard. However, the codification of powers to enter premises without a warrant by s.17 and the increased powers to search premises after arrest provided by ss.18 and 32, will provide greater opportunity to enter and search premises without a warrant than at present. The inclusion (by s.8) of a magisterial power to issue a warrant to search for *evidence* of an offence, as opposed to articles unlawfully possessed, will not add greatly to the reliance of the police upon the magistracy since it is confined to serious arrestable offences and is concerned with persons not themselves involved in such an offence but who innocently possess evidence which is not held in confidence[13]. The vast majority of such persons are likely to surrender such evidence voluntarily and s.8 makes the issue of a warrant conditional upon attempts to obtain the evidence with consent or the frustration of or serious prejudice to the purpose of a search by such attempts. The Code of Practice governing the conduct of searches of premises requires that consent to a search be obtained in writing and requires that the occupier be 'cautioned' that he need not consent; that anything seized may be used in evidence and that the person be informed if he is suspected of an offence. The effectiveness of this requirement in increasing the dependency of the police upon the magistracy rather than on the consent of the occupier will depend on how well informed the public are of the police powers under the 1984 Act. Given the kind of people with whom the police habitually deal there is little likelihood that they will be any better informed than they are now[14].

12. The Code of Practice governing search and seizure under the Police and Criminal Evidence Act 1984 requires that when there is no lawful authority to search premises and reliance is placed upon consent, that consent must be in writing. The occupier must be 'cautioned' that he need not consent and that anything seized may be produced in evidence. If that person is suspected of an offence he must be told this. This is unlikely to reduce the ability of the police to obtain consent.

13. Schedule 1 of the Police and Criminal Evidence Act 1984 provides a procedure for obtaining an order for the production of evidence of an arrestable offence which is held in confidence, and the issue of a warrant if the order is not complied with or is inappropriate. However, such application must be made to a circuit judge. A lack of faith in the magistracy led to attempts during the passage of the Bill to make a circuit judge the issuing authority under s.8 as recommended by the Royal Commission on Criminal Procedure.

14. Of 201 entries to search premises during the study, 184 (92 per cent) were in respect of a dwelling house and of these 70 per cent were council owned dwellings. It is the occupiers of such dwellings who form the majority of actual or suspected offenders with whom the police deal.

Conclusion

The magistracy have an important, though changing, role to play in the pre-trial criminal process for not only are the other parts of the process dependent upon them for the efficient operation of the system, the public are equally dependent upon them to maintain the integrity of the system. As lay representatives of the public in a system staffed by professionals they must resist the temptation to let the professionals take over. On the other hand the role of laymen in such a system must be clearly defined. This means ridding the system of historical anachronisms which give to magistrates roles which are not viable in a changed system. It is a nonsense to expect laymen to review the decision to initiate a prosecution made by professional policemen and, in the future, to be confirmed by an independent Crown Prosecutor. The role of the lay magistrate in the pre-trial process is to act as an independent and objective judge of the facts, and in doing so to act as a check on the possible abuse of power by the professionals who, because of the pressures under which they operate, may take a different view of the facts. The issue of warrants, to arrest, to search premises, to commit persons to prison, in the near future to detain persons suspected of having committed a serious arrestable offence, and the decision to remand a person in custody or to release him on bail, all call for an objective appraisal of the facts and an independence of mind. Without such independence, interdependence slips easily into dependence, in this context upon the views of the police or prosecutor. Magistrates then cease to be a safeguard, the criminal justice system then appears to be operating efficiently but is in truth out of balance and ineffective as a system of justice.

6 Police force cautioning: policy and practice

GLORIA LAYCOCK AND ROGER TARLING

It has long been known that there is considerable discrepancy in the use of cautioning between different police forces. Various bodies, including the Royal Commission on Criminal Procedure (1981) and the Parliamentary All-Party Penal Affairs Group (1981) have commented on this discrepancy and there have been calls for the greater use of cautioning. The research reported on in this paper[1] was set up in connection with the Home Office Working Group on Police Cautioning to describe more fully the reasons for the current variations in practice in order to assess the scope for change.

Some background data

A formal police caution for notifiable offences[2] generally takes the form of a reprimand, at a police station, from a uniformed officer of at least the rank of inspector. A record is kept by the police and it is current practice in the case of juveniles to cite previous cautions in any subsequent proceedings in a juvenile court.

Information on police use of formal cautioning is published annually in *Criminal Statistics England and Wales*. Some of that information for 1982 is summarised in Figure 6:1 and clearly illustrates the main discrepancies which exist; the difference in juvenile and adult cautioning rates and the wide variation in practice between the 43 police forces.

Juvenile cautioning rates have not always been as high as shown in Figure 6:1: they rose sharply in anticipation, and following the implementation, of the Children and Young Persons Act 1969 which was interpreted as giving encouragement to the police to keep children out of the courts as far as possible. Since about 1971 they have levelled off. While much of the initial increase was attributable to juveniles being diverted from court appearance, it has been shown (Ditchfield, 1976) that a significant part of this increase was brought about by many juveniles being cautioned who would otherwise have been dealt with informally, an effect frequently described as 'net widening'. In marked contrast, the rate for adults has remained relatively low and stable over the last 20 years.

---

1. An earlier version of this paper appeared in *The Howard Journal of Criminal Justice*, Volume 24, Number 2.
2. Previously labelled indictable, triable either way or serious offences in *Criminal Statistics England and Wales*. The police also have the power to deal with an offender informally, or, in the case of traffic offences, to issue a warning. Neither is considered in this chapter.

Figure 1 *Average, maxima and minima of police force cautioning rates for 1982. (All 43 police forces, England and Wales.)*

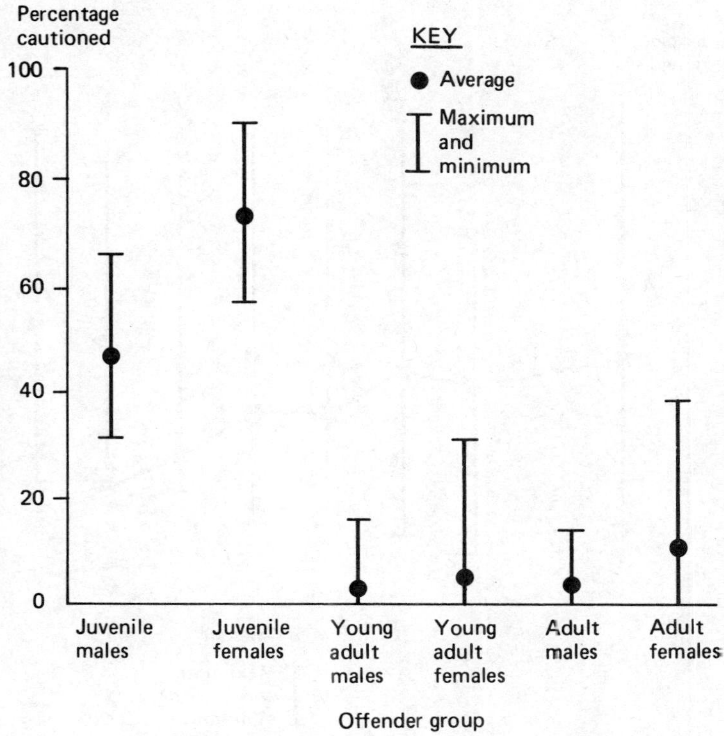

Source: Criminal Statistics England and Wales 1982 (Home Office 1983)

Disparities in cautioning rates, though still large, have in fact over the years decreased. This is illustrated in Figure 6:2 which shows the range in juvenile male cautioning rates over all forces from 1974 to 1983. The average cautioning rate over all forces in any given year is also shown and as can be seen it remains reasonably stable at between 44 and 51 per cent. In contrast, the differences between force rates have narrowed steadily, although not dramatically, during the period. The reduction in the range has been caused mainly by an increase in the minimum rate.

Nonetheless substantial differences in force cautioning rates and differences between adult and juvenile cautioning rates continue. Little previous research has sought to illumine these variations. Several researchers have considered the criteria for cautioning in specific police force areas, for example, Bennett (1979), Landau (1981 and 1983), Farrington and Bennett (1982), and Fisher and Mawby (1982). And Mott (1983) has recently completed a small comparative study of six forces. The organisational arrangements adopted by

Figure 2 *Juvenile male cautioning rates: average, maxima, minima and range. (All 43 police forces, England and Wales.)*

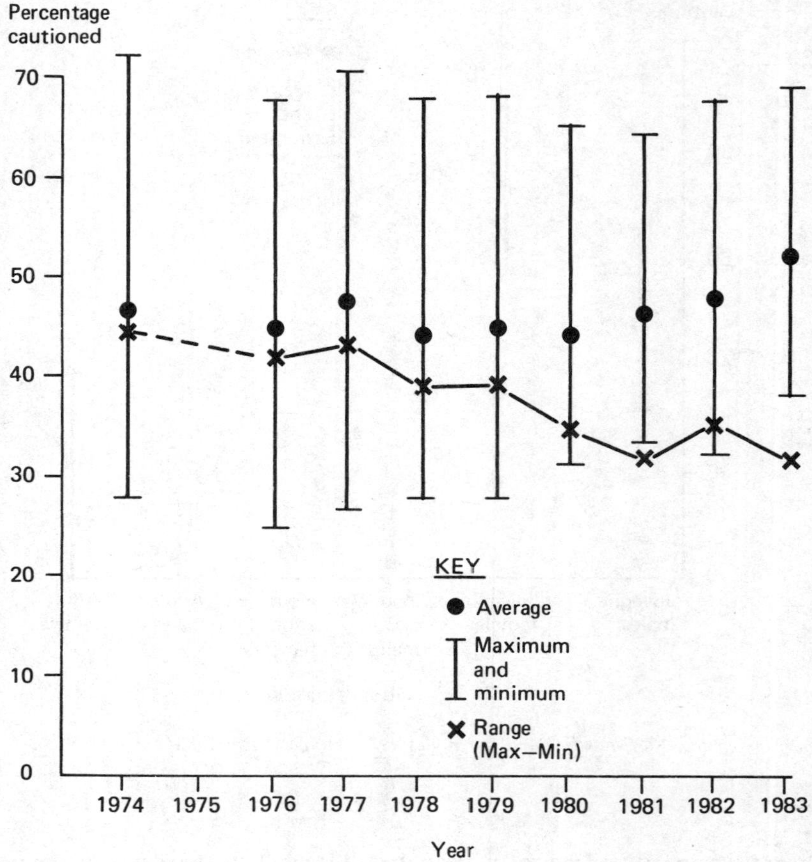

Source: Data provided by Home Office Statistical Department (except for 1975 where data was not available).

individual forces have been described by Redmond-Pyle and Stevens (1983), Miller (1983), and by Mott (1983). Gemmill and Morgan-Giles (1980) have also raised the possible connection between cautioning and other police procedures, in particular arrest, charge and summons.

Ditchfield (1976) is the only researcher to have examined cautioning rates for different groups of offenders and the differences between force areas specifically and in any depth since the changes brought about by the 1969 Act. He showed that different crime patterns accounted for a significant proportion of the actual variation in cautioning rates. He suggested that most of the remaining variation was due to differences between forces in prosecution policy: 'given similar offenders who had committed similar offences, forces apparently differed as to whether or not they would be cautioned' (p.18). Ditchfield could not himself make any direct assessment of police policy nor did he have available any detailed information about offenders, in particular whether they were first offenders or recidivists.

The study described here was designed to fill these gaps. Each chief constable of the 42 police forces in England and Wales and the Commissioner of Police of the Metropolis completed a questionnaire as to policy and practice, forwarded copies of force standing orders, and any other relevant policy documents to the Home Office, and also nine forces were able to provide additional data on offenders cautioned. The results of this exercise are described in the remainder of this chapter. Variations in expressed policy are first described and some effects on practice indicated; secondly some variations in procedure and organisational arrangements are described and discussed. In a final section the implications of these findings for future actions to reduce discrepancies are discussed.

Police force policy

Differences between age groups

Standing orders and other relevant documents show that clear differences in policy underlie differences in cautioning rates between age groups. It is the policy of almost all forces to prosecute young adults and adults unless there is good and sufficient reason not to do so. The major mitigating factor is age – offenders over 60 or 65 years (or those described as 'elderly') might be considered suitable for a caution provided they are also of previous good character (generally taken to mean having no previous or recent cautions or convictions) and the offence is trivial. Other adults considered eligible for a caution are the mentally ill, those disturbed, for example, by recent bereavement, or individuals clearly in great need, for example, 'a mother stealing food for a hungry child'.

On the other hand cautioning of juveniles is encouraged, at least for trivial first offenders. Although not all forces listed the criteria applied when deciding whether or not to caution, the vast majority reported that the offence has to be admitted, has not to be serious, and that the offender has to be prepared to accept the caution and the parents to witness it. Also, the evidence available should be sufficient to support a prosecution in normal circumstances (that is, the conditions set out in Home Office circular 70/78). Twenty-eight forces also noted that they consult the complainant although they do not feel necessarily bound to take notice if there is objection to a proposed caution.

Differences between forces

Although the presumption in favour of prosecuting adults was the policy in all forces, there were differences which contributed to the observed variation in rates between forces. In the Metropolitan Police little discretion is allowed. Force policy is that 'where there is clear evidence of other than a very trifling offence, use of the caution is not justified and the only consideration should be whether to prosecute or not'. The cautioning rate for the Metropolitan Police for all adult offenders was nil (since this research was undertaken the Metropolitan Police has revised its cautioning policy). The stated policy of most other forces was to allow cautions to be given in the special, mitigating circumstances outlined in the preceding section and their cautioning rates reflect this greater permissiveness. The range of cautioning rates for young adult and adult males is relatively small (see Figure 6:1). With the exception of three forces the cautioning rate for these two groups was less than 10 per cent.

For no force was a distinction made in stated policy between adult males and females (despite the fact that Figure 6:1 shows a wide difference in practice). It would appear, therefore, that policy is fairly strictly adhered to in all forces for male offenders, but is interpreted very differently for females in some forces. Much of the difference in cautioning rates for females is attributable to the fact that in some forces shoplifting (which accounts for a large proportion of female offences) is cautioned whilst in others it is not.

The policy documents offer other pointers to the reasons for variation in the cautioning of juveniles. First there was a noticeable difference in the implied approach to cautioning. Many forces stressed flexibility in decision-making thus leaving the decision to caution relatively open. For example 'precise criteria are not laid down to indicate the type of offender and offence as the philosophy is to consider the circumstances of each individual juvenile' (Metropolitan Police) and 'it should be clearly understood that the decision to caution an offender will be made on the individual merit of the case, and will not become a routine response to offences committed by any group or class of offender' (Merseyside Police). These forces both show relatively low juvenile cautioning rates. This policy approach can be contrasted with the approach of forces with high cautioning rates where policy documents express a clear presumption in favour of cautioning 'unless . . .'. For instance, Devon and Cornwall policy is expressed as follows: 'generally a first offender will be cautioned unless the offence is particularly serious or particular local feeling has been aroused' and Essex police policy runs: 'when a juvenile commits an offence which is not serious and this is the first occasion he has come to notice, he will be dealt with by way of an official caution unless the background circumstances indicate that care proceedings should be taken'. Both forces show relatively high cautioning rates.

Despite these differences in implied approach, the policy in all forces is to encourage cautions for juvenile first offenders. It follows therefore that the proportion of offenders who are first offenders will affect cautioning rates. However, the expressed policy on awarding second cautions varies. Eight forces were more explicit in permitting second cautions and amongst this group were the forces with the highest cautioning rates.

The cautioning of first or second offenders

In order to test the effect of these factors some forces were asked to provide more detailed breakdowns of their juvenile cautioning statistics. Unfortunately many forces do not collate their data in such a way as to make the necessary detailed breakdown available. But seven were able to provide the data in the form requested. Information was also available from research studies carried out in two further forces. The forces concerned are listed in a footnote to Table 6:1 below.

The data gathered showed that the proportion of all offenders who were first offenders in any given force was related to actual cautioning rates.

Table 6:1 *Proportion of juveniles cautioned and proportion of first offenders and recidivists cautioned in selected police forces*

Police force	Proportion of offenders cautioned per cent A	Proportion of offenders who were first offenders per cent B	Proportion of first offenders cautioned per cent C	Proportion of recidivists cautioned per cent D
Norfolk	67.5	68.2	84.2	31.7
Suffolk	62.5	76.4	73.0	28.3
Nottinghamshire	60.1	46.2	94.1	31.0
Essex	59.7	60.3	88.6	15.9
Hampshire	56.3	61.9	81.3	15.7
Greater Manchester	48.3	56.0	77.4	11.2
Merseyside	46.6	52.8	69.9	20.5
Cheshire	45.0	54.2	69.0	16.6
Metropolitan Police	37.3	47.1	70.9	7.5

Notes (i) The proportion of offenders cautioned is not the same as the cautioning rate presented in *Criminal Statistics*; it differs in several respects. First the data above includes all juveniles prosecuted even if the case was dismissed or the offender acquitted whereas the cautioning rate includes only those found guilty at the court. Second the offences included differ to some extent both in themselves and possibly in the way they were counted.

(ii) Suffolk, Essex, Merseyside, Cheshire and the Metropolitan Police provided data on all juveniles dealt with for indictable offences in 1982; Nottinghamshire for a similar group dealt with in three months in 1983 and Greater Manchester for the first two months of 1984. The Hampshire data are for 1980 and were obtained from Giller and Covington's current research project (from a personal communication). Norfolk data were obtained from Miller (1983).

As column C (Table 6:1) shows, more than two-thirds of first offenders were cautioned in all nine forces. But the proportion of all offenders who were first offenders varied markedly across force areas from a high 68 per cent and 76 per cent in Norfolk and Suffolk to a low 47 per cent in the Metropolitan Police (column B). The variation in actual cautioning rates (column A) shows that these tended to be high in forces with a high proportion of first offenders and low where first offenders accounted for a smaller proportion of all offenders (column B); (although there are some anomalies – such as the Nottinghamshire rate – which will become clearer when 'second cautioning' is considered below).

This research did not investigate why the proportion of first offenders should differ so markedly by area but there are many possible and obvious reasons including demographic factors, the level of crime and criminality, the proportion of crime that is minor and police practice. Some of these will be subsumed under the variable 'type of crime' which Ditchfield (1976) has already shown to be influential. The point of the analysis from the perspective of this study is to show that variations in actual cautioning rates, though affected by, are not totally dependent on, variations in cautioning policy.

The data gathered were further examined to see the effects of variation in the cautioning of second offenders on cautioning rates. Column D (Table 6:1) shows quite wide variations ranging from 8 per cent (Metropolitan Police) to 32 per cent (Norfolk) in the proportion of recidivists who were given a caution. These variations are roughly in line with stated policy. Suffolk for instance, with 28.3 per cent of recidivists cautioned has standing orders which read 'proceedings will normally be taken if the juvenile has been formally cautioned on TWO separate occasions or has made a court appearance for a similar offence'. Merseyside (recidivist cautioning rate 20.5 per cent) formally states that a second caution may be considered provided the offender has not recently (within three years for a caution or five for a conviction) been dealt with for a similar offence.

Comparison of columns A and D shows, as expected, that forces with low cautioning rates tend to be those who caution low proportions of second and further offences. It can be seen that Nottinghamshire, for instance, which had a surprisingly large proportion of all offenders cautioned (60.1 per cent column A) bearing in mind its low proportion of offenders who were first offenders (46.2 per cent column B) might achieve this high cautioning rate because of the high proportions of second offenders cautioned within that force (column D).

The cautioning of groups of offenders

One other variation in stated policy which can affect cautioning rates must be dealt with before turning to the effects of less formally stated practices: policy for dealing with groups of offenders.

Whilst the overwhelming majority of forces adopt the policy of treating each individual case separately a few respond to all offenders in a group uniformly and in line with the worst individual. Thus in the case of Cleveland 'those offences not thought suitable for a caution are . . . where a juvenile is concerned with an adult in the commission of a crime or antisocial offence'. Bearing in mind that an adult could be as young as 17 this could have an effect on the cautioning rate. The policy can be contrasted with the line taken in

Essex for example (which is more typical): 'where a number of juveniles are concerned in the commission of an offence the adjudication in respect of each of them may well differ'. Whilst this quotation refers to other juveniles rather than adults the principle of the acceptability of different treatment for individuals within a group is an important one.

Procedure and organisational arrangements

In order to achieve a particular objective, policy not only has to be formulated and communicated but the necessary arrangements and procedures need to be made and any impediments removed. It has often been suggested that the initial procedure adopted by the police once a suspect has been apprehended influences his chances of eventually being cautioned. Some possibly relevant organisational arrangements were examined to assess their effects on force cautioning rates.

Summons or charge

If an offender is arrested and charged then the case will probably go to court. The decision to charge a suspect can be taken at a relatively low level usually by the sergeant at the police station. On the other hand if the suspect is not immediately charged but is reported to higher authority to consider appropriate action then the opportunities for cautioning are increased: first because the initial decision is deferred and all subsequent decisions (summons, cautioning, no further action, etc.) have to be ratified at relatively senior levels (for example, superintendent) and, second, because once a person has been reported it may be more economical of police time and manpower to caution him than to summons and prosecute him. It has hence been suggested that 'charging' forces have not kept open an easy option to caution and that this contributes to the low cautioning rates of some forces.

This assertion, if true, would have obvious relevance for any strategy to reduce discrepancies. It has, however, never been directly tested; data on the proportion of offenders summoned are not published. They were made available for this study (for all police forces in England and Wales) by the Statistical Department of the Home Office and also by police forces directly. Results from the analysis indicate that the possible relationship between the use of summonses and of cautions may have been overstated, at least for juveniles. While the correlation between summons rates and cautioning rates for adults was about 0.4 ($p < 0.01$) suggesting a possible connection between the two, the correlation for juveniles was about 0.3 and not statistically significant. (Furthermore, the correlation for juveniles dropped to about 0.2 when two forces with extremely low summons rates were omitted). Also, the vast majority of juveniles taken to court arrive there by means of a summons in most forces. Although the corresponding figures for adults are lower, there remains a substantial number of adults arriving at court from most forces for whom a cautioning option was presumably kept open.

How far summons/charge and cautioning procedures are causally connected is in any case difficult to establish and the little research that has been conducted shows that the link is not straightforward. Gemmill and Morgan-Giles (1980) found that in Bootle, a division of Merseyside Police, 21 per cent of juveniles initially charged went on to be given a formal caution – the charges being dropped after further enquiries. These data shed doubt on the suggestion that forces which prefer to charge offenders necessarily close down their options to caution.

Administrative arrangements
Administrative arrangements vary somewhat between forces, but in the case of juveniles all but two forces operate through a juvenile bureau (or similar organisation), juvenile liaison officers, or other specifically assigned staff who are located at division, sub-division, or force headquarters. However, there did not appear to be any connection between the organisational arrangements adopted and force cautioning rates.

Nor was there a relationship between cautioning rates and whether or not the police consult outside agencies. Before deciding whether to caution juveniles, consultation is both common and extensive under normal circumstances (the exception being where offenders qualify for an early or 'instant' caution as discussed below). On the other hand, it is not common practice for the police to consult other agencies when deciding whether or not to caution adults, although it may happen on rare occasions, and again there was clearly no relationship between the presence or otherwise of consultation arrangements and cautioning rates.

Special early cautioning schemes
One recent innovation which has been adopted or experimented within a number of forces is the special early cautioning schemes, often known as 'instant' cautioning. Their common feature is that the caution may be given within a short period, in most cases a matter of hours of the offender being apprehended. The purpose of such schemes is to reduce the delay in deciding whether to caution, and to avoid many of the time-consuming administrative procedures that would otherwise be necessary (cf. Mott 1983; Frankenburg and Tarling 1983). Prolonged anxiety for the offender associated with waiting for a decision is also reduced. The decision process is also speeded up by the delegation of authority to caution to a lower level than usual and by a clear statement of the criteria to be applied.

Typically the groups now eligible for an early caution are the elderly, those suffering from mental stress, and the young apprehended for the first time for very minor offences. An early caution is given to the elderly because prosecution is not felt to be in the public interest and, following the caution, the offender may be referred to the appropriate social or medical services or relatives may be alerted to the problem. Generally, for juveniles, outside agencies are not consulted before the decision is taken but merely notified after the event. Although some commentators regret the exclusion of probation officers and social workers from the decision-making process, in fact many of these schemes have been drawn up in consultation, and with the agreement of such officials. Furthermore, Mott's (1983) research has shown that for most minor first offenders the social agencies have no prior information on the child to contribute to the decision. At the time of this survey early, immediate or instant cautioning schemes (the name varies though the procedure is much the same) had been introduced or were under active consideration in 14 forces and more recently this number has grown.

Early cautioning schemes have not been in operation long enough to gauge their effect on force cautioning rates. However, they are unlikely to increase overall cautioning rates dramatically or to reduce disparities between forces as the procedure is reserved for very minor or specific cases which, invariably, would have resulted in a caution anyway. Nevertheless, they will have some impact for particular groups. For example, since the introduction of early cautioning in Hampshire, the percentage of elderly offenders cautioned for shoplifting has risen from 68 per cent to 85 per cent.

Discussion

This chapter has presented some fresh data on the question of what underlies differences in cautioning rates. The differential treatment of juveniles and adults is obviously due to policy considerations. The Children and Young Persons Act 1969 and the Home Office's guide to Part 1 of the Act encouraged police forces to consider the welfare of the child and to keep him out of the court as far as possible. These views are clearly reflected in force standing orders; when considering the welfare of the child virtually all forces routinely consult other social agencies, except for first time trivial offenders who qualify for an early caution.

In contrast there is a general presumption in favour of prosecuting adults, although there is an increasing tendency to make special arrangements for the elderly. In addition, some forces have adopted a more lenient approach to young adult and adult female offenders, especially shoplifters. It is with respect to female offenders that the greatest discrepancies and lack of uniformity in practice seem to occur. Without some special effort from the centre similar to that made in the past for juveniles, it is unlikely that the use of cautioning for young adults or male offenders, or for women in some forces will increase.

Not all variation between force practices in cautioning is due to policy. Two predominant factors explaining the observed differences between force cautioning rates for juveniles is the type of crime (Ditchfield, 1976) and the proportion of first offenders in the areas concerned, which varies considerably from force to force. Given such wide variation it is not surprising that cautioning rates differ so markedly. This factor clearly puts a limit on the extent to which differences in force cautioning of juveniles can be reduced. Such differences have been narrowing in recent years but are unlikely ever to disappear completely. Nevertheless the detailed examination of policy documents suggests that some forces could increase the use of cautioning of juveniles, especially by increasing the use of second cautions. Policy regarding groups of offenders could also be clarified and standardised.

It will always be unrealistic to expect all forces to have the same cautioning rates, but each force could be encouraged to evaluate its own practice to see whether force policy is being implemented effectively and whether it should be amended or more precisely defined. Such evaluation depends on the careful collation of statistics. In most forces at present policy is monitored only through internal meetings or conferences and the only information available is from routine statistics showing the number of offenders cautioned or prosecuted by age and offence. The situation is changing. Some forces do, or are intending to, collate more detailed information about the circumstances of the offence and the previous record of the offender. The results of such exercises have enabled these forces to assess more accurately the occasions on which cautions are given and to provide further guidance to officers where necessary. Such assessments may help to reduce variations in force cautioning practice but, given variations in the type of crime and in proportions of all offenders who are first offenders or recidivists some variation must inevitably remain.

7 The prosecution process

ANDREW SANDERS

In this chapter I will relate the pattern of police prosecutions in England and Wales to the way in which prosecutions are organised. A second, and related, aim is to examine the interdependence of police, prosecutors, and court processes. Prosecutions will be shown to occupy a definite structural position in the criminal justice system. This has important implications for reform: altering the powers of prosecutors or individual prosecution arrangements will have little effect if other crucial components of the criminal justice system remain unaltered. I hope, therefore, to establish some general propositions about prosecutions in England and Wales which will remain valid even after the introduction of major changes in the prosecution system.

The research on which this discussion is based took place between 1980 and 1983 and was financed largely by the Economic and Social Research Council (formerly SSRC)[1]. Three police forces were selected. They were picked for their different prosecution procedures, charge:summons ratios, and prosecution:caution ratios. One was a large metropolitan county force (URBAN), one a small rural force (RURAL), and the other policed both rural areas and a city (RURBAL). In URBAN and RURBAL salaried prosecuting solicitors handled all cases, whereas in RURAL there were none. With the police's full cooperation 200 adult non-motoring cases were collected from two divisions or sub-divisions in each force, making a total sample of 1,200 cases. As I was interested in all post arrest/report decisions, the sample should ideally have been constructed from all cases where there were charge decisions (to charge or to refuse charge) and summons decisions. However, refused charges could not be collected, so the sample comprised charged cases and cases in which there was a decision whether or not to summons. Access to the prosecution files and to the officers and prosecuting solicitors involved in decision-making made it possible to probe their criteria for prosecution decisions.

This chapter will examine these criteria principally in relation to adult non-motoring cases, although the same principles apply in juvenile and motoring cases. I shall then go on to discuss how prosecutors exercise their discretion, and the types of control that police and prosecutors exercise over each other.

---

1. The grant of £15,109 (ref. E/00/23/0050/1) was supplemented by a grant of £750 from the Nuffield Foundation. I would like to thank these bodies for this generous financial assistance, and the police forces and Prosecuting Solicitors' Departments which cooperated with me. Of the many colleagues who helped me in this research, I am particularly grateful to Ian Scott and George Cole for their support in its early stages.

Finally I shall examine some of the consequences for court processes. First of all, however, the legal and organisational framework surrounding prosecution decisions needs to be outlined.

The legal framework

Before 1829 neither local nor central government accepted responsibility for day to day law enforcement. Suspects were generally prosecuted, if at all, by the victim, but prosecutions could be initiated by anyone. Then came the new local police forces. Police powers of arrest, search, and interrogation were originally hardly greater than those of the citizen, and no special prosecution powers were provided. So as victims gradually came to expect the police to initiate and conduct prosecutions, the police did so on the same basis as private citizens.

Extra arrest powers have been provided to the police to facilitate their role in prosecutions but the *private* prosecution is still the concept underlying the *police* prosecution. Hence the police, like citizens, have no duty to prosecute any particular case. Unlike in civil law countries, like West Germany, the police need not prosecute every case and no one has the authority to tell the police not to prosecute a particular case. In fact under the doctrine of 'constabulary independence' every police constable has an original, not delegated, prosecution power. In principle the police are answerable for their prosecution decisions and policies, if at all, to the courts alone. Otherwise, police officers have total discretion as to whether or not to prosecute[2]. There are a small number of offences for which prosecutions are controlled by the Attorney-General and Director of Public Prosecutions but this need not concern us here.

Police accountability to the courts was affirmed in *R* v *Commissioner of the Metropolis Ex Parte Blackburn*[3]. In this case the policy of the Metropolitan Police not to prosecute gaming clubs who breached the Gaming and Lotteries Act 1963 was challenged. Lord Denning said that the courts could, in principle, countermand general policy decisions by the police to not prosecute whole classes of offence; but in practice neither in this nor in any other cases have police policies been successfully challenged in the courts. This accountability principle does not apply to decisions to prosecute (or not to prosecute) individual cases at all[4].

The practically unlimited discretion possessed by police in prosecutions was confirmed by the Attorney-General in guidance to the police, when he quoted Lord Shawcross with approval as follows:

---

2. For extended discussions see Marshall (1965) and Jefferson and Grimshaw (1984).
3. 2 WLR 893 (1968).
4. *R* v *Chief Constable of Devon and Cornwall Constabulary ex parte CEGB* (1981). 3 All ER 826.

'It has never been the rule in this country – I hope it never will be – that suspected criminal offences must automatically be the subject of prosecution. Indeed the very first Regulations under which the Director of Public Prosecutions worked provided that he should ... prosecute "wherever it appears that the offence or the circumstances of its commission is or are of such a character that a prosecution in respect thereof is required in the public interest". That is still the dominant consideration.'[5]

The police's right to refuse to prosecute provides the main reason why the citizen's right to initiate private prosecutions has been defended so vigorously. Even now, non-police prosecutions are a significant minority of all prosecutions, although the number of genuine private prosecutions is rather small[6]. The important consequences for this discussion are the enormous variations produced across the country that Laycock and Tarling discuss in Chapter 6.

There are other variations too. Some forces (for instance the Metropolitan Police) leave shoplifting prosecutions to the stores, while in some other forces (for example the West Midlands) 'simple drunkenness' is not prosecuted if the offender is willing and able to attend a 'wet shelter'[7].

The legal framework, then, is as follows. The police effectively have total discretion whether or not to prosecute, as do private and non-police prosecutors. This discretion also extends to the manner in which prosecutions are initiated and handled thereafter. Most are initiated either by way of summons or by arrest without warrant followed by charge and then bail or custody pending the suspect's appearance in court. Prosecutions for most offences – theft, assault, criminal damage and so forth – can be brought in either way. It is not surprising to see that, again, there is considerable discrepancy between police forces. In 1981 11.9 per cent of non-summary adult police prosecutions were by way of summons, but the percentage varied from 63.8 per cent in Dyfed to 0.3 per cent in Cleveland[8]. The legal consequences of each are identical, but we shall see that the consequences for prosecution patterns are not.

Following the decision to prosecute, the police may literally prosecute the case themselves, they may use private solicitors instructed on a case by case basis, or they may hand the case over to a salaried prosecuting solicitor working exclusively for that police force. The latter now predominate and will form the

5. See *Attorney-General: Criteria for prosecution* (Home Office Circular 26/1983).
6. See Lidstone *et al.* (1980).
7. Other variations are noted by Brogden (1982), Chapter 5.
8. Unpublished Home Office statistics.

basis of the Crown Prosecution Service soon to be introduced[9]. Until then the police may choose which cases to give prosecutors. They also decide at what stage in the development of a case (prior to its first appearance in court) the prosecutor should be involved – and this will remain true of most cases even when Crown Prosecutors are introduced, although the latter will have additional powers to, for instance, drop those cases.

Police discretion: structure

In adult non-motoring cases suspects are generally dealt with in four ways, as shown in Figure 7:1. Cases dealt with in boxes 2, 3 and 4 are all classified for the purposes of the criminal statistics as 'detected'.

Figure 7:1 *Prosecution decisions: the main choices*

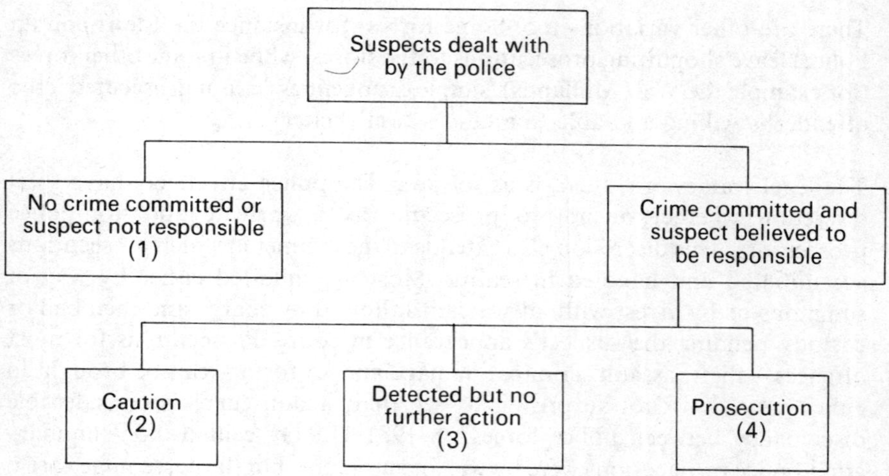

Table 7:1 illustrates the variation between police forces in this research. The overall caution rate (3.5 per cent) corresponds roughly with the national caution rate in adult non-motoring cases. There are no national figures on 'no crime' and 'no further action' rates, but in Gemmill and Morgan-Giles' samples some 12–15 per cent of adult non-motoring suspects apprehended by the police fall into these categories[10]. In juvenile cases much higher percentages are not prosecuted.

9. Under the Prosecution of Offences Act 1985. This is based, with modifications, on the White Paper: *An Independent Prosecution Service for England and Wales* (1983), and the Royal Commission on Criminal Procedure's recommendations. See its Report (1981).
10. R Gemmill and R Morgan-Giles, 1981, Table 3.7.

Table 7:1 *Prosecutions and non-prosecutions**

	(1) No crime/ suspect not responsible	(2) Caution	(3) Detected, but no further action	(4) Prosecution	TOTAL
RURAL	15	25	3	357	400
URBAN	4	11	2	383	400
RURBAL	18	9	4	369	400
Total	37	45	9	1,109	1,200

*Since refused charges were not collected column (1) could give a misleading impression of non-prosecutions, although the caution rate is not affected by this.

Clearly, the decision whether or not to prosecute is rarely a foregone conclusion. But neither this, nor the great variation in caution rates, should distract our attention from the primary prosecution pattern. This is, for adults, a prosecution rate, at its most variable, of 75–85 per cent, with most police forces clustering near the higher figure[11]. There is then, in all forces, a propensity to prosecute.

This observation might seem unremarkable: of course most suspected offenders are prosecuted. But there is no 'of course' about it. Motoring offences are habitually cautioned, informally and formally.

Admittedly these offences are often trivial, although not necessarily more so than drunkenness and prostitution, which the police readily prosecute. Nor are the majority of offences dealt with by non-police agencies like the Factory Inspectorate and Inland Revenue more trivial than those with which the police deal. Yet those bodies' prosecution patterns form a mirror-image of those of the police: they have a propensity to *not* prosecute. Instead, a variety of administrative sanctions are used, perceptively described by one report as a system of 'extended cautioning'[12]. And in many other countries the police are not expected habitually to prosecute[13].

The police propensity to prosecute therefore needs to be explained, rather than taken for granted. Explanation has two components: why? and how? The former could not be systematically probed in the research reported here although the next section will shed some light upon it. But we can consider 'how' in some detail.

11. *Ibid.*
12. Law Commission: Strict liability and the Enforcement of Factories Act (1970). For a detailed comparison of police and non-police prosecutions, see Sanders (1985b).
13. See Leigh and Hall-Williams (1982).

The organisational framework in which adult CID decisions are taken varies, as Figure 7:2 shows in a simplifed form. Other police forces probably structure their decision-making in other ways, but these three forces are similar in their essentials and doubtless this is true of all forces. The underlying principles, at least as far as summons procedures are concerned, are also present in juvenile and motoring cases.

Summons cases

The report for summons usually involves the officer in charge (usually a detective constable) presenting a full written file to his detective sergeant, who would then recommend a decision and pass the file (if it is satisfactory) to the detective inspector (DI). The DI can decide to prosecute. If however he does not wish to prosecute he has to refer the case to his superior (DCI) – who also has the power to prosecute but not to refrain from prosecuting. This is usually the prerogative of the detective superintendent (D.Supt.)[14]. Thus the decision to prosecute is generally taken at a relatively low level while the decision to not prosecute is taken at a relatively high level. To not prosecute requires at least three senior officers to agree, while to prosecute requires the unilateral decision of only one (and any one) of those three officers. So police summons procedures create a propensity to prosecute. In 14 of 120 positive summons decisions (over 10 per cent) the three senior officers failed to agree. Twelve of these were in RURAL out of that force's 74 summonses (16 per cent). In a further six cases the officer in charge's recommendation was overruled, although there were another eight cases where the reverse occurred. But the basic principle is 'when in doubt, prosecute':

> (WN194) (RURAL) The suspect, aged 48, was a shop cleaner. She admitted stealing £4, but had denied stealing money that had gone missing earlier. Cautions were recommended by the officer in the case, his sergeant, and the DI on the grounds of her clean record, lack of education, and absence of evidence that she was responsible for the earlier thefts. The DCI however, thought that she 'was persistently stealing from her employer . . . I cannot see any mitigation.' She was summonsed[15].

These procedures are designed to minimise corruption. Accusations of the kind of behaviour that led to the dismissal of Stanley Parr, Chief Constable of Lancashire, who in the 1970s interfered in the prosecution of a friend's son, are feared. Thus the police centralise decisions to not prosecute but they have no similar concerns with regard to positive prosecution decisions, despite frequent criticism that they prosecute too readily. The police argue that it is

14. In many forces inspectors may decide to administer an 'instant caution'. Where this is contemplated there may be no written file. However these are only the more obvious cases for caution – usually juveniles and old age pensioners. See the discussion in the Home Office Consultative Document on cautioning (1985b) and Home Office Circular 14/1985.

15. Minor details in these cases have been changed in order to preserve their anonymity.

Figure 7:2 *Advice and decision making (CID cases) (adults)*

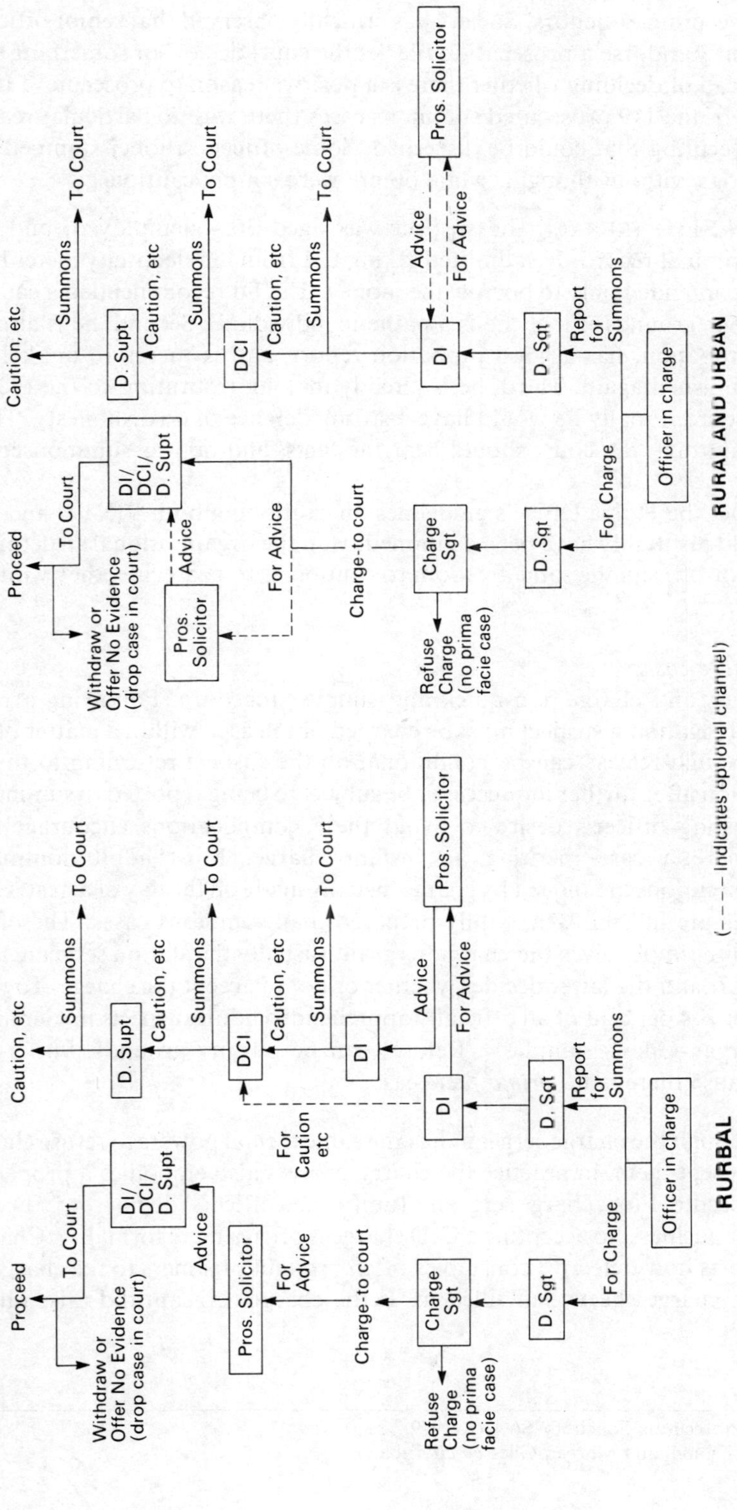

for the court, not the police, to decide upon guilt and innocence. Indeed, the Prosecuting Solicitors' Society has critically observed that senior officers frequently endorse a prosecution file 'let the court decide' or something similar, instead of deciding whether there is a positive reason to prosecute[16]. In forty-two of the 119 prosecuted summons cases there was no particular reason for prosecuting that could be discerned. Some officers 'rubber stamped' prosecutions without thought, while others were simply cautious:

> (WS131) (RURAL) The suspect was aged 36, unemployed, and with a criminal record. He admitted taking £31 from his electricity meter but said he intended only to borrow the money. The DI recommended a caution on four grounds. First, 'he is a pathetic individual'. Second, he is already on probation, has a good probation report, and is therefore unlikely to be punished again. Third, he is already making restitution to the Electricity Board. Finally he would have a strong defence of no dishonesty. The DCI said that 'the court should hear the facts' and he was summonsed.

Under the Home Office's guidelines on cautioning both WN194 and WS131 could justifiably have been cautioned. Had the organisational structure given junior officers the same freedom to caution as to prosecute, they would have been.

Charge cases

Arrest and charge is a quick and simple procedure. Following arrest and interrogation a suspect must be charged or released within a matter of hours. Although release can be conditional on the suspect returning to the police station after further inquiries, or be subject to being reported to summons, the arresting officer's desire to avoid these complications encourage him to prepare a case meriting an instant charge. Most adult non-motoring prosecutions are indeed by charge, usually made on the day of arrest. Charged cases are inevitably less fully prepared than summons cases. The officer in charge simply gives the charge sergeant (usually the station sergeant) an oral report and the latter decides whether or not to accept the charge. To refuse is rare: 2–4 per cent of all officially apprehended adult suspects in Gemmill and Morgan-Giles's samples[17]. Refusal can be on any grounds, but is usually because there is no *prima facie* case.

Although the charge sergeant has the same formal powers to refuse charges as to accept them, in practice the charge process also embodies a propensity to prosecute. First, charge sergeants (uniformed officers) do not see CID work as their business, so accepting a CID charge is often a mere formality. Chatterton reports how detective constables often brought prisoners to the charge office with charge sheets half filled in. If the charge sergeant did raise questions

16. Prosecuting Solicitors' Society (1979).
17. Gemmill and Morgan-Giles *op cit* Table 3.7.

about the evidence he was usually mollified by the assurance of a guilty plea or a confession[18].

Secondly even charge sergeants who wish to screen cases effectively find it impossible. Nearly all evidence on which they base their evaluation is presented orally by the officer(s) asking for the prosecution to take place. As the Prosecuting Solicitors' Society has said 'The view of the charge sergeant . . . must therefore be gained from what he is told by the investigating officer. As an independent check this must be almost without value'[19]. Here is an example:

> (ED115) (RURBAL) P, a 39-year-old with no criminal record, shoplifted goods worth £9. She confessed, saying she took them to cheer up her daughter following the death of her other daughter. Following her arrest and charge the DI asked whether the defendant had medical problems and whether the circumstances had been explained to the charge sergeant. The arresting officer replied that, unknown to the charge sergeant, P did have medical problems. Although most of the police officers involved felt that P should not have been charged, they did not feel the process should be stopped on the grounds of sympathy. But the case was in fact dropped.

Thus, information which could lead to caution or no futher action on grounds of too little evidence can be easily concealed from the decision maker – either deliberately, accidentally, or because it was simply not known at that early stage of the case. Hence 23 (out of 989) charge cases were positively identified as cases that would not have been prosecuted had they been reported for summons. There was an unknown number of others which would, or could, have not been prosecuted. They are unknown precisely because the arresting officer did not need to discover or to disclose the relevant information to the charge sergeant.

Thirdly, a charge sergeant will occasionally refuse a charge because the case is clearly cautionable. This however does not end the case – it simply re-allocates that case to the summons channel where it runs the gauntlet described earlier. Cautionable cases submitted for charge, then, need the agreement of four officers if there is to be no prosecution.

Summary

The question 'how do most adult non-motoring cases come to be prosecuted?' can now be answered. The police structure their decision-making to this end. This is the inevitable result. We have seen that there is nothing in the law to require this. It is therefore their choice.

---

18. See Chatterton (1975) and his paper in King (ed.) (1976).
19. Prosecuting Solicitors' Society, *op cit* para 3.3.

Consider the organisational framework of decision-making in non-police agencies – which prosecute as rarely as the police caution. In the Factory Inspectorate, for instance, a Factory Inspector (the equivalent of the officer in charge) who takes official cognisance of an offence can do one of four things. He can take no action or informal action (an unofficial caution), or issue an enforcement notice (extended caution). All these actions may be taken without authorisation from his superiors. Only if he wishes to take the fourth course of action, to prosecute the offender, need he prepare a report for his Principal Inspector.

Thus while any one police officer (from Inspector level upwards) can authorise a summons, but more than one have to agree if there is not to be a summons, in the Factory Inspectorate any one inspector can decide to not summons, but two must agree if there is to be a summons. Disagreements in the Factory Inspectorate lead to no prosecution, while in the police force they do lead to prosecution. The divergent prosecution patterns of the two types of agency are therefore inevitable and far outweigh the differences between particular police forces or between particular non-police agencies[20].

Police discretion: criteria for prosecution

Since the police are under no obligation to prosecute what criteria should they use in exercising their discretion? As part of the movement towards a Crown Prosecution Service operating consistent criteria, the Attorney-General issued *Criteria for Prosecution* in 1983. They are intended to guide both police officers in their initial prosecution decisions and prosecutors in later stages[21]. The Home Office Guidelines on Cautions broadly endorse their structure.

Weak cases

The Guidelines state the first question to be whether there is sufficient evidence. This is taken, in normal cases, to be a reasonable prospect of conviction (the DPP's '51 per cent rule') rather than just a *prima facie* case. The aim here is to reduce acquittals as there is a considerable body of evidence to suggest that weak cases are a major source of acquittals[22]. The research was carried out before these Guidelines were issued. To see whether they are likely to have any effect we need to consider why weak cases arise in the first case.

First there are 'resource charges' (Chatterton, *op cit*). These occur where the prosecution is not an end in itself, but a by-product of policing public order problems.

20. For a fuller discussion see Sanders (1985b).
21. The Guidelines and their probable effects are critically analysed by Sanders (1985a).
22. See, for instance, McConville and Baldwin (1981), Chapter 5, and Royal Commission on Criminal Procedure (1981a) (paras 6.18 and 6.22).

(EC129) (RURBAL) A group of football supporters were throwing stones at a car with rival supporters. The group included the defendant, who denied throwing anything. He was arrested and charged with threatening behaviour. The defence asked if this could be dropped if the defendant agreed to be bound over. The prosecuting solicitor advised the police to accept this and they did agree. The prosecuting solicitor described the charge as 'a bit thin . . . just enough evidence . . . being at a football match he starts with a disadvantage . . . it's a classic case of a charge before we've had a chance to advise'. He considered the case had a less than even chance of success. The same prosecuting solicitor in another case (which he lost) in the same disturbance said 'the police in RURBAL don't take section 5 seriously enough'.

In this kind of case, weakness is inevitable not so much because the police don't take these cases seriously but because they have in mind sorting out their public order problems rather than the eventual decision in court. However these weak cases do not inevitably fail, for many defendants plead guilty[23]. These cases are a special type of 'policy prosecution', a term originally coined by McCabe and Purves (1972b). There are many other types of policy prosecutions.

(MC121) (URBAN) The suspect (C) reported his car stolen, along with £82. When the police found the car with the money missing he admitted that he had made the story up: he had hoped to hide the fact that he had spent the £82, which he owed to the company for whom he worked part-time. The detective sergeant recommended a caution because the company did not want to see him prosecuted, because of C's generally good character, and because the police had wasted little time over the incident. But the DI decided to prosecute for the theft of the £82 for he deserved to be prosecuted for wasting police time. Also the company did not wish to prosecute because they did not want it known that they employed people (like C) who were claiming social security. The detective sergeant said that the case would cause problems, as they would not be able to prove that the money belonged to the company, but this deterred neither his superior officers nor the prosecuting solicitors. The prosecution would, said the latter, scare people like C and the company in future. The defence successfully submitted there was no case to answer following legal submissions at the trial.

Many weak cases are simply the product of hasty charges or carelessness. Weaknesses are revealed only after the charge is made because of the charge sergeant's limited role:

(EC075) (RURBAL) The suspect took a taxi with a friend. On arrival at the destination he said he had no money, was clearly drunk, and left. He was

23. This was true of both this project and others. See, for instance, Baldwin and McConville (1977).

arrested and charged with making off without payment under the Theft Act 1978. He was held in custody. It later became clear that he had written his name, address, and '£2.50' on a card for the taxi driver. The prosecuting solicitor wrote to the police: 'I feel very strongly that this is not a matter we should proceed with. We cannot prove the dishonesty element as he gave his name and address.'

The charge process is inevitably less efficient in screening out weak cases than is the summons process (where supervising officers consider written files at leisure). So police officers wishing to press resource charges will use the charge process *in order that* these weak cases can be prosecuted. This can be equally true of policy prosecutions in general. Thus while the fundamental flaws of the charge process remain, weak cases will continue to be prosecuted no matter what guidelines there may be. Forces that habitually charge, as distinct from summons, then, will inevitably prosecute higher numbers of weak cases than will other forces.

Policy prosecutions are prosecutions aimed at operationalising policing policies. Prosecution is therefore frequently an adjunct to *policing*, and policing priorities shape prosecution patterns[24]. The source of the police propensity to prosecute therefore lies in the police's law enforcement priorities. Non-police agencies have different aims and seek to further them in different ways: their prosecution patterns are accordingly different. Clearly it is too simplistic entirely to separate different law enforcement functions in units within a particular agency: interdependence between policing 'on the ground' and police prosecution practices is as important as that between the police and other agencies. In directing their attention at police prosecution, rather than police law enforcement, processes the Attorney-General's Guidelines ignore the source of our current difficulties. As such they are likely to have little impact on the prosecution of weak cases.

'The public interest'

The Guidelines state that if there is a reasonable prospect of conviction a second question must then be asked: whether prosecution would be 'in the public interest'. The relevant factors are: the likely penalty, staleness, youth, old age and infirmity, mental illness or stress, whether the victim was a willing party in sexual offences, and the attitude of a complainant. The more serious the offence, the more overwhelming these factors have to be to justify a caution. If, following these considerations, there is doubt about the desirability of prosecution, the accused's character, the community's attitude, and the prevalence of the offence are all to be taken into account. If doubt still remains 'the final arbiter must be the court'.

24. Similar conclusions are reached by Chatterton, *op cit* and Bittner (1979). The pattern of non-prosecutions is shaped in the same way. See Sanders, *op cit*, page 13.

Juvenile cautioning is approached entirely differently, with a pro-caution presumption, in the Home Office Guidelines. But the Home Office Guidelines on adult cautions also modify the Attorney-General's harsh approach. The 'offender's previous record and character' is to be a reason for caution in itself, subject (as are all the criteria) to the seriousness of the alleged offence. This is just as well, as some police forces already take this factor into account. The problem is that some do not, and some do more than others. Table 7:2 shows the reasons for not prosecuting in my own research.

Table 7:2 *Reasons for not prosecuting*

Reason	No crime/ suspect not responsible	Detected but no further action	Caution	Total
Weak case (insufficient evidence)	21	1	3	25
Factors associated with victim: that undermine the case, victim's wishes etc	4	3	13	20
Suspects attitude, character and age	3	2	15	20
Triviality of offence	4	2	10	16
Other	4	1	5	10
Total	36	9	46	91

This is broadly consistent with Steer's (1970) findings[25]. However, the different forces were not consistent with each other (or indeed within themselves). For instance, RURAL gave as many cautions because of the suspect's character (seven, excluding those cautioned on the grounds of age) as the other two forces put together. Similar offences, and similar offenders, are simply dealt with differently. Compare these cases, all involving young men with no previous convictions:

> (WN098) (RURAL) G, a 17-year-old shop worker, shoplifted chocolate worth 14p. He was cautioned because he appeared remorseful and because of its low value.

> (MC163) (URBAN) R, a 17-year-old West Indian, was seen taking a newspaper (worth 14p) from outside a shop. He was arrested and charged with theft. The DI endorsed the file: 'though a small amount involved this is a regular crime in the area and I find PC P's action commendable in view of being off-duty'. He was fined £10.

25. Note that cautions are sometimes given because of insufficient evidence, in direct contradiction to all official rules.

(ED050) (RURBAL) H and X caused £10 worth of damage to a road sign, which X hid under his jacket. They denied intending to damage or steal it. They were drunk. The DCI decided that a prosecution was not worth the effort, especially as H and X might plead not guilty: 'I feel like making an example of yobbos like this but we will caution . . . it's the easy way out.'

(WN147–150) (RURAL) Four drunken youths were carrying a road sign. Three confessed to intending to steal it, but the fourth denied this. He was backed up by the other three. All four were prosecuted. The DCI regarded all of them as 'hooligans'. Even if the fourth were acquitted he would have been 'taught a lesson'. All four pleaded guilty and were fined.

Since cautions are rarely considered appropriate for adult males there is little scope for inconsistency. Even so these cases show how disparate different forces', and different individuals', cautioning policies are. Decision-making on female suspects, particularly in shoplifting cases, was even more inconsistent.

Another common type of case involved youths driving friends' cars without a licence. The youths told the police that they had told their friends they had licences. This protected their friends but was, if true, technically an offence under the Theft Act 1968. None of the three cases of this type in RURBAL were prosecuted. RURAL was less sympathetic, prosecuting most of them.

Guidelines are intended to provide a basis for superior officers' changing the decisions or recommendations of junior officers. The question, as with weak cases, is whether junior officers' desire to prosecute cautionable individuals can be effectively restrained. The summons procedure certainly provides that opportunity, although inconsistency is not thereby removed: WN147–150 and ED050 (above) are both summons cases. But the charge procedure provides no such opportunity. The facts that make a case cautionable may be unknown or unrevealed to the charge sergeant who, as we have seen, is not easily able to inquire into the case or to set the cautioning machinery into motion. ED115 (above) is an excellent example of the charge process allowing the relevant information to be obscured.

Just as it is inevitable that forces with high charge:summons ratios have higher percentages of weak cases than other forces (and Table 7:3 below supports this assertion), so those forces will have higher prosecution:non-prosecution ratios. It is true that, as Tarling and Laycock point out (in Chapter 6) there is only a weak correlation between adult summons and cautioning rates, and none in juvenile cases. But Table 7:1 shows that although RURBAL cautions fewer cases than either URBAN or RURAL, its overall non-prosecution rate (shown in Table 7:4 below) was 8 per cent (as against 4 per cent and 11 per cent respectively). In short, in cases that RURAL would have cautioned, RURBAL decided to not prosecute in other ways. Significantly, RURBAL's charge:summons ratio was nearly as low as RURAL's, while URBAN's was very high. In discussing the relationship between summons, charge, and prosecution rates we need to remember that cautioning is only one way of avoiding prosecution. No guidelines intended to alter prosecution rates can succeed without attending to other policing matters such as law enforcement and organisational policy.

The prosecutor

Crown Court prosecutions are conducted by barristers instructed, as always, on a case by case basis. Most police prosecutions in magistrates' courts are now conducted by salaried prosecuting solicitors. Because of the nature of police prosecutions (their legal character being that of private prosecutions) salaried prosecutors are in a solicitor/client relationship with the police in the same way that other solicitors would be. Thus prosecuting solicitors cannot stop cases which they think should not be prosecuted. At best they can simply refuse to prosecute any such case, leaving it for the police themselves to prosecute. The Prosecuting Solicitors' Society has observed that, although rare, this does occasionally happen[26].

Police forces use their prosecuting solicitors in different ways. Figure 7:2 shows that URBAN and RURAL rarely seek advice from prosecutors prior to deciding whether to prosecute or indeed after guilty pleas in the magistrates' courts[27]. To do so is, anyway, difficult in charge cases where there is no file on which the prosecuting solicitor can advise before charge (and often no full file at any time). Thus most forces seek advice only rarely. RURBAL is unusual in regularly seeking advice at as early a stage as possible. Combined with its lower charge:summons ratio this means that a relatively high percentage of its cases are advised upon prior to the initial prosecution decision. As to what the police may do with this advice the situation is clear:

> 'The solicitor may offer advice but the final decisions on who should be prosecuted for what offence rests with the police. This is equally true if any question arises whether a prosecution should be withdrawn at any stage.'[28]

As Weatheritt reported in her empirical study for the Royal Commission on Criminal Procedure:

> 'On occasions the police feel unable to follow the advice of prosecuting solicitors. It was stressed that these occasions were rare. The most common source of disagreement seems to be over sufficiency of evidence . . . there are also disputes about the law.'[29]

26. Prosecuting Solicitors' Society, *op cit*.
27. This discussion is true only of the largest prosecuting solicitors' area in URBAN, and at the time of the research. Since then advice has become increasingly common in URBAN.
28. Royal Commission on Criminal Procedure (1981b), para 143.
29. Weatheritt (1981), paras 2.39 and 2.40.

The practice of different police forces – in asking for advice and acting upon it – depends, in part, upon their relationships with their prosecutors:

> 'Because good relationships are essential to the successful functioning of a prosecuting solicitors' department, both the chief constables and the chief prosecuting solicitors lay great emphasis in their replies on the avoidance of conflict, the importance of compromise and consensus, and the ability of the two parties to get on well with each other. If prosecuting solicitors' departments do achieve an independence, it is because the police are willing to trust them with it.'[30]

A 'no-win' situation arises: independent decision-making and advice giving is only possible if the police habitually use prosecuting solicitors at an early stage. Yet this atmosphere of trust only develops if prosecuting solicitors provide palatable advice or, at the least, willingly and enthusiastically prosecute cases in which their unpalatable advice has been rejected.

One might think that future prosecutors' new powers will free them from the need to compromise in order to cultivate independence. This is certainly the stated aim of the government's legislation. In future, all cases which the police decide to prosecute, apart from minor motoring, will be handled by salaried prosecutors (Crown Prosecutors). They will have the power to drop any cases they wish[31]. There is, though, reason to believe that prosecutors' weakness rests far more upon their structural position in the criminal justice system than upon their formal powers.

First, prosecutors can only exert limited influence over cautioning if they do not see cautioned cases. Any inconsistency stemming from some police forces being more caution-minded than official policy dictates will remain. Prosecutors cannot achieve consistency with regard to cases that they will never see.

Secondly we have seen that prosecutors may advise on cases before the initial prosecution is taken as well as after – but only at the discretion of the police. The difference is important. As one prosecuting solicitor put it: 'Your advice has to be given with regard to whether the case is charged or not.' Edwards observes that even the DPP makes this distinction[32]. To stop a case before a decision to prosecute has been made is relatively easy. The case is cautioned or otherwise not prosecuted. But to stop a case following a decision to prosecute is rather more difficult. No evidence is offered in court, and the defendant is acquitted, or the case is withdrawn in court, with a similar effect. Thus Weatheritt suggests that:

---

30. Weatheritt, *op cit*, para 2.47
31. In fact this power is subject to a judicial veto in the Crown Court, on cases being dropped. (See Sanders, 1985c.)
32. Edwards, 1984, Chapter 14.

'Once the wheels of prosecution have been set in motion by the police and the presumption is in favour of prosecuting, it may be easier for a prosecuting solicitor to continue to trial with a case than to seek to drop it.'[33]

Prosecutors prefer to disassociate themselves from a potentially bad case, rather than to tangle with the police, become involved in an acrimonious row, and (even if they win that particular battle) put themselves in a weak situation in the future. It is not worth the effort of fighting, especially as many cases succeed despite their evidential shortcomings:

(ED099) (RURBAL) V and W were arrested and charged with burglary. The prosecuting solicitor's 'advice' to the police regarding V was: 'I'm pleased to see that DC* mentions in his report that this accused has intimated a guilty plea. As the file stands there is not a scrap of evidence against him apart from the admissions made by the co-accused' (who could not be compelled to give evidence against V).

Dropping such cases in court embarrasses the police and amounts to what the police regard as unnecessary public criticism. Weeding out weak cases and bringing low cautioning forces like Cheshire (1 per cent in adult indictable cases) up to the average (3.5 per cent) would currently involve dropping thousands of cases, in public, each year in many forces.

The prospects for the future are difficult to predict with confidence. If Crown Prosecutors try to control police prosecutions in this way, they could ruin their relationship with the police. This could, ironically, actually reduce their prosecution role, for the police may be less inclined to involve them in the process at the early stage at which they could influence the prosecution pattern. On the other hand, prosecutors who are prepared to flex their muscles could thereby persuade the police that to have prosecutors 'interfering' at an early stage is preferable to them doing so when the case comes to court. This could become an interdependent relationship of the greatest delicacy, for it cannot be easily legislated for. The charge process, for instance, makes pre-prosecution advice very difficult. Thus in relation to one case with which a prosecutor had problems (EC073) I asked the prosecuting solicitor: 'Shouldn't the police report (for a summons decision) cases that are difficult like this?' He replied: 'It's because they are difficult that they don't let us see them first . . . perhaps that's too cynical.' This was from RURBAL, where there was a high rate of summonsing, pre-prosecution advice, and a co-operative relationship.

The Prosecution of Offences Act does attempt, in a piecemeal way, to deal with these problems. For instance, in certain cases the police will have to seek

---

33. Weatheritt, *op cit*, para 2.19.

pre-prosecution advice (s.8). This is intended for complex and sensitive cases. Also, discontinuance of proceedings by Crown Prosecutors will be possible, in some circumstances, without the court appearance that can currently embarrass the police (s.23). The difficulty here is that these provisions rely for their effectiveness on potential problems being recognised by constables and sergeants (in relation to s.8) and Crown Prosecutors (in relation to s.23) at a very early stage of the cases in question.

Prosecutors can only exercise discretion if they have information on which to do so. For this they rely upon the police. Yet we have seen that the charge process, in particular, leads to much relevant information never being revealed or discovered. In ED115 (above) the fact that the defendant would certainly have been cautioned had all the facts been known originally did not stop any officers arguing that prosecution should not be stopped. This was not unusual. ED115 was remarkable for the fact that it *was* dropped on these grounds – and, perhaps, for the fact that the relevant facts were known to senior officers at all.

Prosecutorial discretion is therefore constrained more by prosecutors' dependence on the police than by limited powers. The stage at which prosecutors are involved in cases, and the information they are given, are the most important matters. These are, and will continue to be, largely matters for the police. The police are, and will continue to be, influenced in these matters partly by their own law enforcement concerns and partly by the way the prosecutor handles the police and their cases.

The importance of procedures rather than powers is highlighted by the fact that although prosecuting solicitors can refuse to prosecute cases they consider are brought improperly (if, for instance, there is no *prima facie* case) they never did so in my research or in Baldwin and McConville's (1981), despite occasional but clear absence of minimal evidential standards. The DPP has always had the power to drop any case, but as we have seen he too is constrained by his position of dependence upon the police. Similarly Moody and Tombs found that prosecutors in Scotland, who have more formal powers than English prosecutors will have, had little freedom of action in practice: the police set the agenda and so 'in most cases not to proceed would be out of the question'[34]. One final case illustrates many of these points:

> (MC119) (URBAN) A and X were involved in a fight. Both were charged with wounding. When the full file reached the prosecutor, some three months after A had been charged, the officer in charge wrote 'it may be felt that there is *insufficient evidence against* A in view of the fact that at the time of the incident the complainant was suffering from the effect of drink and it is only his evidence that indicates that A struck him with the hammer . . .'. The emphasised phrase was underlined by the prosecuting solicitor who wrote 'Too true'. He told the police that 'there is insufficient evidence to justify

34. Moody and Tombs, 1982, page 58.

proceedings' and it was agreed to offer no evidence against A. This interview took place between him and myself:

AS: 'Do you think there is a *prima facie* case here?'

PS: 'Not really ... well perhaps just about.'

AS: 'What would you have done if the police had not agreed to offer no evidence?'

PS: 'Not a lot. I'd have done the committal and expected to lose at the Crown Court. The police would have got a lot of egg on their faces.'

Prosecutions and court processes

I have argued that there is a propensity to prosecute in England and Wales which is not a product of the law. It is a product of policies and procedures about which prosecutors can do little because of their dependence on the police. There is however a degree of interdependence because the prosecutor has some freedom of manoeuvre once the case is in court. This argument can be supported with some data on court results. They also illustrate the relationship between prosecution practices and court processes.

Table 7:3 shows that considerably more cases in URBAN than in the other two forces were dropped in court. These are cases where no evidence is offered or which are withdrawn in court (NEO)[35]. This could be because there are more weak cases requiring rejection in URBAN than in other forces, or it could be because URBAN prosecutors zealously weed out cases that would go to trial elsewhere. There is considerably more evidence of the former explanation than the latter.

Table 7:3 *Court results*

	(a) Not prosecuted	(b) No court result (eg defendant did not appear)	(c) Guilty (inc mixed results)	(d) Not guilty (following trial)	(e) Not guilty (NEO)	(f) Total
RURAL	43 (11%)	5 (1%)	318 (79%)	15 (4%)	19 (5%)	400
(EC)	42 (11%)	8 (2%)	324 (81%)	18 (5%)	8 (2%)	
URBAN	17 (4%)	15 (4%)	308 (77%)	14 (4%)	46 (11%)	400
(ED)	20 (5%)	16 (4%)	336 (84%)	6 (2%)	22 (6%)	
RURBAL	31 (8%)	12 (3%)	330 (83%)	12 (3%)	15 (4%)	400
Total	91 (8%)	32 (3%)	956 (79%)	41 (3%)	80 (7%)	1,200

*EC is the rural and ED the urban division of RURBAL. The figures shown for EC and ED are *double* the actual numbers to provide direct comparison with URBAN and RURAL.

35. In these tables cases are classified as complete acquittals (following trial or NEO) if this was true of the complete case in the research sample. Some of these cases were, however, part of a series of charges in reality.

First, Table 7:3 shows that all three forces had similar numbers of acquittals following trial (taking magistrates' courts and the Crown Court together). Hence URBAN's NEOs are not *instead* of unsuccessful trials, but in addition to them.

Secondly, NEOs were more often a result of intrinsic weakness in URBAN than elsewhere, as Table 7:4 shows.

Table 7:4 *Reasons for NEO*

	Weak cases (insufficient evidence)	Factors associated with victim	Plea bargaining	Triviality	Suspect's age	NK composite reasons	Total
RURAL	6 (32%)	1 (5%)	3 (16%)	1 (5%)	0	8 (42%)	19
(EC)	4 (50%)	2 (25%)	0	0	0	2 (25%)	(8)
URBAN	15 (33%)	5 (11%)	9 (20%)	3 (7%)	0	14 (30%)	46
(ED)	12 (54%)	2 (10%)	0	0	8 (37%)	0	(22)
RURBAL	8 (53%)	2 (13%)	0	0	4 (27%)	1 (7%)	15
Total	29 (37%)	8 (10%)	12 (15%)	4 (5%)	4 (5%)	23 (29%)	80

Now, both weakness and the associated high acquittal rate in URBAN may be associated with, quite simply, its *urban* character. We might expect *urban* crime to be different from *rural* crime. To test this we can compare RURAL with the rural division of RURBAL (EC), and URBAN with the urban division of RURBAL (ED) (a city with similar characteristics to URBAN, though on a smaller scale). This does indicate an urban/rural dimension, but not one that adequately explains the differences between our police forces (see Tables 7:3 and 7:4).

Thirdly, if prosecutors zealously weed out weak cases they would be expected to do so as soon as possible. Table 7:5 shows that this was generally true of RURBAL (and RURAL where, of course, actual police officers often prosecuted), but not true of URBAN. In URBAN, cases were dropped at the last, rather than the first, moment. MC119 (above) is a typical example, where this was largely due to the prosecutors not having the information on which to base NEO decisions until a later stage. In other cases, however, prosecutors hung on hoping for a guilty plea. This happened in the other forces too, but less often.

Table 7.5 *Number of court hearings for NEO cases*

	Number of hearings			
	1 or 2	3	4+	Total
RURAL	11	4	4	19
URBAN	15	12	19	46
RURBAL	12	2	1	15
Total	38	18	24	80

Putting these points together, it seems that forces which habitually arrest and charge produce more weak cases than those with higher summons:charge ratios, leading to a higher overall acquittal rate in the former forces. Unfortunately there is no statistical evidence on this question as research on acquittal rates has never analysed summons:charge ratios.

The vetting process involved in summons procedures weeds out weak cases which would often fail in court were they prosecuted. Simply having professional lawyers as prosecutors does not ensure that this weeding process is carried out even after the prosecutor receives the case. What matters are the roles those prosecutors are given by the police. Final confirmation of this is given if in Table 7:3, we add column (a) (not prosecuted) to column (e) (NEO) in each police force.

This produces totals of 'dropped' cases, before and after the prosecution decision, as follows: RURAL 62; URBAN 63; RURBAL 46. In other words, cases that are not dropped before prosecution commences tend to be dropped afterwards. But not always and not easily: some defendants, such as ED099, plead guilty and some defendants will have to suffer numerous court appearances.

In conclusion, it can be seen that although most police forces choose to organise their prosecution systems such that there is a propensity to prosecute, some do so to a greater degree than others. The consequences for many defendants are clearly adverse. In addition this ties up considerable court, prosecution, and legal aid resources. It is in everyone's interests to change this prosecution pattern. At present we can only speculate about whether the Crown Prosecution Service will manage this. However, the propensity to prosecute is a consequence of specific *procedures*, inseparable from the structure of the criminal justice system in police cases, rather than limited *powers*. Consequently the prospects for change in the future are, in this writer's opinion, poor.

8 The effectiveness of committal proceedings as a filter in the criminal justice system

PETER JONES, ROGER TARLING AND JULIE VENNARD

Committal proceedings were originally conceived of as a constitutional safeguard against the citizen being brought to trial on insubstantial evidence. In theory at least, committal proceedings also benefit the criminal process by providing a judicial screening of evidence, thereby saving valuable court time on the trial of such cases. However, the effectiveness of committal proceedings as a 'filter' within the criminal justice system is currently a topic of much debate, particularly as several recent developments in the criminal justice field – including the proposed introduction of an independent prosecution service and the replacement of the *prima facie* test with the 'reasonable prospects of conviction' test – have a significant bearing on this issue.

Almost all offences tried in the Crown Court are preceded by committal proceeding at the magistrates' court. The primary purpose of these proceedings is, according to the Divisional Court, to ensure that no person stands trial until a *prima facie* case has been made against him; that is, until the court is satisfied that there is a case for the defence to answer[1]. Thus, in theory at least, committal proceedings are intended to act as a filter within the criminal justice system, removing those cases in which the prosecution case is thought to be unmeritorious or inadequately prepared. Until the 1967 Criminal Justice Act 'full' (often termed 'old-style') committal proceedings were required in every case, with the examining justice having to consider the evidence and any statement by the accused. The 1967 Act introduced a second form of committal proceeding, the 'paper' committal, whereby a person could be committed to the Crown Court for trial by an examining justice without consideration of the evidence (though in certain cases the magistrate will consider the written statements following a submission that they disclose insufficient evidence to put the accused on trial by jury)[2]. Since the Act an ever-increasing proportion of committals have been of this latter form, a trend which prompted the Royal Commission on Criminal Procedure (1981a) to question the continued effectiveness of committal proceedings in preventing inadequately prepared and selected cases from reaching the Crown Court.

---

1. *R v Epping and Harlow JJ, ex parte Massaro* [1973] 137 JP 373; [1973] 1 All ER 1011.
2. Currently full committals are committals under the Magistrates' Courts Act 1980, s.6(1) and paper committals are committals under the Magistrates' Courts Act 1980, s.6(2).

One problem with any assessment of the effectiveness of committal proceedings is that it is extremely difficult to define in precise terms what are 'weak' or unmeritorious cases. The effectiveness of committal proceedings in filtering out recognisably weak cases from the criminal justice system is often simply measured in terms of the final outcome of the case – with acquittal rates being the main criterion adopted. However, acquittal rates, as such, are of little value as indicators of weakness in a case since they fall into two very different groups; jury acquittals and acquittals by judge. Only the latter group have relevance to the question of whether the evidence justified bringing cases to trial in the Crown Court.

Although acquittals are fully discussed by Sid Butler in Chapter 13, a brief summary is given here to set the discussion of committal proceedings in context. Acquittals by judge comprise two basic types. First, the judge may order an acquittal – the normal course should the prosecution intimate that it does not wish to offer any evidence against the defendant on a particular charge or charges. Alternatively, the judge may direct the jury to acquit – a decision taken after he has heard some or all of the prosecution evidence and decided it is insufficient for a decision to be left to the jury. While these types of outcome are the best available indicators of weak cases both have their shortcomings. Directed acquittals may well result in cases which were not recognisably weak prior to the trial (see McConville and Baldwin, 1981). Similarly, ordered acquittals can result from an acceptance by the judge of alternative charges rather than from an inherently weak case. Nevertheless, in the absence of detailed knowledge of individual cases ordered and directed acquittals remain the best general indicator of instances where the filtering system has failed, allowing unmeritorious cases to pass through to the Crown Court. Consequently, the definition of weak cases employed in this study comprises cases which resulted in ordered and/or directed acquittal(s) on all counts.

The report of the Royal Commission (*op cit*), in attempting to assess the effectiveness of committal proceedings as a filter for weak cases, noted that in 1978 some 2,000 of over 84,000 defendants subject to committal proceedings had their cases discharged at the committal stage because there was not sufficient evidence to put them on trial in the Crown Court. However, the report also noted that of those cases which reached the Crown Court in which defendants entered a plea of not guilty about 40 per cent resulted in an acquittal by judge (ie ordered or directed). Thus, while it is clear that magistrates do discharge some defendants during committal proceedings, the high proportion of 'acquittals by judge' in the Crown Court indicates a very limited effectiveness by committal proceedings as a screening procedure. In 1981, the year for which data in this study were collected, *Judicial Statistics*, produced by the Lord Chancellor's Department, reveal that acquittal by judge comprised 43 per cent of all acquittals (8 per cent of all defendants dealt with in the Crown Court).

Aims of the study

In the absence of any large scale or national survey data on committals the primary aim of the study was to provide detailed information on committal proceedings – the number of defendants discharged, the proportions of full and paper committals, the number of each type to reach the Crown Court, the final outcome of cases committed via the two routes and the waiting time involved in the committal process.

The study method and sample

Data were provided by the Home Office Statistical Department on all committal proceedings which took place during a one month period (January 1981) at all magistrates' courts in England and Wales. The sample included information on all cases – those discharged at the committal stage as well as those actually committed to the Crown Court – and the data collected included the date of the committal hearing, details of the charges, the Crown Court to which the case was committed and the date of completion of the case.

Further information was obtained from magistrates' courts on the date of first appearance at the magistrates' court, on the type of committal and on which party instigated the full committal if this took place. Finally, a third source of data was obtained: the Crown Court provided information on the outcome of each charge.

Inevitably, given the various data collection stages of the project, a certain amount of information was lost. While both magistrates' courts and the Crown Courts were extremely helpful they were not always able to provide the additional information required on each case.

Type of committal

During the study period, January 1981, there were 5,553 persons subject to committal proceedings at the magistrates' courts. Information on type of committal proceeding was available for most cases and shows that the large majority (92.4 per cent) were paper committal proceedings and just 7.6 per cent were full committal proceedings (Table 8:1). This latter figure is considerably larger than that reported in several smaller local studies (though comparison with such studies is complicated by the fact that most did not include discharged cases in their sample). Bottoms and McClean (1976) found that only one of the 356 defendants in their Sheffield sample was dealt with by full committal, and evidence presented to the James Committee in 1975 found 10 out of 440 cases committed for trial during one year in Teesside were full committals. A more comparable figure is presented by Lidstone (1983), who found that 8.5 per cent of the 970 committals in a London court during 1982 were full committals.

However, in the same report data for two provincial courts showed full committals comprised only 0.5 per cent and 4.5 per cent of all committals. The suggestion from such results, that courts vary in the proportion of cases involving full committals, is supported by the present survey. The figures for full committal proceedings varied from over 12 per cent in the Western circuit to just 4 per cent in the Midland and Oxford circuit (Table 8:2).

Table 8:1 *Type of committal proceeding*

	Number	Per cent
Full	394	7.6
Paper	4,758	92.4
Total	5,152	100

Missing data n = 401

Table 8:2 *Type of committal proceeding by court circuit*

Type of committal:	Crown Court circuit: MIDLAND OXFORD	NORTH EAST	NORTHERN	S.E. PROVINCE	S.E. LONDON	WALES	WESTERN	Total
full	4.2	4.8	4.8	5.9	10.0	7.0	12.5	7.6
paper	95.8	95.2	95.2	94.1	90.0	93.0	87.5	92.4
Total number	949	901	6	623	1,195	284	432	5,152
per cent	100	100	100	100	100	100	100	100

Missing data n = 401

Of the 394 cases in which magistrates considered all the evidence (full committals) 48 (12 per cent) were discharged as having no case for the defence to answer (Table 8:3). Of the 4,758 paper committal proceedings all but 60 (1 per cent) were committed to the Crown Court. Of these 60 cases, two thirds (40) were discharged because the prosecution withdrew the case and one third (20) involved a successful submission by the defence that there was insufficient evidence to put the defendant on trial by jury. There were 401 cases in which outcome was known (113 discharged, 288 committed) but no information was available on type of committal proceeding.

Table 8:3 *Type of committal proceeding and outcome of case*

	Type of committal proceeding: Full		Paper	
Outcome:	n	%	n	%
Defendant discharged	48	12.2	60	1.3
Committed to Crown Court	346	87.8	4,698	98.7
Total	394	100	4,758	100

Missing data n = 401

Who requested full committal proceedings

Lidstone (*op cit*) argues that prosecuting solicitors and police officers would only request a full committal in cases involving identification of the accused by witnesses, a domestic assault or similar case, in which they have reason to suspect the witnesses may not come up to proof. He adds that defence solicitors will also opt for full committal proceedings in such cases. Less commonly full committal proceedings are requested as a means of fully appraising the evidence via a rehearsal for the trial. This practice has been criticised in several judgments particularly when the aim appears to be that the defence can test their cross-examination of prosecution witnesses with a view to using the results to their advantage in the Crown Court (see Harris, 1983). A further reason suggested in Lidstone is that solicitors use full committal proceedings simply to boost their income at the expense of the legal aid fund.

While the data in this study cannot provide any insight to the reasons why full committals were requested they do give an indication of the source of the request. Magistrates' courts were asked to provide, wherever possible, information on which party had requested full committal proceedings (Table 8:4). This information was not always available and consequently the data refers to less than half the total number of full committal proceedings (186 of the 394 cases). Nevertheless, the results indicate that between one fifth and one quarter (22 per cent) of full committal proceedings were requested by the prosecution and two thirds (67.8 per cent) by the defence. The remaining one tenth (10.2 per cent) arose because the defendant was not legally represented, in which case full committal proceedings are automatic.

Table 8:4 *Who requested full committal proceedings*

	Number	Per cent
Prosecution request	41	22.0
Defence request	126	67.8
Defendant(s) not represented	19	10.2
Total	186	100

Missing data n = 208

Outcome

As noted above, of the 5,553 cases in the sample 5,332 were committed to the Crown Court (though full information was not available for 320 of these).

The overall acquittal rate in the sample was 15.6 per cent. While this is slightly lower than the published annual figure of 18.4 per cent (*Judicial Statistics*, 1981) the relative proportions of jury, ordered or directed acquittals are similar[3]. In the sample the figures are 56.7 per cent acquitted by the jury[4], 22.2 per cent acquitted by order of the judge and 21.1 per cent acquitted by direction of the judge. A detailed breakdown of the outcome of cases reaching the Crown Court is shown in Table 8:5.

Table 8:5 *Outcome of case by type of committal proceedings*

		Full %	Paper %	Total %
Convicted on all charges		55.1	73.2	72.9
Mixed outcome – acquitted and convicted		11.4	11.5	11.5
Acquitted on all charges by jury		18.5	8.9	9.5
Acquitted on all charges by judge		15.0	5.4	6.1
Total	number	341	4,643	4,984
	per cent	100	100	100

Missing data n = 348

Employing the definition of weak cases outlined above (ie only those ending in ordered and/or directed acquittals) 309 of the 5,012 cases where outcome was known (6.2 per cent) can be identified as 'weak'. If one accepts that such cases provide an indication of the efficiency of the criminal justice system in filtering out weak cases then it might be felt that 6 per cent does not represent a very bad 'failure rate'.

One might expect that full committal proceedings would be relatively effective at identifying and weeding out any weak cases. The evidence of Table 8:5 offers little support for the latter expectation. Acquittals by judge occurred in 15 per cent of full committal cases, a considerably higher proportion than the 5.4 per cent of cases involving paper committals. This may be because full committal proceedings tend to take place in cases which are more problematical than those normally dealt with in paper committal proceedings, for instance, where proof of the defendant's guilt hinges on the reliability of identification evidence from prosecution eyewitnesses.

Time taken

One of the criticisms levelled at committal proceedings is that they introduce an additional delay in the already lengthy waiting times experienced by defendants. However, there is no published information on this. The data on waiting times published in *Judicial Statistics* measures only the time which elapses between date of committal and final disposal. In 1981 the average time for defendants committed for trial was 15.7 weeks. Additional statistics show

3. As data on plea were not recorded the acquittal rate represents the proportion of all defendants tried in the Crown Court rather than of those pleading not guilty to one or more charges.
4. In *Judicial Statistics* all mixed acquittals – involving a jury acquittal as well as an ordered and/or directed acquittal – are coded as a jury acquittal. The same procedure is adopted in this study.

that 38 per cent of defendants were disposed of in less than 8 weeks, and 73 per cent in less than 20 weeks.

In this study additional information was collected on the time which elapsed between first court appearance and committal proceedings. Some knowledge of this time is of relevance to the issue of time limits discussed in Chapter 11. Table 8:6 shows that the average time taken from first appearance to committal hearing was 8.9 weeks and the median 7 weeks[5].

Table 8:6 *Time between first court appearance and committal proceedings (in weeks)*

Time taken (weeks):	Per cent	Cumulative per cent	Number
Less than 4	17.3	17.3	831
4 < 8	37.2	54.5	1,788
8 < 12	22.6	77.1	1,088
12 < 16	11.0	88.1	528
16 < 20	5.1	93.1	243
20 < 24	2.3	95.4	109
24 < 32	2.4	97.8	115
32 < 40	0.9	98.6	42
40 < 48	0.6	99.2	27
48 and over	0.8	100	38
Total	100	100	4,809

Average time 8.9 weeks
Median time 7 weeks

Note: Cases discharged by the magistrate are included. Data on the time between first court appearance and committal proceeding were unavailable for 263 defendants.

Separate analysis by type of committal reveals that the average time for full committal was 15.3 weeks, considerably longer than the average of 8.4 for paper committals. The median times for full and paper committals were slightly less divergent at 12 and 7 weeks respectively. Adding the two time periods together gives a total waiting time that covers the period from first court appearance to final disposal. The sample total waiting times for England and Wales indicate an average of 23.7 weeks and a median of 20 weeks, though these mask considerable variation between the different court circuits. In the South East (London) circuit the average total waiting time was 34.7 weeks and the median 33 weeks whereas in the North Eastern circuit the average was just 16.1 weeks and the median 13 weeks.

5. Since the sample contains a small number of cases which took a very long time the average waiting time can be inflated, thus becoming a poor indication of the waiting time experienced by the majority. In such situations the median (the time in which exactly half the cases have been dealt with) offers a useful statistical alternative.

the median 33 weeks whereas in the North Eastern circuit the average was just 16.1 weeks and the median 13 weeks.

Conclusions

Committal proceedings are intended as a mechanism for ensuring that cases are dismissed where there is insufficient evidence to put the accused on trial in the Crown Court. However, their effectiveness in fulfilling this function is increasingly being called into question. The results of this study are inconclusive though they offer some insight into the impact of committal proceedings on the criminal process.

It could be argued, for example, that full committal proceedings represent an effective filter within the Criminal Justice System since 12 per cent of such cases resulted in a discharge. As a counterbalance to this, however, is the fact that the proportion of cases involving a full committal which resulted in an acquittal by judge on all counts was considerably higher than for paper committals – 15 per cent and 5 per cent respectively. This might be taken to indicate some reluctance by magistrates to dismiss weak cases even when they preside over full committal proceedings, though without analyses of the evidence on which such cases went forward the figures are only suggestive. Flaws in the prosecution case may have emerged in the Crown Court which were not apparent at the committal proceedings. Of course, from the perspective of the Crown Court such differences may matter very little since full committals are relatively rare and, in terms of absolute numbers, the majority (253 of the 309) of weak cases arrive via the paper committal route.

Looked at another way 221 cases were removed at the committal stage while 309 weak cases got through. Therefore, committal proceedings did prevent 221 out of 530 (42 per cent) from reaching the Crown Court.

In terms of waiting times the study shows that committal proceedings, especially full committals, add a significant amount to the time taken to complete cases – the overall average was nine weeks, the average for full committals 15 weeks. However, since the listing of a case at the Crown Court can only take place after the prosecution statements are available it is difficult to estimate how much (if any) of this time could be saved should committal proceedings be discontinued.

9 Advance disclosure of the prosecution case

FLOYD FEENEY

Historically the evidence in both civil and criminal cases was produced at trial and not before. During the past half century, however, many have come to believe that disclosure in advance of trial reduces surprise, aids fairness, assists in producing prompt dispositions and lowers costs. Advance disclosure has consequently become quite common in civil matters (Sunderland, 1933). Advance disclosure has had a more chequered history, however, in criminal cases.

The fundamental principle of the Anglo-American accusatory system of criminal justice is that the prosecution must prove its case and that it must do so without compelling testimony from the accused. This principle inhibits the kind of mutual disclosure that takes place in civil cases and makes a simple transfer of the concepts developed there difficult. Concerns about such problems as witness tampering and intimidation are also stronger in criminal cases and have contributed to a cautious approach.

While the concept of disclosure has been slow to develop in criminal cases, as a practical matter there has been a considerable amount of disclosure by the prosecution in the most serious criminal cases for over a century. This disclosure has come about largely as a by-product of changes in the committal proceeding, however, rather than through any explicit intention to provide advance disclosure.

The committal is an ancient procedure, dating at least to the fifteenth century. Prior to 1830 the purpose of the proceeding was almost wholly to gather evidence against the accused. The accused was generally allowed neither to be present at the hearing nor to know what evidence was adduced (Stephen, 1933).

With the establishment of professional police forces in the early 1800s, the police began to take over the investigatory function previously performed by the magistrates and the committal began to become more judicial. The Prisoners Counsel Act 1836 permitted defendants for the first time to inspect the depositions taken at committal proceedings, while the Indictable Offences Act 1848 went even further, requiring witnesses to be examined in the presence of the accused and granting the accused the right to question witnesses, have an attorney present and receive a copy of the depositions (Stephen, *op cit*).

The theory of these new rights was not to provide information to the defence in advance of trial but to create a check against unwarranted prosecutions.

The basic idea was that the accused should not be forced to endure the rigours of trial by jury and all the pressures that that entailed unless there had been an earlier judicial determination that there was a strong case against him[1]. The prosecution was not required to present all its witnesses or evidence, but the new method of committal nonetheless provided a great deal of information about the prosecution case[2]. The right to cross-examine the prosecution witnesses and to receive a copy of the depositions proved particularly helpful in this regard.

Whatever the original theory and practice, by the middle of this century it had become clear that one of the major functions served by the committal proceeding was to inform the accused about the prosecution case. The extent to which this purpose had become the dominant reason for the committal proceeding was demonstrated in the Criminal Law Act 1967. This Act retained the old-fashioned method of committal in which evidence is presented in court and the magistrates determine whether that evidence is sufficient to warrant binding the accused over to the Crown Court for trial. The Act also, however, created a new form of paper committal in which witnesses are not examined orally in court but rather have their written statements delivered to the defence. In this new form of committal the magistrates are not required to read the statements unless so requested by the defence. The fact that over 90 per cent of all committals now use this new paper system (see Chapter 8) provides the clearest possible indication that disclosure has replaced judicial testing of the evidence as the dominant practical purpose of the committal proceeding[3]. Even where the old-fashioned form of committal is used, its purpose may be disclosure rather than an attempt to have the case against the accused thrown out (see, eg, Lidstone, 1983, and Napley, 1966).

Along with the development of advance disclosure as the dominant purpose of the committal proceeding, additional rules requiring disclosure of the prosecution case have developed in the Crown Court requiring proceeding and evidence to be used at trial but not brought forward at the committal proceeding (cf. Royal Commission on Criminal Procedure, 1981). These developments are, of course, very much in keeping with the course of changes that have been taking place in civil cases in the past half century.

Despite the transformation of the committal proceeding, the development of additional disclosure rules for criminal cases in the Crown Court, and the major changes that have been made in civil cases, advance disclosure has been slow to come to cases handled wholly in the magistrates' courts. These cases

1. See, for example, Royal Commission on Criminal Procedure, (1981a), 180–181, and (1981b), 70; and Halyk (1967/68), 181.
2. See, for example, *R v Epping and Harlow JJ, ex parte Massaro* (1973) 1 QB 433, reaffirmed in *R v Grays JJ, ex parte Tetley* (1980) 80 Cr App R 11.
3. See Royal Commission on Criminal Procedure, *op cit*.

are particularly important, as they now make up over 80 per cent of all indictable cases and over 95 per cent of all cases including motoring cases (*Criminal Statistics England and Wales*, 1983). Until the Magistrates' Courts Act 1957 there was no required disclosure at all for these cases, and this Act changed the situation only slightly, requiring a brief statement of facts – usually only a sentence or two – in the very minor cases in which guilty pleas are invited by post[4].

This lack of legally required disclosure has been softened to some extent by informal systems in which the prosecution voluntarily – either for reasons of fairness or for pragmatic reasons such as possibly inducing a guilty plea – chooses to disclose all or part of its case to the defence. More recently, some jurisdictions have introduced a pre-trial review procedure – a new form of voluntary disclosure in which the prosecution systematically discloses its case to the defence in cases listed for contested hearings in the magistrates' court as part of a process of discussion with the defence about the case (see Baldwin, 1985, Desbruslais, 1982 and Barnatt, 1983). A controversial part of some of these pre-trial review schemes is a duty on the part of the defence to reciprocate by disclosing some information about the defence case (*Law Society's Gazette*, 1983). Despite these various informal practices, however, it seems clear that advance disclosure is both less frequent and less extensive in the magistrates' courts than in the Crown Court.

Efforts to extend the principle of advance disclosure to the magistrates' courts on a more systematic basis began at least as early as 1965 when the Law Society's Standing Committee on Criminal Law argued that the person tried on indictment in the magistrates' courts should have the same information available as he would if tried by jury (Law Society, 1983). In 1966 Justice, the British Section of the International Jurists Association, made similar arguments (Justice, 1966), and in 1973 there was an attempt on the floor of Parliament to amend the Criminal Justice Act 1973 to require such disclosure. This amendment was withdrawn, however, when the Solicitor-General agreed to look into the matter.

The first intensive examination of the issue was that undertaken by the James Committee. After reviewing the arguments and the evidence available, the Committee concluded in 1975 that advance disclosure should be extended at least to the more serious cases in the magistrates' courts (James Committee, 1975). In the Committee's view such an extension would both increase the fairness of the criminal justice process and would have important efficiency benefits. Among other things the Committee suggested that providing advance disclosure prior to the mode of trial decision would reduce waiting times, the number of elections for trial in the Crown Court and costs.

4. Magistrates' Courts Act 1957, ss. 1–2. These provisions have since been re-enacted as Magistrates' Courts Act 1980, s. 12.

Two years later Parliament responded with section 48 of the Criminal Law Act 1977. This section gave the government the authority to require more advance disclosure if it wished to do so. The government had concerns about the cost of doing this, however, and immediately announced its intention to delay implementation of the Act. This concern about costs arose largely from the fact that many police forces did not routinely produce statements of the sort used in committal proceedings until there was an election for trial. Providing such statements prior to the mode of trial decision, as suggested by the James Committee, could be expected to require thousands of additional statements. Suggestions that disclosure be provided by the use of brief summaries of the evidence instead of statements were viewed sceptically by many. The Law Society and others argued that the information provided would be too skimpy and too biased to assist the accused. Police forces which did not produce summaries were concerned about the cost and feasibility of beginning a new procedure. Those forces which did already produce summaries for their own internal purposes had reservations as to whether these were sufficiently uniform and accurate to be disclosed externally. There were also concerns about the effects of disclosure on witnesses and the outcome of cases.

In 1981 the Royal Commission on Criminal Procedure again reviewed the issues relating to advance disclosure. Reaching essentially the same conclusions as the James Committee, the Commission recommended that section 48 be implemented, at least as to cases triable either way. A working party convened by the Home Office to consider the problem was unable to reach a clear-cut solution, however, and recommended the creation of a pilot scheme to help assess the cost and operational effects of introducing disclosure. In response two such schemes were begun: one in the Northumbria force testing the use of case summaries, and one in East London testing the use of written statements. The Northumbria scheme began in November 1982 and the East London scheme in August 1983.

Based on the results then available from the pilot schemes, the Home Secretary in May 1984 announced his intention to issue rules implementing section 48 within a year. In May 1985 rules of this kind were put into effect. These rules require that advance disclosure of the prosecution case be provided in all either way cases when so requested by the accused or his attorney. The decision as to whether the disclosure is made in the form of written statements or by case summaries is left to local discretion for the present, but the Home Secretary has announced an intention to mandate one system or the other in the near future and stated his inclination to mandate a system of disclosure based on statements.

The new rules obviously represent a major development in the handling of criminal cases. They greatly improve the amount and quality of information available to defendants for making decisions about either way cases, particularly three critical decisions related to how the case will be heard:

- whether to elect trial by jury in the Crown Court;
- whether to plead guilty or contest the issue in the magistrates' court;
- how best to conduct the defence in the magistrates' court.

The rules fall considerably short of providing either way defendants who elect to stay in the magistrates' courts with the full amount of disclosure provided in the Crown Court but are a major step toward placing the two courts on the same footing. While section 48 also authorises extending advance disclosure to purely summary matters, the rules do not extend disclosure to these cases at this time.

It will no doubt be a considerable time before it will be possible to determine whether the James Committee was correct in thinking that disclosure would improve fairness and efficiency or to assess fully the impact of the new rules on such things as workload and costs. The results from the pilot schemes provide some important insights, however, into these and related questions.

The Newcastle pilot scheme

The Newcastle pilot scheme began on 1 November 1982 and continued through 31 October 1983. Under the scheme legally represented defendants in either way cases received summaries of the prosecution case upon request. As the Newcastle division already produced summaries of the prosecution evidence for internal use, it had no need to institute major new procedures for producing case summaries. It sought to prevent disclosure of the name and address of witnesses, however, by devising a new form which allowed this information to be put on the back of the summary. The division also sought to improve the thoroughness and accuracy of summaries through a special training programme.

During the scheme the Newcastle division handled over 3,700 either way cases. Defendants in 2,600 of these cases were legally represented, and thus eligible to request disclosure of the prosecution case. Over 870 of these represented defendants did so request. Thus over 30 per cent of those eligible and over 20 per cent of all either way defendants sought disclosure. Requests increased from fewer than 20 per cent of those eligible in the early months of the scheme to 40 per cent in the later months.

Having planned the scheme carefully at the outset, the Newcastle division encountered little difficulty in supplying the summaries requested. Disclosure requests were addressed to the divisional prosecutions department and vetted by a detective inspector. As experience was gained, the vetting was largely delegated to a constable. Whilst the police retained the authority to withhold sensitive information, they found no need to do so during the pilot scheme. Similarly there were no difficulties with witness tampering or intimidation.

In order to determine the effects of the pilot scheme disposals during the scheme were compared with those for a four-month period prior to its beginning. The most valid comparison was that for the first five months of the scheme[5]. This comparison showed that elections for trial in the Crown Court decreased from 30 to 25 per cent in either way cases, while guilty pleas in the magistrates' courts increased from 53 to 57 per cent.

Other analyses confirmed these effects. There was no change in elections for trial or guilty pleas for unrepresented defendants (who were not eligible for disclosure) whilst elections for represented defendants decreased from 42 to 36 per cent and guilty pleas increased from 35 to 40 per cent. Either way cases from Gateshead, a division of the Northumbria force which was not part of the pilot scheme, also showed a sharply different pattern of disposals. Elections for trial went up in Gateshead while declining in Newcastle.

The views of the more active defence solicitors in Newcastle also suggest the same conclusion. When asked to describe the effects of the pilot scheme, they said that it had not greatly altered disposal patterns but that it had decreased the number of elections for trial and increased guilty pleas.

Taken together these analyses provide a strong indication that the decrease in elections for trial and the increase in guilty pleas was caused by the introduction of advance disclosure. The pilot scheme also appears to have had a beneficial effect on waiting times. Whilst the time to disposal in the magistrates' court was essentially unchanged, the decrease in the number of elections for trial resulted in a decline in overall waiting times.

In order to determine the long-term effects of advance disclosure the more active defence solicitors were asked why they requested disclosure in some cases and not in others. One group of solicitors said they always requested disclosure because it was difficult to evaluate the case purely from what the accused said. Other solicitors took a much more focused approach, requesting disclosure only for cases in which they were unclear as to whether to elect jury trial.

Both groups of solicitors indicated that the one page summary provided by the police was somewhat uneven in quality and that it occasionally overstated the prosecution case. The general view, however, was that the summaries were well done and very helpful. The solicitors nonetheless indicated that if it were possible to have statements instead of summaries, they would prefer statements.

5. Data were collected for the remaining seven months of the experimental scheme. These do not appear to be comparable to those for the first five months, however, as the percentage of prosecution committals increased during this latter period.

Aside from the research and evaluation costs associated with the pilot scheme, the principal costs incurred by the Newcastle division were the training at the outset of the scheme and the cost of vetting and responding to disclosure requests. The cost of vetting and responding to disclosure requests declined as the division became more familiar with disclosure and by the end of the scheme had dropped to no more than £2 per disclosure.

As the cost of a guilty plea in the Crown Court is three to four times that of a guilty plea in the magistrates' court, the scheme resulted in considerable savings to police, courts, the legal aid fund and other agencies. Police and prosecution savings alone – in reduced appearances and case preparation – were more than ten times the cost of vetting and responding to disclosure requests.

The Metropolitan Police pilot scheme

The Metropolitan Police pilot scheme was designed to test the use of witness statements as a method for providing advance disclosure. Conducted in H District in an East London area served by the Thames Magistrates' Court, the scheme began on 1 August 1983 and continued through 31 July 1984. Under the scheme defendants charged with either way offences were given a notice indicating that disclosure would be provided upon request. In order not to discourage early guilty pleas notices were not given to defendants whose cases were disposed of at first appearance in court. Road traffic offences were also excluded because they are administered differently from other cases. To help prevent an increase in waiting times as a result of the scheme, the period of police bail for either way cases was reduced from 21 to 7 days. Officers were also instructed to prepare witness statements in all either way cases going past first appearance. In addition to the disclosure to be made upon request prior to the mode of trial decision, the pilot scheme provided for automatic disclosure to defendants who elected a contested summary hearing in the magistrates' court.

During the period of the scheme H District handled approximately 3,100 either way cases. Over 2,000 of these cases proceeded past first appearance and were thus eligible for disclosure. Disclosure was requested in 151 cases. Thus 7 per cent of those eligible for disclosure and 5 per cent of all either way defendants sought disclosure. This percentage increased from 4 per cent of those eligible in the early months of the scheme to 14 per cent in the final month.

Police stations encountered few difficulties in providing disclosure under the scheme. The methods for doing this, however, varied from station to station and time to time. Initially two of the three H District stations directed that officers prepare statements immediately in all either way cases, whilst the third station required preparation only for those cases going past first appearance. Initially also the detective chief inspectors reviewed each set of statements prepared so that the statements could be speedily disclosed if requested.

It soon became apparent, however, that statements were being prepared and vetted in many more cases than disclosure was being requested, and detective chief inspectors soon began to cut back on the number of reviews undertaken. Initially they cut back to reviewing only those cases going past first appearance. Later they began to review only those cases in which requests for disclosure were received. Gradually also the task of vetting the files was delegated – first to the detective inspector and later to other staff. The instruction requiring officers to prepare statements immediately was never rescinded but gradually the practice changed so that statements were generally prepared only when a request for disclosure was received. As in the Newcastle scheme the police retained the authority to withhold sensitive information but did not have to use this authority. Similarly, there were no problems of witness intimidation or tampering.

In order to determine the effects of the pilot scheme disposals for two three-month periods during the scheme (September–November and January–March) were compared with those for the same two periods in the year prior to the scheme. This comparison showed that cases in which no evidence was offered increased from 3 to 8 per cent during the scheme and guilty pleas from 57 to 58 per cent. Summary contests declined from 14 to 10 per cent while committals for trial declined from 24 to 22 per cent.

A separate analysis of cases going past first appearance and thus eligible for disclosure indicated that virtually all the change in guilty pleas, summary contests and committals was in cases going past first appearance. Guilty pleas for this group increased from 37 to 41 per cent, while summary contests decreased from 24 to 15 per cent and committals from 36 to 34 per cent. The increase in cases with no evidence offered, however, occurred both in cases disposed at first appearance and in cases going past first appearance.

As in the Newcastle pilot scheme the views of the defence solicitors tended to confirm the statistical findings. When asked about the effects of the pilot scheme, the more active solicitors indicated that the scheme had had no great effect on either committals or guilty pleas. Most, however, said that it had led to some decreases in committals and some increase in guilty pleas. Defence solicitors also indicated that in a few instances disclosure had led them to contest cases that they would not otherwise have contested.

As might have been expected from the small number of requests for disclosure received during the scheme, the analyses do not indicate any large effect on case outcomes. The pilot scheme has probably resulted in some decrease in summary contests and possibly slight changes in committals and guilty pleas. It is less clear whether the pilot scheme is responsible for the increase in cases with no evidence offered. In the early months of the scheme detective chief inspectors reported a number of instances in which the additional vetting created by the pilot scheme had resulted in a withdrawal of charges. The number of such instances reported, however, was too small to account for the increase shown in the analysis.

Waiting times in the magistrates' court increased slightly during the pilot scheme (from 57 to 64 days for committals and 33 to 35 days for other cases). Because of the much greater time required for final disposal in the Crown Court no reliable information is available concerning changes in Crown Court waiting times.

As in the Newcastle scheme defence solicitors were asked why they requested disclosure in some cases and not in others. The solicitors with the most active practices in the Thames Magistrates' Court indicated that they generally requested disclosure in cases in which they were uncertain about the desirability of electing for a jury trial. A number said that because there was already a great deal of informal disclosure at the Thames Magistrates' Court there was generally no need to request formal disclosure in cases in which the defendant was planning to plead guilty in the magistrates' court. Solicitors with active criminal law practices spread over many different courts said that they had heard of the scheme but that they requested disclosure only occasionally. Solicitors on the duty solicitor rota but who rarely appeared in the Thames Magistrates' Court also said that they knew of the scheme but that they had never used it.

The principal costs incurred in the scheme were those involved in taking statements that would not otherwise have been taken and in typing, photocopying, vetting and transmitting these statements. These costs varied considerably from station to station and time to time.

It is particularly difficult to estimate the extent to which statements would have been required in the request cases in the absence of the pilot scheme. It seems likely, however, that statements would have been required in at least 60 per cent of the cases going past first appearance, as 36 per cent of these cases in the pre-scheme period ended in committal and 24 per cent ended in a summary contest.

Based on an average of 8 pages per case the cost of preparing, typing and vetting statements can be estimated at more than £70 per case. Two thirds of this cost is incurred in entering the particulars in the officer's notebook in the first instance, however, and is a cost whether statements are prepared or not. The incremental cost of preparing statements is therefore approximately £25 per case. As statements are already prepared for other reasons in 60 per cent or more of the disclosure cases, the incremental cost of disclosure can be estimated at approximately £15 per disclosure.

The principal savings from the pilot scheme come from the decrease in summary contests. As each such contest which becomes a guilty plea saves at least £100 on average, this decrease results in considerable savings to the police, the prosecution, the courts and the legal aid fund. These savings may amount to more than £70 per disclosure.

Analysis of experimental results

The first argument advanced by the James Committee for providing advance disclosure of the prosecution case to either way defendants was that it would improve the fairness of the system. It was not possible to measure this directly in the two pilot schemes as there is no easy way to measure fairness. Defence solicitors in both areas, however, were asked whether they believed that the new procedure had had any effect on fairness in the cases they handled. They were unanimous in saying that the new procedure had improved fairness. The most common comment was that disclosure had provided assistance in understanding the case, but a few also indicated that disclosure had led them to contest some cases where they would not otherwise have done so. Police and prosecuting solicitors also tended to feel that fairness had been improved, but raised questions as to why, if the procedure did improve fairness, disclosure was not requested more frequently than it was.

The second argument advanced by the James Committee for providing advance disclosure was that it would increase guilty pleas, decrease elections for trial and improve waiting times. Whilst the two schemes vary somewhat in their results, both appear to have brought about increased guilty pleas and decreased elections for trial figures. These effects were stronger in the Newcastle scheme where advance disclosure was requested more frequently than it was in East London. Whilst less clear, there is also some evidence that advance disclosure reduced the number of contested hearings in the magistrates' courts and encouraged early analysis of the evidence available for the prosecution.

There does not appear to have been any strong effect on the waiting time between charge and disposal in the magistrates' courts. The decreased number of elections for trial, however, means that some cases that formerly went to the Crown Court are now disposed of in the magistrates' courts, thus leading to a decline in the average overall waiting time. No problems of witness intimidation or other improper use of information disclosed were reported during the pilot schemes.

One of the most important conclusions from the pilot schemes is that it appears feasible for the prosecution to provide advance disclosure either by summaries of the case or by witness statements without great administrative difficulty. Such disclosure is probably easiest when provided by case summary by a force that already produces case summaries. The experience in the Metropolitan Police with the use of witness statements, however, suggests that this method of providing disclosure is also administratively feasible. Careful advance planning obviously also greatly assists in reducing the amount of administrative difficulty whatever the method for providing disclosure.

The pilot schemes also suggest that advance disclosure may lower the overall cost of processing criminal cases. The out-of-pocket cost of providing disclosure by summary was £2 per disclosure and that by witness statements £15 per disclosure, and in both schemes disclosure costs tended to decrease as the police became more familiar with the procedure. In both schemes these out-of-pocket costs appear to have been more than offset by the savings generated by disclosure. As the cost of proceedings in the Crown Court far exceeds that in the magistrates' courts, the decreased number of Crown Court cases brought about by disclosure produces major savings in police, prosecution, court and legal aid costs. Taken together these savings exceed the out-of-pocket costs of providing disclosure. Taken by themselves police and prosecution savings alone also appear to exceed the out-of-pocket costs of providing disclosure. Somewhat similar savings are also produced when cases that would have been contested summary trials result in guilty pleas instead.

Both the cost and the method of providing disclosure is likely to be affected by other developments such as the creation of an independent prosecution service and tape-recording. If the creation of an independent prosecution service results in the preparation of a full file of witness statements in each case or in more cases, disclosure by witness statements will obviously become easier and cheaper. Similarly, as statements relating to interrogation of the defendant now make up a substantial part of statements that are disclosed, tape-recording can also be expected to affect the method and cost of disclosure.

Costs, savings, police workload, and effects such as increased guilty pleas and decreased elections for trial, all appear to increase as the number of disclosures requested increase. It is difficult to project the rate of request from the two pilot schemes, however, because their experience was so different. The rate of request in East London was only 5 per cent of the either way cases while that in Newcastle was 25 per cent. In both schemes the rate clearly increased as the defence solicitors became more familiar with the procedure.

As interviews with defence solicitors in East London suggest, lack of familiarity with advance disclosure was a factor in the lower rate of requests and as the issuance of national rules will help to make the procedure better known it seems probable that the rate of request under the national rules will be closer to that in Newcastle than that in East London.

It is not clear what effect the new disclosure rules will have on pre-trial review schemes in the magistrates' courts. The rules themselves take a neutral stance and are not intended to discourage either the use or further development of pre-trial review schemes. They are highly likely, however, to have some effect.

One of the principal motivations for many defence solicitors to participate in such schemes has been the disclosure they received from the prosecution in either way cases. As the defence will be entitled to advance disclosure without participating in the pre-trial review scheme, it is likely that the defence will feel less inclined to participate in pre-trial review. Pre-trial review schemes also serve other functions, however, and it seems likely that such reviews will continue although perhaps on a reduced scale. Among other things they provide the parties with an opportunity to discuss the case, a purpose that is often useful to both sides.

Summary

The new rules constitute an important new chapter in the development of disclosure in criminal cases. Many questions remain, however, and it seems likely that there are still chapters to come. Some of these questions concern relatively short-term issues. Will the police choose to implement the new system through the use of case summaries or by providing witness statements? Will national implementation prove to be as easy as the pilot schemes? How will disclosure be affected by developments such as tape-recording and the independent prosecution service? When the time comes to issue more permanent rules will the government follow through on its announced preference for the use of witness statements?

There are also longer range and more basic questions. How do defence solicitors and barristers actually use the information that they receive from disclosure? To what extent is such information used for case preparation or to spot holes in the prosecution case and to what extent is it used to force the accused to be more realistic with himself as to what he has done and with his attorney as to what his realistic chances are in a contest? Should advance disclosure be extended to purely summary cases? If so, should this extension be to all summary matters or only to those such as assault on a constable, etc, which are frequently contested? Should there be a greater amount of defence disclosure? Could this be done without impinging on basic rights? Should advance disclosure in the magistrates' court explicitly track that in the Crown Court in order to upgrade the quality of justice in the magistrates' courts and produce a more uniform system. Are there new forms of disclosure such as inspection of the prosecution file that should be considered? How should advance disclosure fit in with such procedural devices as pre-trial review schemes?

These and other questions will not be quickly answered. Major development is under way, however, and the system is not likely to return to its former state.

10 Remand decisions at magistrates' courts

PETER JONES

Introduction

During the six years 1976–1982 the daily remand population in British prisons increased by almost 50 per cent. This dramatic rise was the result of a combination of two factors – the steadily increasing number of defendants being remanded in custody by the courts and the general increase in the length of stay of defendants in custody. The Home Office, aware of such trends, has responded by looking carefully at measures to improve efficiency and reduce delay in the courts. One of the initial problems to be faced is the considerable variation that exists between magistrates' courts in the granting of bail. What is not clear however, is whether these variations simply reflect the different types of caseload faced by the courts or real differences in magisterial decision-making across the country. It is this question which is addressed in the study described here.

Background

The issue of court remand has been the subject of critical debate for the last two decades. In the early 1970s a series of reports and published papers suggested that a large number of defendants were being remanded in custody unnecessarily (King, 1971; Bottomley, 1970). It was argued that one of the reasons for this was that magistrates had insufficient information on the defendant other than that supplied by the police. It was no coincidence therefore that the remand decision of the court frequently mirrored the earlier remand decision and recommendation of the police.

An attempt was made in the Criminal Justice Act 1967 to persuade magistrates of the need to increase their use of bail and reduce the number of remands in custody. In the period immediately after the Act the bail rate did rise, though the extent to which this was a direct consequence of the legislation is questionable. In their study of the effects of the 1967 Act on court bail decisions Simon and Weatheritt conclude that the Act 'as it stood . . . could not be expected greatly to increase the courts' use of bail through the restrictions it placed on magistrates' powers to refuse bail. These restrictions were such as to have very little practical value. The main contribution of the Act to the general rise in the use of bail probably occurred because the discussion and passing of this legislation encouraged magistrates to adopt a more liberal policy.' (Simon and Weatheritt, 1974.)

However, the introduction of the 1967 Act did little to resolve the controversy which continued to surround the issue of court bail. Consequently, in 1971 the Home Office announced the setting up of a Working Party on Bail Procedures in Magistrates' Courts. The Report of the Working Party recommended a change of attitude in the granting of bail by magistrates but proposed no radical changes to the way the bail system actually operated in the magistrates' courts (King, 1981). The subsequent Bail Act 1976, whilst introducing some important changes to the bail system – there was now to be a presumption in favour of bail – brought about no long term reduction in the proportion of defendants remanded in custody. The number of persons received into custody fell slightly in 1977 and dropped sharply in 1978, the year in which the Bail Act was actually implemented. However, in the following years the number of defendants remanded in custody rose steadily, though at different rates in different regions (see Morgan, 1984). This rise in custodial remands, coupled with the general increase in the average length of stay of defendants in custody, had the effect of increasing the daily remand population in prisons by almost 50 per cent in six years, from 4,800 in 1976 to 7,200 in 1982.

The Home Office responded to the rise in the remand population by looking carefully at measures to improve efficiency and reduce delay in the courts. One of the initial problems to be faced is the considerable variation that exists between magistrates' courts in the granting of bail. What was not clear however, is whether these variations simply reflected the different types of caseload faced by the courts or real differences in magisterial decision-making across the country.

Design of the study

The focus of this study is the remand decision made by the court following the defendant's first court appearance. Therefore, the sample in this study comprises only those defendants who were not dealt with at their first court appearance (ie it includes those who were either committed to the Crown Court or had their cases adjourned). This is an important point since it means that the sample does not represent either the total number of defendants remanded by the police (since many will be dealt with at first court appearance) or the total number dealt with by the magistrates' court.

The data on which the analysis was based were derived from information originally prepared from the 1980 *Criminal Statistics* by the Home Office Statistical Department for developmental work on the Home Office Research and Planning Unit's Criminal Justice Model. The original data comprised all those defendants charged or summonsed on indictable or triable either way cases during 1980 – a total of some 533,000 defendants. For the purpose of the present study all defendants dealt with at first court appearance were removed from the sample, leaving a total of 222,000 remanded defendants (41 per cent). Of these almost 33,000 defendants (15 per cent) were remanded in custody[1].

Most previous studies of bail in this country have involved detailed analyses of relatively small samples of cases, often collected over a short period of time (Bottomley, 1970; King, 1971; Zander, 1971; Simon and Weatheritt, 1974; Bottoms and McClean, 1976). One exception to this was the work of Melvin and Didcott (1976), where the database of almost 10,500 defendants represented all accused persons granted bail and/or committed to custody pre-trial in Scotland during 1972. One result of these early studies has been the identification of a series of factors which consistently emerge as being closely associated with the remand decision – these include the police remand decision, type of offence and the age, sex and criminal record of the defendant. However one factor which previous studies have not examined in detail is the significance of variations in court practice to the overall remand decision – that is the extent to which court practice varies by area. The present study examines the relationship between the remand decision and a range of factors (including court area) and, using multivariate techniques, attempts to assess the relative significance of each factor to the remand decision. The study also incorporates some analysis of the outcome of the case.

Factors related to the court remand decision

Age and sex of defendant

A crosstabulation of the age and sex of defendants reveals some support for the results of previous studies. It is clear that the court remand decision varies significantly by the sex of the defendant – 17 per cent for men, 6 per cent for women (Table 10:1). Less variation is evident by age group though it is clear that the proportion remanded in custody is significantly lower amongst males aged under 17 (11 per cent) than it is for the other male age groups. For females the age effect shows more of a gradual decline in the proportion remanded in custody as age increases (from 8 per cent for under 17s to 4 per cent for over 35s).

Type of offence

There are two main ways in which an offence can be classified. The first is the standard offence group classification employed in Criminal Statistics. As one would expect the court remand decision varied a great deal across these offence groups, with over 50 per cent of those accused of robbery remanded in custody as compared with 9 per cent of those accused of theft (Table 10:2).

1. In this study the remand decision studied was the first decision made by the court. Thus, 'mixed cases' involving an initial bail decision and a subsequent custodial decision were classified as a bail remand. Similarly, those involving an initial custody decision and a subsequent bail decision were classified as custodial remands. This differs from *Criminal Statistics* where all mixed decisions are classified as custodial remands.

Table 10:1 *Defendants remanded in custody by age and sex*

	Age: under 17	17–20	21–24	25–34	35+	Total %	n
Male	11.0	17.9	18.8	17.9	16.4	16.8	189,747
Female	7.8	7.5	7.3	6.0	4.0	6.2	29,964
Total %	10.7	16.8	17.3	16.2	19.4	100	
n	28,302	65,131	35,902	47,858	42,518		219,711*

*Information on age or sex was not available in 162 cases.

However, contained within each offence category are crimes of varying degrees of seriousness. One way of discriminating more serious from less serious offences is to further subdivide them by the second type of classification: indictable and triable either way. (The categories robbery and theft cannot be divided in this way as all robberies are indictable and all theft offences are triable either way.) As illustrated in Table 10:2 a crosstabulation of both these variables shows quite clearly the extent to which the rate of court custodial remand varies even within the standard offence classification. Thus for offences of violence, 8 per cent of defendants in triable either way cases were remanded in custody whereas for those involved in indictable cases the proportion remanded in custody was over five times greater at 43 per cent.

Table 10:2 *Proportion of defendants remanded in custody by offence group and offence type*

	Offence type: Indictable (%)	Triable either way (%)	All (%)
Violence	43.3	8.3	12.4
Sexual	53.4	15.8	24.8
Burglary	45.0	26.8	27.1
Robbery	50.6	—	50.6
Theft–Handling	—	9.3	9.3
Fraud	20.5	13.3	13.8
Criminal damage	44.4	18.8	20.2
Motoring	7.0	12.7	15.1
Other	19.7	14.4	12.7
All offences %	41.5	13.8	15.4
n	12,413	207,460	219,873

Charge or summons

There are two main procedures by which a defendant may be brought to a first appearance at court – charge and summons. Normally summons cases involve relatively minor offences and very few are remanded by the magistrates' court. As a result of this summons cases comprise only a very small proportion of the total sample in this study (3 per cent) and are unlikely to figure largely in any general analysis of court remand decisions. Nevertheless, it is worth noting that the type of proceeding does appear to play a part in the court remand decision. Analysed separately for each offence group it is clear that the proportion of defendants receiving a custodial remand is consistently higher when the proceedings were by charge rather than summons (Table 10:3).

Table 10:3 *Proportion of defendants remanded in custody by offence group and proceedings type (N = 219,711)**

	Proceedings type: Charge (%)	Summons (%)
Offence group:		
Violence	12.6	4.2
Sexual	25.5	4.6
Burglary	27.4	15.8
Robbery	50.8	28.2
Theft–Handling	9.4	3.4
Fraud	14.1	5.2
Criminal damage	20.8	7.4
Motoring	11.3	6.4
Other	6.0	3.8
All offences %	15.7	6.2
n	213,293	6,418

*162 cases involving summons other than by the police were removed from the sample.

Police remand decision

The study by Simon and Weatheritt (1974) found that the police bail decision was probably the most important single factor in determining the granting of bail by magistrates. The same conclusion is drawn from this study (see Table 10:4). In cases where the magistrates' court bailed a defendant no fewer than 89 per cent had previously been bailed by the police. Similarly, in cases where the magistrates' court remanded defendants in custody 90 per cent had previously been remanded in custody by the police. This relationship was noted by the Home Office Working Party, whose report (1974) commented that 'a high correlation between the views of the police and the decisions of the courts is to be expected, since the considerations which each should have in mind are in many respects similar' (para 91). Bottoms and McClean (1976), whilst expressing some doubt over this particular explanation, agree that magistrates do normally accept the police view and suggest that this fact explains the discrepancies that exist in court practice – that is, the variations amongst courts simply reflect variations in police practice with regard to bail.

Table 10:4 *Police and court remand decisions*

	Court decision: Bail	Custody	n
Police decision:			
Bail	89.0	11.0	162,743
Custody	11.0	90.0	49,867
Total %	100	100	
n	179,345	33,085	212,430*

*All cases where a defendant was arrested, bailed and re-arrested (n = 1236) or where defendants were not arrested or released without bail (n = 6207) are excluded from the analysis.

So far the study has examined, in turn, the nature of the association between a range of factors and the court remand decision. The next stage therefore, is to add one more factor – area[2] – to the list and to try to identify which of this group of factors is the most significant in 'explaining' court remand decisions. In order to undertake this analysis log linear modelling techniques were employed[3]. Briefly, the aim of the analysis was to explore the degree to which the variation in court remand decisions could be accounted for by one or more independent factors. The influence of these factors is indicated by the 'goodness of fit' or G-square statistic. The comparative size of the reduction in G-square therefore provides an estimate of the relative importance of each factor or combination of factors.

The analysis showed quite clearly that the police remand decision was by far the most significant factor in the 'model' of court remand decisions. The second factor in the model was the offence group. Between them these two factors alone accounted for a great deal of the variation in the court remand decision, though one other factor did enter the model – this was area. This suggests that over and above the important influence of the police remand decision and the offence mix, courts do have different policies and practices when deciding whether to remand defendants in custody or on bail. More detailed inspection of the results of the analysis also suggested that while the influence of the offence mix on court remand decisions remained constant across area the same is not the case for the police remand decision. The statistical model showed that the extent to which the police remand decision influences the subsequent court decision varies significantly by area.

After taking these three factors into account it was clear that the remaining factors – the age and sex of the defendant, whether the proceedings were by

2. To assess geographic variation in remand decisions all courts were grouped together by the police force area within which they are located.
3. For a description of the log linear modelling procedure see Bishop *et al.*, 1975

charge or summons, and the indictable/triable either way dichotomy – were marginal in their influence on the court remand decision.

Variation between areas

Column 1 of Table 10:5 illustrates quite clearly the extent to which magistrates' courts differed in the proportion of defendants they remanded in custody – from less than 10 per cent in some areas (Bedfordshire 7 per cent; Gwent 8 per cent; Hertfordshire 9 per cent) to over 30 per cent in others (Dorset 31 per cent; North Yorkshire 37 per cent).

Of course there are several possible reasons why such geographic variation might exist. The most obvious, bearing in mind the results of the earlier analysis, is that police forces might differ widely in their use of custodial remands and, since the police and court decisions are so closely associated this will inevitably lead to differences in the court rates of custodial remand. Similarly, it was shown earlier that type of offence affects the remand decision, therefore areas with a large proportion of robberies or burglaries, for example, might be expected to have a high rate of custodial remands.

Conversely areas with a high proportion of thefts might be expected to have a low rate of custodial remands. A third possible reason is that the police remand decision and/or the offence mix do not fully explain rates of custodial remand in each area, suggesting that even when these two factors have been taken into account magistrates' courts still differ significantly in their policy on remand decisions.

There is another important point to consider. The differences shown in column 1 of Table 10:5 might merely reflect differences in the proportion of cases that are remanded and not dealt with at first court appearance. It will be recalled that the rates in column 1 show the proportion of those cases remanded that are remanded in custody. Thus, in areas where most cases are dealt with at first court appearance only a few, perhaps the more serious cases, are adjourned, with a higher proportion of them resulting in custodial remands. In contrast, in areas where a high proportion of cases are adjourned proportionately few will be remanded in custody. However, this possibility can be dismissed. The rates of custodial remands shown in column 1 were correlated with the proportion of all cases coming to court that were remanded, and there was no significant association between the two ($r = 0.07$).

The same analysis did show offence mix to be closely associated with the area rates of custodial remand. In particular, areas which dealt with a high proportion of offences of burglary and robbery had a high rate of custodial remands and vice versa ($r = 0.53$) and, conversely, areas which dealt with a high proportion of theft offences tended to have a low rate of custodial remands ($r = -0.44$).

Table 10:5 *Variations in court remand decisions by area**

	Court custody rate (%)	Police custody rate (%)	Court custody rate A–E†	Police–Court ratios C–C (%)	custody B–B (%)	Total no. of defendants
Area:						
Bedfordshire	7	20	–6.8	66	84	1,637
Gwent	8	8	0.2	96	99	1,212
Hertfordshire	9	10	–0.2	86	98	233
Lincolnshire	11	14	0.6	89	87	1,752
Surrey	12	13	–0.1	95	98	1,591
Merseyside	12	17	–2.5	96	93	17,895
S. Wales	12	11	–0.8	69	96	4,012
Suffolk	12	13	0.3	98	99	1,255
Metropolitan	12	24	–4.0	92	85	64,579
Kent	12	13	2.6	80	96	392
Essex	13	13	1.8	82	98	3,705
Nottinghamshire	14	14	0.9	69	95	6,575
W. Midlands	14	15	–1.3	95	98	8,384
Northumbria	14	21	–4.8	86	90	8,379
Durham	15	15	0.3	93	98	1,787
Derbyshire	15	24	–3.8	90	88	3,476
Avon–Somerset	16	35	–6.0	96	76	3,788
West Mercia	16	26	–1.2	90	86	2,599
Cumbria	16	15	0.7	78	97	121
Hampshire	16	19	1.4	87	94	6,246
Cambridgeshire	16	20	2.8	95	95	1,460
Northants	17	20	–2.9	84	93	1,851
Warwickshire	17	19	–2.6	92	96	912
Dyfed-Powys	17	13	5.7	64	97	200
Thames Valley	18	20	2.1	89	95	5,813
Leicestershire	18	19	0.7	98	98	3,541
Gtr. Manchester	18	33	–5.7	91	79	18,509
N. Wales	19	33	–7.6	86	79	1,012
Humberside	19	26	–2.8	93	90	3,912
Gloucestershire	19	22	1.8	95	95	647
City of London	21	32	0.4	95	85	623
Lancashire	21	28	–0.4	98	92	2,234
W. Yorkshire	22	29	–4.3	93	89	8,361
Cheshire	22	24	2.4	98	97	3,614
Norfolk	24	29	4.3	95	92	1,877
Staffordshire	25	33	0.8	87	85	2,567
Sussex	26	30	4.8	92	92	3,364
S. Yorkshire	28	30	2.8	85	92	3,894
Cleveland	28	29	0.3	99	98	1,289
Wiltshire	29	39	–1.4	92	82	1,147
Devon–Cornwall	29	34	4.3	89	89	2,378
Dorset	31	35	8.1	95	92	1,444
N. Yorkshire	37	35	8.9	78	91	1,072
All areas %	16	23		90	89	212,430
S.D.	6.6	8.4		8.9	6.0	

*All cases where a defendant was arrested, bailed and re-arrested (n = 1,236) or where defendants were not arrested or released without bail (n = 6,207) are excluded from the analysis.
†Actual rate of custodial remands minus the expected rate.

However, even when both the police remand decision and the offence mix were taken into account they did not fully explain the marked differences in the overall rates of court custodial remands. It is clear therefore, that although court remand decisions are closely associated with the earlier police decision and with the offence mix for that area, these factors alone do not fully explain the considerable variation which exists between areas in the propensity to remand defendants in custody.

Given the data on police remands in custody and the offence mix it was possible to estimate for each area an expected rate of court remands in custody based on 'average' practice for the country as a whole. The figures in column 3 of Table 10:5 give some indication of the different policies in each area with regard to remands in custody – they show the extent to which the actual rate of custody differed from the 'expected' rate in each area. Thus, in Bedfordshire the actual court custody rate of 7 per cent is 6.8 per cent less than might be expected given the police custody rate and the offence mix. Similarly, the actual court custody rate for Gwent is just 0.2 per cent higher than might be expected.

Taken as a whole the data in columns 1–3 of Table 10:5 allow some basic classification of areas. Thus, there is a group of areas in which the rate of court custodial remand is higher than expected – this group comprises North Yorkshire, Dorset, Dyfed-Powys, Sussex and Norfolk. Conversely, there is a group where the policies of the courts appear quite different and the rate of custodial remand is considerably less than expected – a group which includes North Wales, Bedfordshire, Avon and Somerset, Greater Manchester, Northumbria, West Yorkshire and the Metropolitan area.

Police and court remand decisions

Further evidence on the extent to which court decisions correspond to police decisions is shown in columns 4 and 5 of Table 10:5. The first of these represents the proportion of defendants remanded in custody by the magistrates' court who had previously been remanded in custody by the police. The second repeats the procedure for the much larger category of bail. If the argument propounded by Bottoms and McClean were correct, that variations in court practice simply reflect variations in police practice, then one would expect a very high degree of association between the remand decision of the courts and that of the police. While the figures for both bail and custody are high – overall 90 per cent of defendants remanded in custody by the courts had previously been remanded in custody by the police and 89 per cent remanded on bail by the courts had previously been remanded on bail by the police – there are considerable variations in these figures by area.

Using both these indices it was again possible to classify areas – this time into three broad groups. In the first group were those areas – for example, Gwent, Surrey, Suffolk, the West Midlands, Leicestershire, Gloucestershire, Cheshire and Cleveland – where both the court and police remand decisions were almost always the same (approximately 95 per cent or more of defendants remanded by the courts had received the same remand decision from the police). In the second group were those areas – South Wales, Nottinghamshire and Dyfed-Powys – where there was considerable agreement between the police and the courts over the bail decision (over 95 per cent of defendants given court bail had previously been given bail by the police), but little agreement over custody (less than 70 per cent of defendants given custody by the courts had been given custody by the police). Finally, in the third group came those areas – such as Avon and Somerset, Greater Manchester and North Wales – where the situation was reversed and close agreement existed between the police and courts over custodial remands but not with regard to bail. Only one area – Bedfordshire – clearly fell outside this categorisation. In this particular area marked differences existed between the police and the courts with regard to both bail and custody decisions.

The outcome of the case

An important feature of the remand process is the degree to which the remand decision of the court compares with the eventual outcome of the case. One might expect for example that in most cases involving a custodial remand the court would be likely to impose a custodial sentence. Unfortunately, the present study is restricted in the analysis that can be made of outcome since the data source does not contain information on the eventual outcome of those cases committed to the Crown Court. Consequently no precise figure can be put on the number of bail remands ending in a non-custodial sentence or the number of custodial remands ending in a custodial sentence. Despite this difficulty, however, some general information on outcome can be provided.

Table 10:6 compares the outcome of cases where the defendant had been remanded on bail or custody. While 27 per cent of bail cases are committed to the Crown Court (2 per cent for trial and 25 per cent for sentence) the figure for custodial remand cases is 60 per cent (14 per cent for sentence and 46 per cent for trial).

Table 10:6 *Outcome by type of remand*

	Type of remand: Bail (%)	Custody (%)	Total (%)	n
Non-custodial sentence	49.5	17.4	44.6	97,975
Custodial sentence	10.3	19.0	11.6	25,548
Not guilty	5.4	0.9	4.7	10,443
Case not proceeded with	3.3	1.6	3.0	6,580
Committed for sentence	2.2	14.1	4.0	8,887
Committed for trial	24.8	45.8	28.0	61,565
Failed to appear	4.5	1.2*	4.0	8,875
Total %	100	100	100	
n	186,045	33,828		219,873

*The remand classification was based on the remand decision at first court appearance. Cases classified as failed to appear despite a custodial remand therefore mostly comprise cases involving a subsequent change to bail.

The number of defendants who abscond while on bail is often interpreted as a measure of the 'failure rate' of the bail system. In this study 4 per cent of defendants failed to appear at court, a figure which is broadly comparable with figures reported in other studies but does tend to overestimate the actual absconding rate for most areas. Indeed, the average rate of 4 per cent only existed in seven large-city areas – the Metropolitan area, the City of London, Lancashire, Greater Manchester, Leicestershire and Derbyshire. Generally the rate was well below this and in eleven court areas it was actually below 1 per cent.

If all committals and absconding cases were removed from the sample one is left with those cases which were actually dealt with by the magistrates. Restricting the analysis to this sub-sample of cases suggests that the remand decision is not always a particularly good indicator of eventual case outcome. For example, 15 per cent of defendants remanded on bail received a custodial sentence (Table 10:7). More significantly, of the defendants remanded in custody 45 per cent received a non-custodial sentence, 4 per cent had their cases dismissed and 2 per cent were found not guilty.

Table 10:7 *Outcome by type of remand for cases dealt with in the magistrates' court*

	Type of remand: Bail (%)	Custody (%)	Total (%)	n
Non-custodial sentence	72.3	44.8	69.8	97,975
Custodial sentence	15.0	48.9	18.1	25,548
Not guilty	7.9	2.3	7.4	10,443
Case not proceeded with	4.8	4.1	4.7	6,580
Total %	100	100	100	
n	127,401	13,145		140,546

Conclusions

The study examined three main issues. First, what factors appeared to be most significant in 'explaining' the court remand decision for individual defendants. Second, how much variation existed between areas in the rate of custodial remands and what factors might have determined this. Third, what was the outcome of the cases in the sample and how did they correspond with the previous court remand decision.

The results strongly suggest that the most significant factors in the court remand decision are the police remand decision, the offence group and court policy. Other factors such as the age and sex of the defendant and the type of proceeding (charge or summons), though associated with the remand decision, tend to be of marginal significance in the overall explanation of individual court remand decisions. Furthermore, while the influence of type of offence on the court remand decision appears to be independent of area the same is not the case for the police remand decision. It is clear that despite an overall close association between police and court decisions the degree to which the court decision agrees with the police decision varies from area to area.

The analysis also showed that considerable variation did exist between areas in the overall proportion of defendants remanded in custody by the courts. Much of this variation can be accounted for by variations in the proportions remanded in custody by the police and in the offence mix. However, after allowing for these factors there are areas in which the court rate of custodial remand did not approximate to that which might be predicted.

It would appear that the variation between areas can usefully be perceived in two ways. First, it is possible to categorise areas by the extent to which the court decision agrees with that of the police. Thus, Gwent, Suffolk, Leicestershire and Cleveland would emerge as four areas where the courts had quite different rates of custodial remand but a similar propensity to follow very closely the remand decisions of the police. Conversely, areas such as Bedfordshire, the Metropolitan area, Avon and Somerset, Greater Manchester and North Wales were characterised by court remand decisions which were at some variance with those of the police.

Second, it is possible to group areas through a comparison of their actual rate of court custodial remand with their expected rate given the police rate of custodial remand and the offence mix. From this perspective areas in which the court rate of custodial remand seems high would include North Yorkshire, Sussex, Dorset, Norfolk and Dyfed-Powys. Those areas where the rate seems comparably low would comprise Greater Manchester, the Metropolitan area, Northumbria, West Yorkshire, Bedfordshire, Avon and Somerset and North Wales.

Finally, the study showed that of those defendants dealt with in the magistrates' courts the vast majority (85 per cent) either received a non-custodial sentence or were acquitted. However, of those defendants who were remanded in custody only 49 per cent actually received a custodial sentence.

11 Speeding up justice

ROGER TARLING and JULIE VENNARD

There is general agreement that delay in dealing with defendants works against the ideals of justice. The Streatfeild Committee (1961) noted that 'all the benefits which flow from justice being done will be more potent when it is done quickly'. Public confidence in the effectiveness of the judicial process can be undermined if delays are lengthy; and the significance of a sentence in terms of deterrence, both to the defendant and the general public, may well diminish with time.

There are other reasons why lengthy delays should be avoided. Many defendants, particularly if they are remanded in custody, may suffer unduly from long delays, especially if they are not subsequently given a custodial sentence. (Approximately 40 per cent of defendants remanded in custody are either acquitted or given a non-custodial sentence.) Chapter 10 showed how defendants remanded in custody put pressure on the prison system, with the population of male defendants remanded in custody increasing by 50 per cent, to 7,200, in the six years to 1982. Repeated adjournments also entail substantial economic costs for the police, magistrates and courts' staff as well as the prison service. Witnesses or victims, particularly of unpleasant events or of substantial financial loss may also suffer prolonged anxiety due to protracted proceedings. Last, but by no means least, the likelihood that a trial will provide an effective means of ascertaining the truth may diminish with time. Butler (Chapter 13) suggests, at least for Crown Court cases, longer waiting times are associated with higher acquittal rates.

The desirability of dealing with defendants as expeditiously as possible and the pressures on the criminal justice system have given rise to a good deal of debate on the strategies that might be pursued to minimise delay. For example, there is growing interest in statutory time limits similar to the 110 day rule in Scotland or those brought into being in the United States by the Speedy Trial Act. The research described in this chapter looks, first, at the nature of delay and at ways in which delays might be reduced through changes in organisation. Second, the effect of the speedy trials legislation in the United States is discussed, to see what lessons might be drawn from the US experience in relation to statutory time limits.

Pre-court time

Research suggests that the average time for cases to reach magistrates' courts (including juvenile courts) has, in recent years, been between two and three months. (Nightingale, 1979; Vera Institute of Justice, 1979; Bowden and

Stevens, 1980; Gemmill and Morgan-Giles, 1980; Lupton and Roberts, 1982; Frankenburg and Tarling, 1983). In their study of 685 juveniles dealt with at six juvenile courts, Frankenburg and Tarling were able to sub-divide the pre-court stage into three identifiable stages. The first, the time from the commission of the offence to the juvenile being arrested or reported, took on average 1.4 weeks. The second stage, the time from arrest or report to charge or summons, ie the period in which the police decide whether or not to prosecute, took on average 4.0 weeks. And the third stage, the time taken to bring the juvenile to court once the police had decided to prosecute took on average 3.0 weeks.

Average time taken for cases to reach court masks considerable variation. The length of time between apprehension of the suspect and first court appearance depends largely on whether the police proceed by means of charge or summons. The Vera Institute of Justice, Gemmill and Morgan-Giles, and Frankenburg and Tarling all found that cases where the police charged suspects reached court between three and four times more quickly than cases where a summons procedure was used.

Court time

Court time, the period between first court appearance to the final disposition of the case, is more complex and is dependent on many factors. Adjournments, each adding to the time taken to complete the case, can occur for several reasons and at different points in the process; for example, to enable the defendant to seek legal representation, to fix a date for a contested hearing, for reports to be prepared and so on. Therefore the length of time taken will vary considerably according to the complexity of the case. So it is important to consider the number of court appearances, the intervals between them and the reasons for adjournments.

The majority of cases appearing before magistrates' courts are completed quickly. *Criminal Statistics* 1979 stated that approximately 60 per cent of indictable triable either way cases are concluded at the first court appearance. From data collected by the Home Office Statistical Department on 8,000 cases remanded at magistrates' courts in May to October 1978 (to study the working of the Bail Act 1976) it can be estimated that a further 19 per cent of cases require two hearings; 11 per cent three hearings, and 10 per cent four or more.

Frankenburg and Tarling found that proportionately fewer cases involving juvenile defendants were dealt with at first appearance – only 41 per cent – whereas 34 per cent required two hearings, 17 per cent three and 8 per cent four or more.

Measuring total time spent on remand (for those cases not dealt with at first appearance before the case was completed) it was found from the data collected following the Bail Act that 32 per cent of defendants spent up to three weeks on remand, 35 per cent 4–7 weeks, 19 per cent between 8 and 13 weeks and 15 per cent spent more than 13 weeks on remand (*Criminal Statistics* 1979, Table 8.17).

Persons remanded in custody were on average remanded more often than those on bail but their time on remand tended to be less. The average duration of each remand was about four complete weeks for persons remanded on bail throughout, but about one week for those remanded in custody. (This difference is to be expected because of the statutory limitations on the duration of remands in custody.) In accordance with the above findings. Frankenburg and Tarling found the average duration between remands for juveniles was 4.7 weeks (very few juveniles being remanded in custody).

Further analysis of both these sets of data revealed two other factors which contributed to the time taken. First, time taken varied according to the type of court. Defendants at both the Inner London courts and the larger (city centre) courts tended to spend longer total times on remand, and intervals between hearings were also longer, although they did not adjourn cases any more often than smaller courts. Second, contested cases seem to pose particular difficulties. Obviously a contested case will take longer than an uncontested case because once a defendant has pleaded not guilty the case will have to be adjourned to hold a trial. Nevertheless, the interval from entering a not guilty plea to holding a trial is much longer than the interval following an adjournment for another reason. For example, Frankenburg and Tarling found that the interval between the defendant pleading not guilty and the trial taking place was 6.9 weeks. (A similar figure was found by Bottoms and McClean, 1976.)

In addition to adjournments to hold a trial, Frankenburg and Tarling recorded the reasons for all other adjournments in their sample of juvenile cases. The results are shown in Table 11:1.

It can be seen that approximately one half of all adjournments were in order to conduct a trial or for reports to be prepared. What is also striking from the table is the many and varied reasons that account for the other 55 per cent of adjournments.

Contrasting these more recent findings with the results of much earlier research by Gibson (1960), shows just how much the picture has changed in the last 20 to 25 years. Gibson's study focused on the length of remands for defendants whose cases were first heard in April 1958. She found that the average remand period was about two weeks for defendants whose cases were dealt with entirely summarily and that only 5 per cent were on remand for more than four weeks compared with 69 per cent today. Furthermore, only 2 per cent of defendants were remanded for reports.

Table 11:1 *The percentage of all adjournments by reason for adjournment*

Reason for adjournment	% of adjournments
To hold a trial	25
For reports to be prepared	21
Defendant's absence	12
To seek legal representation/obtain legal aid	9
Prosecution requested more time to prepare its case	5
Defence requested more time to prepare its case	4
To remand in care/custody	1
Witness's absence	3
To join up with another case for disposal	2
Associated with having co-defendants*	5
Summons not served	2
Not enough court time to hear case	5
Reports not ready	2
More than one reason†	3
Other	2
Total number of adjournments	640

*For example, the co-defendant did not attend court, entered a different plea or sought legal representation etc.

†In the majority of cases the court was considering imposing a custodial sentence so the proceedings were adjourned for reports to be prepared and for the defendant to seek legal representation.

Strategies to reduce delays

Much of the pre-court stage was spent in arriving at a decision to prosecute. Obviously, deliberations and consultations are important and result in many defendants, particularly juveniles, not appearing in court at all, the police choosing to caution them instead. Nevertheless some thought could usefully be given to improving administrative arrangements and procedures in order to speed up the decision. Some steps have already been taken in this direction by the agencies involved – the 'instant cautioning scheme' described in Chapter 6 is one example.

The number of adjournments, the intervals between them and the difficulties encountered with contested cases, particularly at the larger courts, all contribute to the time it takes for a court to dispose of a case. In order to deal with cases as expeditiously as possible and to improve on existing times two broad strategies are open to the courts: first to avoid adjournments which are not essential and second, to cut down the length of adjournments which are necessary and inevitable. As far as inessential adjournments are concerned, 27 per cent of the adjournments shown in the table would have been eliminated by ensuring that the summons had been served, that reports were ready as requested, that there was enough court time to hear the case, that the defendant was legally represented where necessary, and that the prosecution and defence were ready to proceed. While it is fully appreciated that avoiding these adjournments may be difficult to achieve in practice it is nevertheless important to realise how far administrative improvements could go towards minimising delays. Turning to the second strategy adjournments to hold a trial after a defendant had pleaded not guilty are unavoidable, but it may still be possible to reduce the present average intervals. The Home Office Working Group on Magistrates' Courts suggested some procedures that might be implemented by listing officers and justices' clerks and described the steps that some courts have taken to achieve a reduction.

Pre-trial reports have been mooted to avoid adjournments and some courts have explored the provision of such reports. However, preparing reports earlier in the proceedings may not be cost-effective; some reports will prove unnecessary if the defendant is acquitted or if the court would not otherwise have requested one. Furthermore, there is a limit to the inquiries that can properly be made about the circumstances of a defendant who has not been found guilty or who intends to contest the charge(s). Nevertheless, pre-trial reports could usefully be prepared in cases where a guilty plea is expected and where a report can be accurately predicted.

Although research has not identified a simple or universal way of reducing the time taken to deal with defendants, it has isolated a number of aspects of police and court procedures where time could be saved without prejudice to the proper administration of justice. The findings, important in themselves, could assume still greater significance if time limits were to be introduced, so that improvements which are in any event highly desirable were to become essential in order to meet statutory requirements.

Speeding up justice in the United States

In the United States, concern to reduce delay in bringing cases to court led to the federal Speedy Trial Act of 1974. Speedy trial rules have also been introduced in the state courts, where the nature of cases dealt with placed programmes of delay reduction in a rather different context – generally the issues at stake are simpler than in cases dealt with at federal level. The state courts deal on the whole with police-processed offences originating from citizens' complaints, whereas the federal courts receive most of their cases from enforcement agencies such as the Federal Bureau of Investigation or Internal Revenue services. Major offence categories are robbery, embezzlement, fraud, drugs and narcotics. While caution is needed in drawing inferences from other jurisdictions about the efficacy of time limits, there is much that can be learned from the American experience.

A review of the American speedy trial rules addressed three questions:

a. whether, and if so to what extent, time limits have reduced delay in bringing cases to trial;

b. what effect, if any, the introduction of the sanction of case dismissal has had on the level of compliance with the time strictures;

c. how frequently, and for what reasons, extensions beyond the 100 day limit are granted by the courts; and

d. what existing sources reveal about the costs and benefits of the Act for judges, court administrators, the prosecution and defence.

The sources of data included empirical studies of federal and state speedy trials requirements and more general studies of court delay, statistical data compiled by the Administrative Office of the United States Courts (AO) and the reports of the Speedy Trial planning groups which were set up in the district courts to monitor the impact of the time limits. Personnel at the AO who were closely involved in the implementation and administration of the Act were also consulted.

The federal Speedy Trial Act of 1974

As amended in 1979, the Speedy Trial Act requires courts to bring cases from arrest to trial within 100 days (90 days where defendants are remanded in custody). The 100 day time limit was phased in over a four year transition period (which ended in 1979) and a sanction of dismissal for failure to comply was imposed in July 1980. Flexibility was built into the Act through so-called excludable time provision. That is, the Act stipulated that certain reasons for delay – ranging from specifically defined events to broad 'interests of justice' requirements – shall be excluded from the computation of time taken (see Frase, 1976, for an overview of the Act).

Statistics published on the operation of speedy trials legislation show levels of compliance with the time strictures from 1976 (when transitional time limits were imposed) through to 1982. They report a high compliance rate throughout these years and a progressive increase during this period in the proportion of cases brought to trial within the time requirements. In the year 1981–82, 97 per cent of defendants were indicted in 30 days or less; for the second (indictment to trial) interval, 96 per cent of defendants were tried in 70 days or less. Recording of dismissals through non-compliance with the time limits began in 1980 and the most recent (1982) figures indicate that between 1980–82 only 40 cases were dismissed in these circumstances.

A major problem in interpreting these compliance rates however, is that they represent 'net' processing time and omit periods of excludable time granted by the court. It is not apparent, therefore, whether compliance has been achieved at the expense of heavy reliance on excludable delay. Similarly, although the statistics include information on the number of defendants detained in custody prior to trial and the lengths of their detention, these are 'net' times. They show that, of the (35,400) defendants whose cases were terminated in 1981, 25 per cent were held in pre-trial custody. Of these, only 3.2 per cent exceeded the 90 day 'custody clock'. However, since excludable delay is deducted from the computation, it is not known how long defendants were actually detained prior to trial. Moreover, where defendants were detained beyond the 90 days, it is not possible to tell from the data who was instrumental in delaying proceedings.

Statistical data on the number of cases in which excludable delay occurred, together with recent studies of case processing time under the legislation (Bridges, 1982, and Feeley, 1983), suggest that the increased rate of compliance since the Act came into effect may well be due to the more frequent use of extensions beyond the 100 day limit. For example, of the 35,400 defendants whose cases were terminated in 1981 (the year following the implementation of sanctions), some 40 per cent were reported to have had one or more excludable delay periods applied during the first or second of the speedy trial intervals. This was the largest incidence of excludable delay on record, and constituted a 17 per cent increase over 1976. The reason most frequently cited for granting excludable delay was that additional time was requested by the prosecution, or more often by the defence. In 1981, 53 per cent of extensions were of this type. Continuances granted 'in the interest of justice' comprised the second largest category, accounting for 22 per cent of incidents of excludable time. Whilst inconclusive, these figures tend to support the prediction that the exceptions permitted under the Act would be increasingly used to achieve technical compliance, with no real impact on disposition times.

Without reliable national data on actual time intervals between arrest and trial, both prior to and after sanctions were imposed, the effects of the mandatory time limits on court delay remain a matter for speculation. Valid empirical assessment of the influence of the Act on the speed of disposition would also need to take into account the possible effect on case processing times of other developments in the federal system in the years following the enactment of the speedy trials process, not least of which is the marked downward trend in the number of criminal defendants awaiting trial during the years 1976–82 (a drop from 27,800 to 24,000). Other relevant factors are the increasing numbers of prosecutions for fraud (which because of their complexity tend to involve greater processing time) and an increase in the proportion of contested cases in the federal system. The statistical data are also uninformative on such questions as whether adherence to the time limits is problematic for all, or only certain kinds of offences. If the latter proved to be the case, it would lend support to the argument for extending the 100 day limit for restricted categories of offences, where extension of time is the norm.

State speedy trials provisions

Studies of the experiences of state courts in operating speedy trial rules have reached conclusions which accord with these insights into the federal Speedy Trial Act. A number of states have adopted speedy trial rules, specifying time limits on bringing cases to trial. A 50 state survey of state speedy trial provisions, undertaken in 1982 by the National Centre for State Courts, indicates considerable variation in their formal requirements. As with the federal Speedy Trial Act, reliable statistical data on actual case processing times prior to and after promulgation of the various time standards are lacking. But some information on the question has emerged from more general studies of court delay. In his study of case processing time in state trial courts, Church (1978), for example, undertook some analysis of the relationship between the actual time taken to disposition and state speedy trial requirements. While there was wide variation in disposition times among the 21 courts in his sample, Church observed that the pace of litigation 'was not linked in any direct way to the duration of the court's speedy trial standard'.

In a follow-up study Church (1982) reported that there was a close correspondence between views on how courts *should* operate in particular types of cases and the actual pace of disposition in the four districts. On the other hand time limits did appear to generate support within the court and legal community for a faster pace of litigation, and may have assisted in establishing standards and reducing disposition times. The essential message from the study was that time limits which are sufficiently flexible to meet the requirements of individual cases must be accompanied by a commitment on the part of the judge to enforce reasonable deadlines for the conclusion of pre-trial activities. Feeley's (1983) assessment of state attempts to reduce delay through speedy trial rules is broadly consistent with the inferences which Church drew from his empirical data.

Taken together, these studies of federal and state attempts to expedite case handling suggest that, while time limits have played a part in setting standards or targets according to which courts assess their performance, the real key to success lies in judicial control over a wide ranging programme of delay reduction. A commitment on the part of the court to enforce reasonable deadlines is viewed as an essential prerequisite of such a programme. In addition, the court should seek to achieve an effective consultative machinery to ensure co-operation from the defence and prosecution with the goals of the programme. There is reason to believe that measures to speed up case disposition which lack effective sanctions will have little impact if, as often seems to be the case, the interest of practitioners and their responsibilities to their clients are better served by maintaining the status quo.

Conclusions

Research has helped to identify the nature of delays, and in doing so has pointed to possible ways of reducing them through changes in police and court procedures. The possibility of statutory time limits as a means of reducing delays in England and Wales has stimulated interest in the American experience in this regard. The effects of the speedy trial provisions suggest that legislation offers no panacea for delay, and that safeguards against liberal interpretation of any grounds for exclusion are essential. Given such safeguards, time limits could play a valuable role in reducing delays by encouraging the development of improved procedures for bringing cases to trial.

12 The outcome of contested trials

JULIE VENNARD

The right to claim trial by jury

The allocation of criminal cases between the Crown Court and magistrates' courts is a subject of long-standing debate amongst those involved with or having an interest in the administration of criminal justice. In recent years this debate has centred on the question whether the right to trial by jury ought to be preserved for the less serious types of offence which are at present triable on indictment at the Crown Court. Those who favour a transfer of jurisdiction point to the considerably greater costs of trial on indictment and to the fact that trials in the Crown Court are generally far longer than in magistrates' courts. Time and expenditure on the trial of relatively minor cases in the Crown Court is widely regarded as disproportionate to the gravity of the offences involved. One of the problems associated with the rising caseload in the Crown Court was discussed in Chapter 11 – namely that longer waiting times mean that defendants charged with more serious types of offence are being remanded in custody for increasingly long periods.

Extension of summary jurisdiction over indictable offences has been a significant trend over the last century and a half. Only a small proportion of defendants actually exercise their right to a trial in the Crown Court – some 90 per cent of all criminal cases are tried summarily – and any major shift of work towards the Crown Court must create severe problems for its workload, and costs would escalate. But while few would seek to justify an unrestricted right to trial by judge and jury, there is a lack of consensus as to the categories of offence for which the choice of venue ought to be retained. The report of the James Committee (1975) on the distribution of cases between the two levels of trial recommended the removal from the jurisdiction of the Crown Court of a range of offences which carried the right of election, including theft of low value property. Debate surrounding this latter recommendation brought into focus the strength of public support for the right to choose jury trial and it failed to gain acceptance in Parliament. Other, less controversial, restrictions were adopted in the Criminal Law Act 1977. For example public order offences and criminal damage of £200 or less became purely summary.

The Criminal Law Act also established a more rational basis for the classification of offences. Based on the premise that the most serious offences should be tried only in the Crown Court and the least serious should be triable only summarily, the Act reduced the categories of offence for mode of trial purposes from six to three. For the range of intermediate offences which vary greatly in severity defendants retain the right to elect trial on indictment. Low value thefts and other offences which are widely held to represent a waste of Crown Court resources and are the focus of current controversy, fall within this intermediate category of triable either way cases. Theft and related offences of dishonesty (including handling of stolen goods and deception) form the most numerous class of triable either way offences that come before the Crown Court.

The changes in jurisdiction effected by the 1977 legislation for a time halted the steady upward trend in the total numbers proceeded against for either way offences and the proportion of defendants who are committed to the Crown Court for trial. However, since 1979, the upward trend in cases committed for trial has resumed. The cumulative increase between 1979 and 1983 in the numbers of either way cases committed was 44 per cent[1]. And whereas waiting times in the Crown Court fell in that period, the *Judicial Statistics* for 1984 show that the position has begun to worsen again, with the average for custody cases exceeding 10 weeks.

Choice of forum

Traditionally jury trial has been regarded as superior to trial summarily by virtue of the fact that it offers judgment by a randomly selected group of one's fellow citizens. This supposed representativeness is seen as maximising the chances of a fair and impartial verdict and tends to be contrasted with a magistracy perceived as being heavily weighted towards the middle aged and middle class. It is also widely claimed that juries are a safeguard of civil liberties and a means of checking unpopular or inflexible laws. Whether these ideals are realised, indeed, whether it is a proper function of the jury to give expression to 'extra-legal' considerations in their verdicts, has long been questioned in the writings of jury critics (for example, Marshall, 1975). And while notionally jury trial provides for representative judgment by one's peers, in practice these ideals can be undermined by excusal for service, peremptory challenge by the defence and jury vetting by the prosecution.

Historical and philosophical reasons apart, on a variety of pragmatic grounds trial at the Crown Court is seen as superior to summary trial. For example, whereas defendants tried in the Crown Court are provided with information on the case against them, it is only very recently that formal provision for disclosure of the prosecution case in magistrates' courts has been introduced. Secondly, where the admissibility of evidence is in dispute at summary trial the presiding bench learns of the existence of that evidence even though it may be excluded on the grounds of unreliability. In the Crown Court the judge determines the question of admissibility in the jury's absence. It is also frequently alleged that where they anticipate conviction some defendants elect trial on indictment simply to gain time before the commencement of a

1. See *Criminal Statistics England and Wales* 1983, Table 6.5, for the proportions of either way offences committed for trial in the Crown Court between 1979–83.

custodial sentence and enjoy certain privileges which they will lose after sentence.

For the defendant who pleads not guilty, however, one of the fundamental reasons for choosing trial in the Crown Court is undoubtedly the belief that the prospect of acquittal is higher than if the case were tried before magistrates. This has emerged strongly in the studies of defendants' decisions on venue and in evidence received by the James Committee (see Bottoms and McClean, 1976, and Gregory, 1976). It was against a background of speculation about the respective chances of acquittal in cases commonly tried at both courts that the present study was formulated. Hitherto there has been no attempt to systematically compare the outcome of equivalent cases, controlling as far as possible for differences in the prosecution and defence evidence. Although statistics are published by the Lord Chancellor's Department on acquittal rates in contested cases tried in the Crown Court there are no comparable national statistics on acquittal rates in magistrates' courts[2]. Even if such statistics were available they would not permit meaningful assessment of the differences between the two tribunals in their propensities to acquit. It may well be that cases which go to the Crown Court on the defendant's election are brought on weaker prosecution evidence than where defendants agree to summary trial. The possibility of a higher sentence on conviction after trial in the higher courts would be likely to deter defendants from exercising their right to jury trial unless, on the face of the available evidence, the prospect of acquittal seemed high. To test this premise, the research reported in this chapter examined in detail the evidence on which verdicts were brought in comparable samples of either way cases tried at the two types of court. While other studies over the last decade have addressed the issue whether jury verdicts are in accordance with the evidence (eg McCabe and Purves, 1972 and 1974, Zander, 1984, Baldwin and McConville, 1979) this study provides the first comparative assessment of outcome for the two levels of trial.

An earlier phase of the comparative study described in this chapter (Vennard, 1981) sought to remedy the dearth of information about the adversarial trial in magistrates' courts. For that study it was decided to adopt a new approach – one which would provide a systematic assessment of the evidence as presented in court and of the performance of witnesses under cross-examination. Information was compiled through observation of a sample of contested trials at selected courts. Details of the evidence advanced by the prosecution and the defence were recorded and a method was devised for assessing the impugnment of witness credibility. The latter, although largely overlooked in studies of jury verdicts, proved to be a key factor in explaining magistrates' decisions

2. Between 1976 and 1978 statistics were published by the Home Office showing acquittal rates for cases tried in the magistrates' courts. However, it was discovered that these figures (which suggested an acquittal rate in magistrates' courts of 50 per cent) were inaccurate and that the true acquittal rate was markedly lower (in the region of 25 per cent).

to convict or acquit. The high conviction rate was consistent overall with the fact that the majority of charges were brought on strong evidence implicating the defendant (for example, a confession or eyewitness evidence). The features of the case most strongly related to outcome were the defendant's own performance in giving evidence – whether his account was consistent and generally plausible – and the credibility of prosecution witnesses. For example, where the defendant's credibility was impugned in cross-examination, conviction followed in 93 per cent of the cases. And whereas the magistrates dismissed some 69 per cent of charges where the credibility of prosecution witnesses was impugned, only 18 per cent ended in acquittal where such witnesses were ostensibly credible. Some support was found for the view that the magistrates tend to accept prosecution eyewitness evidence, particularly that of police officers, in preference to the defendant's conflicting account of his part of the alleged offence. Key questions to emerge from this study were whether verdicts in the Crown Court would be correlated with the same sorts of evidential factors – both in terms of the direction and the strength of associations apparent in cases tried summarily.

The present study

The main objectives of the comparative study were thus:

(i) to analyse the prosecution and defence evidence, including the testing of witness credibility, in comparable cases tried in the Crown Court and in the magistrates' courts; and

(ii) to compare the outcome in the two samples, having regard to the type of evidence adduced and the performance of witnesses under cross-examination.

Consideration was also given to the part played by statements of confession in establishing the prosecution case, disputes over the admissibility and accuracy of statement evidence and the procedures for resolving such disputes at the two modes of trial. A report of these aspects of the research has been written up elsewhere (Vennard, 1984).

The research design and sample

A number of factors could, in theory, explain differences in acquittal rates in the Crown Court and in magistrates' courts. On the one hand, a higher acquittal rate in the Crown Court might reflect differences in the strength of the evidence adduced. It might be that lawyers tend to advise their clients to elect trial by jury where they believe the prosecution evidence is seriously flawed and that, as a corollary, their own case is relatively strong. A second hypothesis is that juries look for higher standard of proof than magistrates or are more sceptical of prosecution evidence – particularly from police officers. A third explanation, for which there is some support in the previous research (Baldwin and McConville, 1979) is that juries acquit against the weight of the evidence and that their verdicts are on occasion 'perverse' or irrational.

The above hypotheses were influential in determining the offence selection for the present study. In order to take into account features of the evidence peculiar to the nature of the charge and attempt some assessment of its strengths and weaknesses, it was important to focus on a restricted range of offences triable either summarily or in the Crown Court and attempt to secure sufficient numbers within each offence category. At the same time it was desirable to include in the sample the types of offence which have been suggested as suitable for re-classification as purely summary offences. The sample was thus restricted to the following triable either way offences:

(i) wounding or assault occasioning actual bodily harm (section 20 and section 47 Offences Against the Persons Act 1861);

(ii) shoplifting;

(iii) other theft/handling.

A sample of 305 contested summary charges was achieved from six magistrates' courts (three in London and three in the provincial centres in the North and Midlands and West). A sample of 320 contested Crown Court cases was obtained from the same three provincial centres and one Inner London Crown Court. Although there were some problems in achieving comparable numbers of charges within each offence category, overall numbers were sufficient to permit some comparative analysis within offence of the type of evidence adduced in the Crown Court and magistrates' courts. (The offence distribution is shown in Table 12:1.)

Since the prosecution must establish its case on each individual charge preferred against a defendant, the analysis of outcome in relation to the evidence adduced is expressed in this study in relation to the contested *charge*, not the defendant. In fact, in both the Crown Court and magistrates' courts the large majority of defendants pleaded not guilty to one charge only; multiple contested charges were rather more frequent in the Crown Court (23 per cent) than in magistrates' courts (11 per cent). Certain other differences and similarities between the defendant samples are noteworthy. Those tried summarily were somewhat younger than defendants tried in the Crown Court (45 per cent and 37 per cent respectively were under 30). In both courts the samples were predominantly male; roughly a fifth of charges were contested by women at each venue. The samples were also well matched in terms of the proportion of defendants who were tried jointly with one or more co-defendants (at both courts some three-quarters of the defendants were tried alone). Marginally more defendants tried at the Crown Court had previous criminal records (65 per cent) than defendants tried summarily (60 per cent).

Two thirds of defendants in the Crown Court sample had elected trial; 11 per cent had been committed as a decision of the Bench. For the remainder, information on who chose the venue was unavailable. This rate of election by defendants is considerably higher than has been reported elsewhere (eg

Bottoms and McClean, 1976; Baldwin and McConville, 1979), but it must be remembered that the present sample is restricted to defendants who pleaded not guilty to the charges preferred. Finally, the samples were comparable in terms of legal representation in as much as under 5 per cent (14) of defendants tried summarily were unrepresented by counsel or solicitor advocates.

Verdicts brought at the two modes of trial

Table 12:1 shows the outcome of contested charges heard at the Crown Court and in magistrates' courts within each of the three offence categories included in the study.

Table 12:1 *Types of offence to which defendants pleaded not guilty at the Crown Court and magistrates' courts by outcome*

Nature of charge	Crown Court			Magistrates' courts		
	Number	% of sample	Acquitted %	Number	% of sample	Acquitted %
Wounding or assault	103	32	60	83	27	29
Shoplifting	72	23	58	81	27	24
Other theft/handling	145	45	54	141	46	33
Total	320	100	57	305	100	30

It will be seen that the proportions of charges within each offence category are roughly comparable at both courts, yet for all three categories the acquittal rates are markedly lower for cases tried summarily.

Among the contested charges in the present samples, 9 per cent were dismissed in the Crown Court by direction of the judge. Ordered acquittals would not have fallen into the sample since the field workers were instructed to include only cases in which juries were empanelled and the prosecution evidence was presented. Six per cent of contested summary charges were dismissed in similar circumstances – ie because the prosecution failed to establish a *prima facie* case.

The evidence adduced by the prosecution and the defence

Subject to certain exceptions, the burden of proof is always on the prosecution to prove beyond reasonable doubt all the elements of the alleged offence. To establish the 'facts in issue' the prosecution must prove that the defendant was responsible for the criminal conduct (the *actus reus*), and that the action was accompanied by the requisite criminal intent (the *mens rea*). Evidence of these 'facts in issue' is typically supplied through the testimony of witnesses and may either be 'direct' or circumstantial. Evidence of written or oral confessions, documentary or material evidence, may also form part of the prosecution case.

The earlier phase of this research established strong statistical associations in the predicted direction between four key evidential factors and conviction by magistrates. These were: (i) a statement of confession; (ii) eyewitness evidence implicating the defendant; (iii) prosecution witnesses whose credibility was not manifestly impugned; and (iv) the impugnment of the defendant's credibility on grounds of inconsistency or the implausibility of his testimony. Corroborative evidence produced by defendants and evidence of previous character contributed marginally to outcome differences but were outweighed by the defendant's performance in the witness box. These findings were taken as the starting point in the analysis of the evidence and its relationship to outcome in the comparative analysis reported here. The prosecution evidence was first classified according to: whether witnesses who testified gave eyewitness accounts or circumstantial evidence implicating the defendant in the alleged offence; the content of statements attributed to defendants as a result of questioning by the police; and the impugnment of prosecution witnesses in cross-examination. The classification of the defence case took into account defendant credibility; defendant's previous character; and availability of defence witnesses. Table 12:2 summarises the differences and similarities between the courts on these features of the prosecution and defence case.

Table 12:2 *The evidence in cases tried in the Crown Court and magistrates' courts*

Prosecution factors	Crown Court Number	%	Magistrates' courts Number	%
1 Direct evidence from prosecution witnesses	164	51	152	50
2 Written confession	25	8	38	12
Oral confession	42	13	30	10
Damaging admission	136	43	140	46
3 Prosecution credibility impugned	138	43	69	23
Defence factors				
4 Defendant credibility impugned	235	73	214	70
5 Defendant character not put in evidence	206	64	191	63
6 Credible defence witness	36	12	45	16

A striking feature of Table 12:2 is the close similarity in the evidence adduced in the two modes of trial. The one – very notable – exception is that prosecution credibility was impugned almost twice as often in the Crown Court as in magistrates' courts. The table does, of course, mask differences between offence categories in the sorts of evidence presented by the prosecution. However while some of the more obvious differences are worth noting they do not invalidate comparison between the courts since, as Table

12:1 showed, there was little variation in the proportions of each offence category dealt with by the two types of court. In both courts most charges of wounding or assault were brought on eyewitness evidence, usually that of the victim. Similar proportions of charges were brought on the evidence of police officers who alleged that they were the victims of the alleged conduct (approximately one third). For shoplifting, in over 90 per cent of cases tried summarily and four fifths of Crown Court cases, prosecution witnesses (in the main, store detectives) testified that they had seen the defendant take the goods and leave the store or had apprehended the defendants with goods in their possession for which they had not paid. In contrast, defendants were implicated by direct evidence in only 6 per cent of cases of theft/handling tried in the Crown Court and 10 per cent of those tried summarily. In most cases the prosecution relied for proof of the events and dishonest intent on indirect evidence of one form or another.

Incriminating statements attributed to defendants

Statements attributed to defendants were classified according to whether they contained full confessions, damaging admissions, or denials. The term damaging admissions was used to denote statements which, though short of full confessions, were used by the prosecution for inculpatory purposes, as were defendants' statements made in response to questioning by the police which conflicted with the accounts they gave at trial. Table 12:2 shows that confessional statements were attributed in respect of only a fifth of charges but that a further 43 per cent in the Crown Court and 46 per cent of summary charges were supported by damaging admissions.

In both courts the prosecution relied far more frequently on statements to support charges of theft/handling than where defendants were charged with shoplifting or assault. Full confessions were adduced in approximately a third of charges of theft whereas fewer than 10 per cent of Crown Court and summary charges of assault were supported by confessions. Whether this pattern reflects police questioning practices – specifically a greater propensity to secure statements where proof of the offence was otherwise dependent on circumstantial evidence (typically theft/handling) – is speculative.

While the two courts were very similar in the distribution of incriminating statements within the three offence categories, it is noteworthy that, in the cases tried summarily, those statements were more often written by the defendant than in the Crown Court. Fifty-six per cent of confessions in cases tried summarily were contained in written statements (these were either written or dictated and signed by defendants), compared with 37 per cent in the Crown Court. The importance of this distinction between written and oral statements is that the latter are more open to challenge by the defence. Comparison between the two samples on the extent and nature of challenges to statement admissibility and accuracy confirmed that such disputes were more frequent in cases tried in the Crown Court, particularly in respect of oral statements (see Vennard, 1984).

The credibility of prosecution witnesses

The right to cross-examine witnesses in open court is an established part of our adversary system of trial. Eggleston (1983) notes that 'usually the decision as to the facts depends in the last resort on which of the witnesses the tribunal believes to be telling the truth'. This involves an assessment of the credibility of each of the witnesses called to testify. Hence, the vital role of the prosecution and defence advocates is in establishing the credibility of their own witnesses and attempting to raise doubts about the reliability of the opposing witnesses' accounts.

The assessment of the association between attacks on witness credibility and outcome in the first phase of this research underlined the importance of witness performance under cross-examination. Obviously, there are difficulties in quantifying the grounds on which lawyers endeavoured to discredit witnesses and it is important to bear in mind the limitations of the approach used here to capture this feature of the trial. To minimise the risk of subjectivity the observers were required to refer to a 'check list' of criteria which are widely acknowledged to be the most common tests of witness credibility applied by the courts. These criteria, based largely on Eggleston's (1983) itemisation of the factors which judges take into account when assessing the credibility, are summarised at Appendix A. This technique does not purport to demonstrate whether, and if so on what grounds, witnesses *were* discredited and it is not known whether the challenges brought by advocates influenced magistrates' and juries' verdicts. However, the assessment of witness performance did capture lawyers' attempts to undermine or dilute the testimony of opposing witnesses on such grounds as poor recollection of significant facts, conflict with the facts recorded in earlier statements and other forms of inconsistency, or the general improbability of their assertions. It is reasonable to suppose that decisions to acquit or convict would to some extent reflect this dimension of the prosecution and defence case.

This method of recording and classifying the attempts of defence lawyers to cast doubt on the credibility of prosecution witnesses revealed a statistically highly significant difference between the two courts (Table 12:2). Examination of the grounds on which the defence challenged the credibility of the opposing witnesses indicated that, in both courts, inconsistency was the predominant weakness they were able to expose (factors 1–3 in the check list of criteria at Appendix A). Defence lawyers were twice as successful in disclosing inconsistency in cases tried in the Crown Court than in magistrates' courts.

A related finding was that cross-examination of prosecution witnesses by defence advocates elicited information favourable to the defendant in significantly more Crown Court cases. The use of this tactic by defence advocates is important, not only in building a strong defence case, but as an effective means of suggesting that the prosecution had deliberately kept from the court facts which were in the defendant's favour. The following cases illustrate this point.

Case 151: An employee of a large department store, P, was charged with theft of cigars from the display. Two security officers testified to having seen P remove two packets of cigars without making any attempt to pay for them. P signed a statement written out by the police to the effect that he had stolen the cigars. He was dismissed from his job. While there was no dispute as to these facts, cross-examination of the security officers disclosed that other members of staff, who were still employed by the store, also took cigars and 'had a drink and smoke at the company's expense'. This practice was apparently widely regarded as 'perks of the job'. Notwithstanding ostensibly strong eyewitness evidence and an incriminating statement the jury dismissed the charge against P.

Case 100: G was charged with wounding following an altercation at his home in which the complainant, F, received two small flesh wounds on his wrist alleged to have been inflicted by G with a fencing foil. Cross-examination of F by defence counsel elicited several remarks damaging to the prosecution case: on a previous occasion he had visited G's house in a state of intoxication and had been asked to leave; on the night of the incident in question F was again drunk; he had accosted G earlier in the evening at a club and a fight had ensued. As a result of receiving a slap around the face from G, F and his brother had gone to G's house 'to get him'. G's defence – of self-defence – was consistent with the unfavourable impression created by F under cross-examination. The judge directed the jury that, both on G's own account and that of F, G's use of the foil on his doorstep to protect himself and his family would have been no more than was lawful in the circumstances.

Other features of the prosecution case

The appraisal of the prosecution evidence included certain other evidentiary components, namely the part played by expert witnesses and by documentary and forensic evidence. The analysis disclosed that the prosecution called expert witnesses in very few cases (under 10 per cent in both the Crown Court and in magistrates' courts). In both courts the prosecution seldom adduced material evidence implicating the defendant in the offence. In cases of assault or wounding, for instance, charges were supported by documentary or forensic evidence in only 5 per cent of charges dealt with in the Crown Court and in magistrates' courts. Documentary evidence implicating the defendants was adduced in approximately a fifth of theft charges (the difference between courts was not significant); in other cases of dishonesty the prosecution was able to establish ownership of the property through documentary evidence. Since so-called 'material' evidence is invariably accompanied by witness testimony and depends for its force upon the reliability of those witnesses or other circumstantial facts adduced by the prosecution, it was not included as a component of the prosecution case for the purposes of this analysis. The fact that the availability or otherwise of material/forensic evidence was not associated with differences in outcome at either court, supports this decision. Expert witnesses were too few in number to permit analysis of their impact on outcome.

Summary of prosecution evidence

For the range of offences under investigation therefore, there were more similarities than differences between the courts in the types of evidence on which the prosecution relied. The courts were differentiated to a small degree on the number of written (as distinct from oral) statements and to a more marked extent, on the credibility of prosecution witnesses. On both indices of prosecution strength, the comparison suggests that magistrates were presented with somewhat stronger prosecution evidence than judges and juries. On other factors – the availability of eyewitnesses, expert witnesses and material evidence – there was little or no variation between the sample of cases tried at the two courts. Before considering the contribution of these evidentiary features towards an understanding of verdicts at the two modes of trial the nature of the defence case, including the performance of defendants and their witnesses in testifying, warrants brief description.

Defendants' explanations

For this stage of the analysis the sample of contested charges were reduced by 29 in the Crown Court and 19 tried in magistrates' courts as a result of the prosecution failure to establish a *prima facie* case. These charges having been dismissed at the conclusion of the prosecution case, the defendants were not called upon to give evidence. The substance of defendants' accounts was classified according to whether they contended:

(a) that they were absent from the scene and could not, therefore, have been responsible for the alleged offence;

(b) that they had been at the scene but were not responsible for the offence in question; or

(c) that they were responsible for the conduct but had lacked the criminal intent.

In cases of wounding and assault, most defendants sought to exonerate themselves on the grounds that they lacked the requisite criminal intent and had acted in self-defence. Three fifths of charges brought in magistrates' courts were countered on this type of defence, compared with half of the charges brought in the Crown Court. Conversely, more of the defendants tried in the Crown Court denied the conduct ascribed to them. In cases of shoplifting and other theft/handling a few defendants testified that they had not been at the scene and could not therefore have been responsible. This defence was used in 14 per cent of Crown Court charges and 6 per cent of charges tried summarily, but the defence relied on most frequently at both courts was (c) above – lack of criminal intent.

Defendant credibility

The criteria itemised at Appendix A for recording challenges to witness credibility were applied to the cross-examination of defendants by the prosecution. Table 12:2 above shows that in both the Crown Court and in magistrates' courts the credibility of the large majority of defendants was impugned on one or more of these criteria. This occurred in respect of 70 per cent of charges tried summarily and 73 per cent of those tried in the Crown Court. The two samples were also similar in respect of the grounds on which credibility was called into question by the prosecution. Inconsistency was the most common discrediting factor (criteria 1–3 in Appendix A), recorded in respect of some two fifths of charges heard at both courts. In a further one third of charges cross-examination by the prosecution sought to impair the credibility of defendants by attacking the general plausibility of their explanations (criterion 6). The remainder were impugned on their general credit or reputation.

Evidence of the defendant's character

An important feature of the defence case is evidence of the defendant's previous character. The law recognises that absence of previous convictions on the part of the defendant is relevant to the assessment of his credibility. Indeed, discrediting the character of the defendant is generally acknowledged to be one of the most effective ways of casting doubt on his evidence and overall truthfulness (see for example Cross, 1979). The rules governing the admissibility of evidence do not allow the prosecution to adduce evidence of any previous convictions against a defendant. Since, however, *absence* of a record adds to the strength of the defence case it will almost certainly be mentioned. It follows that the court is likely to infer the existence of a criminal record if there is no mention of the defendant's good character. The few research studies which have examined the relationship between a defendant's prior record and/or mention of good character indicate that this has a marked impact on verdicts, both in magistrates' courts and the Crown Court (see Zander, 1974; McCabe and Purves, 1972; Vennard, 1980).

The present study indicated close similarity between the two samples on this factor. The defendant's good character was not put in evidence in some two thirds of cases tried in the Crown Court and in magistrates' courts.

Defence witnesses

Defence witnesses testified on behalf of defendants in respect of a third of summary and two fifths of Crown Court charges. However, in the Crown Court there were only 36 charges (12 per cent of all charges) in which defence witness credibility was *not* impugned on grounds of inconsistency or other manifestations of unreliability. In cases tried summarily, the comparative figure was 45 (16 per cent). A pre-supposition in this analysis (suggested by earlier research) was that defence witnesses would only increase the chances of acquittal if their evidence stood up under cross-examination.

Summary of defence evidence

Comparison between cases tried in the Crown Court and in magistrates' courts in terms of the substance of the defence case, the performance of defendants and their witnesses under cross-examination and the previous character of defendants, elicited few differences. Notably, in both courts, defendants whose credibility was not impugned and who were of previous good character were in the minority; and in most cases defendants were unable to supply corroboration of their accounts from consistent and otherwise credible witnesses.

Subsequent analysis assessed the extent to which inter-relationships between elements of the prosecution and defence case reported here accounted statistically for the different outcome of cases tried at the two courts. As a first step, the relationship between all of the main components of the prosecution and defence case described above and outcome was examined. The Crown Court and magistrates' courts were compared in terms of the direction and strength of associations between verdict and features of the evidence. Multivariate analysis was then undertaken to explore the interaction between those factors found to be most strongly associated with differences in verdict, and to estimate their relative importance in explaining outcome at each court.

Table 12:3 illustrates the differing acquittal rate at the two modes of trial according to the presence or absence of the five features of the prosecution and defence case which showed statistical associations with the verdict.

Table 12:3 *Outcome by major components of prosecution and defence evidence*

	Crown Court		Magistrates' courts	
	Number	% acquitted	Number	% acquitted
1 Statement of confession	24	36	5	7
No statement of confession	158	62	85	36
2 Prosecution credibility:				
impugned	101	73	39	57
not impugned	81	45	51	22
3 Defendant's credibility:				
impugned	107	46	33	15
not impugned	34	94	36	62
4 Defendant of previous good character	59	69	35	37
Character not put in evidence	94	46	36	19
5 Credible defence witness	26	72	15	33
No credible witness	127	50	56	23

The table demonstrates that, at both courts, the chances of acquittal were considerably higher where: confession evidence was absent; prosecution credibility was impugned; defendants' accounts stood up under cross-examination; and defendants' good character was put in evidence. Evidence from credible defence witnesses also appeared to have some impact on outcome, though to a lesser extent. There was no support for the premise that eyewitness evidence *per se* gave a lower rate of acquittal than circumstantial evidence. This lack of association held for both courts. Indeed, acquittal was rather more likely to follow in the Crown Court where there were eyewitnesses (typically in cases of wounding or assault and shoplifting), than where the evidence was circumstantial.

Table 12:3 also shows that, on each of the key indices of evidential strength/weakness, the acquittal rate in magistrates' courts was markedly lower than in the Crown Court. Thus, in magistrates' courts, under a tenth of charges brought on confession evidence resulted in acquittal compared with over a third of such charges tried in the Crown Court. It will be remembered that there were proportionally more written confessions in summary cases, but this fact would not account for the magnitude of the difference in outcome; only two of the thirty charges supported by oral confessions in summary cases ended in acquittal (7 per cent), whereas for the equivalent group of cases tried in the Crown Court the acquittal rate was 40 per cent.

The calling into question of prosecution witness credibility had a considerable impact on outcome. This relationship was highly statistically significant in both courts. But whereas in the Crown Court disclosure of inconsistency or other weaknesses in prosecution witnesses gave an acquittal rate of 73 per cent, in cases tried summarily the equivalent figure was significantly lower (57 per cent).

Given that verdicts in both courts were clearly influenced by this latter factor, it is all the more noteworthy that the credibility of prosecution witnesses was undermined more frequently in the Crown Court than in cases tried by magistrates. Whether this was because the prosecution evidence was manifestly weaker and thus more open to attack in cases tried in the Crown Court, or because defence lawyers were better equipped to cross-examine prosecution witnesses on their credibility – for example, in having prior knowledge of the prosecution case – is uncertain. There is also the possibility that the longer delay in bringing cases to trial in the Crown Court increased the chances of successful challenge on the part of the defence.

The impact on outcome of the testing of defendant credibility was also very pronounced in both courts. In the Crown Court, with two exceptions, all of the defendants whose credibility was *not* impugned on these criteria were acquitted; less than half of charges resulted in acquittal where the prosecution disclosed inconsistency or other signs of untruthfulness. As will be seen from Table 12:3, in magistrates' courts the differential acquittal rate on this criterion was even greater: three fifths of charges resulted in acquittal where defendant credibility was *not* impugned compared with only 15 per cent where defendant credibility was called into question. Consistent with the pattern running through this analysis so far, however, is the finding that, whether or not defendant credibility was impugned, the acquittal rate was markedly higher in the Crown Court than in magistrates' courts.

The other important dimension of the defence case is evidence of good character. In the Crown Court the acquittal rate for those who were of good character was 69 per cent compared with 46 per cent where this was not mentioned in court. In magistrates' courts the comparative acquittal rates were predictably far lower for both categories. Even so, the chances of acquittal at summary trial where good character was mentioned were twice as high as when this type of evidence was absent. When outcome was examined with reference to official records of the defendants' previous convictions, this confirmed the importance of prior record in accounting for differences in verdicts.

It was premised earlier in this chapter that differences in the type of offence and in the nature and strength of the evidence might explain the higher acquittal rate in cases tried in the Crown Court. The results of these analyses suggest that neither of these factors can account for the magnitude of the difference in outcome between the courts. The Crown Court acquittal rate is higher for all three offence categories and for all the dimensions of evidential strength and weakness measured in this study. The only major difference between the two samples of cases in terms of the evidence adduced was in relation to prosecution witness credibility. Yet even where that evidence was *not* impugned, juries were twice as likely as magistrates to bring verdicts of not guilty.

Certain of the evidentiary factors identified in this preliminary analysis would appear to be significant predictors of outcome in contested cases. To examine their explanatory power more accurately their effects were considered simultaneously through multivariate statistical analysis. By this means, it was also possible to assess in very approximate terms how far type of court is associated with differences in verdict once full account has been taken of variations in the attributes of the prosecution and defence evidence measured in the study.

Composite analysis of the association between outcome, evidence and court

To gain fuller insight into the large differences between the Crown Court and magistrates' courts in outcome the statistical technique of logistical regression (Appendix B) was employed. In essence, this approach indicates the relative importance of the range of factors included in the analysis in explaining outcome.

Using this technique, a two-stage analysis was carried out. The first part was concerned with two questions: whether measures of evidential strength identified in this study are related to outcome at each mode of trial when considered simultaneously; and what is the relative effect of each factor at each type of court. Two separate models were developed to explore these questions, one based on cases tried in the Crown Court, the other on cases tried summarily (Tables B1 and B2 at Appendix B).

The second stage of the analysis involved a further model in which data from both courts were combined and type of court was included as a factor in the model. This permitted an assessment of the effect of court on the acquittal rate when evidential factors had been controlled (Table B3 at Appendix B).

Stage I

While it is not possible to compare courts very precisely on the relative influence on outcome of individual features of the case, the broad pattern of the results is clear. In magistrates' courts, six evidential factors were considered and four retained in the first model as being significantly related to outcome. These factors were in order of importance:

i defendant's credibility;

ii defendant's previous character;

iii prosecution witness credibility; and

iv statement of confession.

The remaining factors – availability of prosecution eyewitness evidence and corroborative evidence from defence witnesses – did not attain statistical significance. These findings broadly confirm the earlier suggestion that the performance of defendants in the witness box, coupled with evidence of previous character, are powerful predictors of outcome in magistrates' courts[3].

The same factors were considered in the Crown Court model. On this occasion the final model comprised just three significant factors:

i defendant's credibility;

ii prosecution witnesses' credibility; and

iii defendant's previous character.

3. The model of outcome in magistrates' courts differed in some respects from that derived from the first phase of this research (see Vennard, 1981). The removal from the sample of offences of public order, assault on a police constable and other purely summary offences, may explain these differences. In bringing these charges, the prosecution had to rely heavily upon direct evidence from eyewitnesses (the majority of whom were police officers), whereas in cases of dishonesty circumstantial evidence, often supported by statements of confession, was far more common. It would seem to follow that, whereas in the earlier model much of the variation in outcome was explained by the availability of direct evidence, in this revised model other features took on more significance.

The addition of eyewitness evidence, confession evidence, and defence witnesses did not add significantly to the explanation of outcome and were therefore excluded. It will be seen that the order of importance of the factors in the two models differed slightly, but that in both courts the performance of prosecution witnesses and defendants under cross-examination, coupled with evidence of defendants' previous character, were powerful predictors of outcome. While other factors may well have played a part in establishing or casting doubt on the prosecution case, these strong and consistent associations suggest that the predominant evidential influences over verdicts may have been captured.

Stage II

Table B3 in Appendix B shows the effect of court on outcome once having controlled for differences in the evidence at each court. Once again, the impugnment of prosecution witness credibility and defendant credibility outweigh the effect of other features of the prosecution and defence case. The type of court emerges as the third most significant factor, followed by previous character and confession evidence. It may be inferred from these results that the court dimension, for reasons which are unexplained in these data, had a highly significant influence on the verdict independent of differences in the nature and strength of evidence measured in the research.

The final part of this report considers some possible explanations that might underlie these differential acquittal rates and their association with indices of the evidence and witness credibility.

Conclusions

To date there has been no empirical basis for assertions regarding the rates of acquittal at the two courts once having allowed for differences in the strength of the prosecution and the defence case. The present study reveals the associations between verdict and quantifiable indices of evidential strengths and weaknesses and provides new insights into the importance of type of court in accounting for outcome differences. The findings tend to suggest that, for the either way offences included in this study, the chances of acquittal are significantly higher in the Crown Court than in magistrates' courts. This remains true even having allowed for important features of the evidence which are known to weigh heavily in the courts' assessments of strength and weaknesses in the prosecution and defence case.

The quantitative approach adopted necessarily over-simplifies the evidential basis of verdicts and leaves unanswered a variety of questions concerning the competence of the two tribunals at arriving at just verdicts. The unexplained differences in outcome which are attributed to court may, of course, be associated with other evidentiary features which the present study was unable to quantify. Moreover, a comparison between courts using a wider range of offences (or, indeed, a different sample of courts) might well find that other factors play a part in accounting for differences in outcome. Certainly, it cannot be inferred from these findings that magistrates are more prone than juries to convict the innocent, or that juries have a greater propensity to acquit the guilty. Bearing in mind these important qualifications, the study offers a firmer factual basis for future debate about the outcome of contested cases at the two tiers in relation to the types of evidence supplied by both parties, than had existed hitherto. In this final section consideration is given to possible interpretations of the findings reported in the previous section. Of necessity, much of what follows is speculative rather than conclusive.

Those who have voiced the criticism that juries are inclined to return verdicts of not guilty against the weight of the evidence (the so-called 'perverse' acquittal), might be reassured by the finding that, for the most part, acquittals corresponded with identifiable weaknesses in the prosecution case or an explanation from the defendant which was not manifestly discredited. Acquittals which were *not* explicable in terms of the balance of the evidence – for example, where the credibility of prosecution witnesses was not impugned – were the minority. Nevertheless, juries were systematically more likely to acquit than magistrates, the differential being greatest where the prosecution had a seemingly strong case – such as a statement of confession or eye-witnesses whose accounts stood up under cross-examination. For example, whereas eyewitness accounts were sufficient to achieve conviction in 71 per cent of assault charges brought in magistrates' courts, this was by no means true of cases tried in the Crown Court. Only 40 per cent of this group of charges resulted in conviction on indictment. In cases of shoplifting, which showed the largest variation in the rate of acquittal between the courts, juries were markedly less inclined to accept the accounts of store detectives as sufficient proof of the defendants' guilt.

It can be assumed that, in bringing convictions on the basis of direct evidence from eyewitnesses, the presiding magistrates were satisfied that those witnesses had accurately observed, recalled and reported the defendant's part in the incident. It will be remembered that identification was seldom in issue, most of the defendants having admitted their presence at the scene; conflict with the accounts of prosecution witnesses was over their conduct or state of mind at the time of the alleged offence. Defendants charged with shoplifting were in most cases apprehended outside the store by security officers within minutes of the alleged incident. Both for this offence and assault – where there were almost invariably eyewitnesses – evidence of the requisite criminal intent was supplied either explicitly, or by implication, in the description of the defendant's conduct.

A number of writers who have commented on the quality of justice dispensed in the lower courts have suggested that magistrates' seeming tendency to rely upon the word of a police officer against that of a defendant is inevitable in a system of trial in which the police play a key part in the decision to charge, in selecting the evidence to be laid before the court and in conducting the prosecution (Wootton, 1978; Jackson, 1979; Williams, 1979; Burney, 1979). Magistrates interviewed by Burney emphasised that it was not unreasonable to accept the evidence of police officers given that they are trained in recording and presenting evidence in court. Since, moreover, the vast majority of cases dealt with summarily are uncontested, magistrates have little occasion to question the reliability of prosecution witnesses, whether police officers, store detectives or civilians. Like police officers, security officers employed by retail stores are trained to observe and record the details of the conduct leading to arrest as soon as possible after the incident. Their testimony tends to stand up well under cross-examination by the defence, not least because they are fortified by notes made up at the time or shortly after the event. This is reflected in the fact that in cases of shoplifting – which were almost invariably brought on eyewitness evidence – the defence were able to impugn the credibility of prosecution witnesses in only 6 per cent of charges tried summarily compared with a quarter of equivalent cases tried in the Crown Court.

While there are no first-hand data on juries' attitudes towards the testimony of police and security officers, research into the deliberations of shadow juries recruited to observe a series of actual trials suggests that they may not be as sceptical of such evidence as jury critics have often asserted. According to McCabe (1975) shadow juries observed in her study were determined to 'give all possible credence to the prosecution case'. While they subjected the accounts of witnesses to close scrutiny, the honesty of prosecution witnesses was seldom questioned. There was a general feeling that they had to accept the evidence of police witnesses because 'they are paid to look after our interests'. In contrast, much attention was given to the character and veracity of defendants. This was seen by the researchers as consistent with the fact that the majority of the defendants, as in the present study, admitted involvement in an incident which, on the face of it, seemed to be criminal. In their evaluation of defences of lack of guilty knowledge/intent, shadow juries looked for credible alternative accounts to counter-balance the prosecution version of events. Though reluctant to doubt the honesty of prosecution witnesses, shadow juries did make reference to inaccuracies and uncertainties in their accounts – particularly in the case of civilians and store detectives. One view of store detectives was that they felt the need to justify their existence by catching shoplifters and achieving convictions and that therefore their evidence had to be treated with caution. The juries were also conscious of the dangers of 'distortion in all our observations and judgements that comes from our own prejudices'. Shadow juries thus gave considerable weight in their deliberations to attempts to discredit witnesses.

In the present study, cross-examination of prosecution eyewitnesses impugned their credibility twice as often in the Crown Court as in magistrates' courts. As a corollary, in cases tried in the Crown Court defence advocates were far more likely to elicit evidence favourable to the defendant in their cross-examination of prosecution witnesses. This fact carries the implication that part of the explanation for the higher acquittal rates in the Crown Court is the extent to which defence lawyers undermined the prosecution case in cross-examination of witnesses, coupled with jurors' and magistrates' differing responses to the impugnment of that evidence. There are a number of possible explanations for the marked variation in prosecution witness performance in cross-examination recorded in the study. First, in cases tried in the Crown Court the prosecution case may have been inherently weaker allowing defence advocates more scope to point to inconsistencies, inaccuracies or other defects in the accounts of witnesses than in equivalent summary cases. A second possible factor, the significance of which could not be quantified in this study, is the disadvantage (now rectified) under which defence advocates in magistrates' courts are placed in not being permitted formal disclosure of the prosecution case prior to trial. The advocate frequently hears the substance of the prosecution case for the first time when oral evidence is being given in court, as a consequence of which he is less well prepared for cross-examination than his counterpart in the Crown Court. Thirdly, longer waiting times in the Crown Court may place defence advocates at an advantage insofar as prosecution witnesses' memories may fade with the passage of time. In the present study some three fifths of cases tried summarily came to trial in less than six months compared with only 18 per cent of Crown Court cases.

All of these factors may contribute towards explaining differences in the impugnment of prosecution witnesses. It is also important not to overlook contrasts in the styles of advocacy adopted at the two tiers of court to which researchers and legal scholars have drawn attention. Indeed, studies of the dynamics of contested trials have led some writers to argue that the determination of a defendant's culpability is in large measure a question of the relative skills of the prosecution and defence lawyers in 'constructing' their case and selecting and defining the 'facts' in the direction that best establishes their version of the incident (eg Bennett and Feldman, 1981). McBarnet (1983) puts forward the proposition that what she terms the 'ideology of triviality', which pervades much of the work of the lower courts, deters solicitors acting for defendants from devoting sufficient time to advance preparation. As a consequence, the level of advocacy is, in her view, notably lower than in the Crown Court (see also Derbyshire, 1985, for justices' clerks' criticisms of the standards of representation among defence solicitors). Others (eg Mungham and Thomas, 1979) have argued that the routine and largely uncontested work handled by solicitors in magistrates' courts allow few opportunities to develop skills in advocacy. The contested trial is for most solicitor advocates the exception rather than the rule: to the barrister who practices in the Crown Court, competence in law and advocacy are paramount.

The comparative quality of advocacy at the two levels of trial was beyond the scope of the study. The results strongly suggest, however, that an examination of trial outcome in contested cases is incomplete without reference to the relative success with which each party established the credibility of its witnesses and undermined the accounts or general credit worthiness of opposing witnesses. From the strong statistical relationship between witness credibility and outcome it can be inferred that this dimension of the prosecution and defence case figured prominently in the judgments of both magistrates and juries.

On the other hand, juries were far more prone to acquit than magistrates even where the evidence of prosecution witnesses was *not* shown to be inconsistent or otherwise defective in cross-examination. Even more striking was the fact that juries acquitted on almost half (107) of charges where defendant credibility *was* impugned (Table 12:3). Juries also acquitted on just under half of charges where defendant's good character was not put in evidence. Magistrates were markedly less likely to acquit in these circumstances. It would seem therefore that other factors come into the reckoning and that one must look beyond the more obvious dimensions of evidential strength and weakness for a possible explanation of these differences in outcome.

Again it is instructive to consider the explanation offered by McCabe (1975) for the high rate of acquittal by shadow juries. While it cannot be assumed that the deliberations and verdicts of shadow juries are equivalent to those of real juries, McCabe found a level of agreement on verdict (75 per cent) which suggests that in most cases the course of discussion may also have been similar. She concluded that, in the face of the shadow juries' determination to give credence to the prosecution and their tendency to view the defendant as having a high 'guilt potential' by virtue of his being in the dock, the propensity to acquit must be due to juries' interpretation of the high standard of proof required to sustain conviction. The research suggested that 'the animus against the police and other prosecution witnesses was manifestly not because they were disbelieved but because they did not provide sufficient evidence to support the shadow jurors' insatiable appetite for evidence that they might believe'. The majority of jurors were of the view that the defendant had a clear right to acquittal if his account was not adequately rebutted by the prosecution. When a defendant, however suspect the circumstances of his arrest, produced an explanation that seemed to be credible, he tended to be given the benefit of the doubt.

This interpretation is consistent with Baldwin and McConville's (1979) finding that, for most acquittals brought by juries in their sample of contested cases, respondents (judges and other trial participants) acknowledged that there was some readily identifiable weakness in the prosecution case or a reasonably convincing explanation from the defendant which justified the verdict. It may be, therefore, that differences in verdict between the Crown Court and magistrates' courts are in part a reflection of their interpretation of the amount of evidence needed to sustain a conviction. Juries may demand a stronger body of evidence from the prosecution in order to be convinced of the defendant's guilt. As a corollary, they may find 'reasonable doubt' in a counter explanation from the defendant which, in the face of eyewitness evidence and/or a self-incriminating statement, would not satisfy magistrates.

A question raised by the James Committee in their 1975 report was whether 'the interests of society can be served fairly and efficiently without some redistribution of work whereby the Crown Court would be relieved of the less serious cases which could properly be dealt with by magistrates' courts'. At one end of the spectrum are many offences – such as minor traffic offences – for which free access to trial by judge and jury would be difficult to justify. Yet as the James Committee observed, for very few offences is there a clear dividing line between the more or less serious instances. Offences of dishonesty are a case in point. There is also the argument that monetary value is not always a realistic guide to the gravity of the offence. It follows that opinion as to the scope for downgrading some of the less serious offences which carry the right to trial on indictment – such as low value theft – is likely to remain contentious. Central to this debate is the issue of public confidence in the two modes of trial and beliefs in the respective chances of acquittal on pleading not guilty.

Although this research did not address the subject of defendants' choice of venue, some of the findings reported here have implications for this issue. The available research, reviewed recently by Ashworth (1984), points to the conclusion that the decision whether or not to elect trial at the Crown Court is influenced by a wide range of factors, some of which are positively favourable to the Crown Court, others reflecting lack of confidence in the thoroughness and impartiality of magistrates' courts. Ashworth considers that the latter set of considerations (and, by implication, the lower chances of acquittal at summary trial) may exert a greater influence over a defendant's unwillingness to accept summary trial than structural differences – such as the wider availability of legal aid and advance disclosure of the prosecution case in the Crown Court. There is some evidence, however, that improvements in summary procedures would result in greater acceptance of summary trial. The pilot study of the impact of advance disclosure by the prosecution in either way cases tried summarily, described in Chapter 9, suggests that this provision is likely to reduce the number of elections for trial in the Crown Court and increase guilty pleas in magistrates' courts. Analysis of the extent and nature of disputes over the admissibility of evidence in cases within the present study indicated that defendants are more inclined to elect trial than have the case heard by magistrates when challenging statements attributed to them by the police. Improvements in the procedures whereby magistrates determine the admissibility of such evidence could be expected to have some impact on Crown Court workloads. Independent verification of statements obtained in custody might also reduce the number of cases in which defendants seek to rebut the evidence in the Crown Court (Vennard, 1984). It must also be remembered that, according to existing studies of decisions on venue, shorter waiting times and the prospect of a more lenient sentence are major incentives to acceptance of summary trial (Bottoms and McClean, 1976; Gregory, 1976).

It is perhaps timely to re-examine the factors which influence defendants' choice between trial at the Crown Court and summary trial and the reasons why a high proportion of defendants plead guilty in the higher courts. The manner in which lawyers' advice features in these decisions would be an important element of such research. Since some 60 per cent of defendants plead guilty in the Crown Court – and as Ashworth (1984) points out, the percentage is even higher on some circuits – it seems likely that lack of confidence in summary trial is just one of a variety of considerations which influence choice of venue and plea. The available research confirms this supposition (Baldwin and McConville, 1979; Bottoms and McClean, 1976) but there is a need for closer examination of such questions as why guilty plea rates are consistently higher in some parts of the country than in others. There may be greater scope for reducing the pressure of work in the Crown Court amongst defendants who plead guilty than where the charge(s) are contested.

Variation in prosecutorial efficiency in screening out weak cases is likely to account to some extent for inter-circuit differences in plea rates and in the chances of acquittal (see Butler, Chapter 13). Research into prosecution practices may help identify measures which will reduce the numbers of cases brought to trial on manifestly weak evidence (Sanders, Chapter 6). With mounting concern at the volume of business in the Crown Court, and changes in prospect in our system of prosecution, the policy relevance of such research is clear.

APPENDIX A

Assessment of witness credibility

Witness credibility was assessed by reference to the following check list of factors:

1. The *inherent consistency* of the story: did the evidence of a witness contain internal contradictions.
2. Consistency with *other witnesses* testifying for the party.
3. *Consistency with undisputed facts* eg documentary evidence, facts admitted by the parties or matters of common knowledge or experience.
4. The *'credit'* of witnesses eg evidence of bias against a party or general reputation of untruthfulness.
5. Factors which might render eyewitness evidence unreliable (such as poor eyesight) and uncertainty over material facts.
6. The inherent *probability or improbability* of the story.

APPENDIX B

Log linear models were employed to examine the degree to which court outcome was associated with factors measuring evidential strengths and weaknesses. The influence of these factors is indicated by the 'goodness of fit' or G-square statistic which has an approximate chi-square distribution. The comparative size of the reduction in G-square provides an estimate of the relative importance of each factor or combination of factors in understanding differences in outcome (for a description of the log linear modelling procedure see Bishop *et al.* 1975).

The particular technique used in the study was logistic regression which is based on the generalised linear model – GLIM (see Baker and Nelder, 1978). This form of analysis fits a model to the data which maximises the amount of variation explained in case outcome by including in the model those factors which produced the largest reductions in unexplained variation (G-square). The method involves a stepwise inclusion of factors until no further significant reduction in variation can be achieved.

In the magistrates' courts model four factors were included in this final stage (see Table B1) whereas for the Crown Court model just three factors were included in the final stage (see Table B2). When both samples were combined and court included as a factor in the analysis (see Table B3) the final model comprised five factors. Only in the Crown Court model was the unexplained variation (G-square) found to be statistically significant. Clearly, outcome in the Crown Court is associated with one or more factors in addition to the three significant factors identified in the analysis.

Table B1 *Analysis of verdict in magistrates' courts by evidence*

Variable	Reduction in G-square attributable to variable	df	p
Defendant credibility	48.1	2	0.001
Defendant's previous character	19.8	2	0.001
Prosecution witness credibility	16.8	1	0.001
Statement of confession	15.0	2	0.001
Scaled deviance = 220.9 df = 278			

Table B2 *Analysis of verdict in the Crown Court by evidence*

Variable	Reduction in G-square attributable to variable	df	p
Defendant credibility	36.3	2	0.001
Prosecution witness credibility	13.6	1	0.001
Defendant's previous character	13.2	1	0.001
Scaled deviance = 339.5 df = 286			

Table B3 *Analysis of verdict by evidence and court*

Variable	Reduction in G-square attributable to variable	df	p
Prosecution witness credibility	59.5	1	0.001
Defendant credibility	46.1	2	0.001
Court	51.2	1	0.001
Defendant's previous character	34.2	2	0.001
Statement of confession	12.9	2	0.005
Scaled deviance = 566.9 df = 568			

13 Acquittal rates

SID BUTLER

As a result of the recommendations of the Morris Committee in 1965 the long-standing property qualification for jury service was replaced in 1972 by a right and duty applying to voters in general, subject to an upper age limit and the exclusion of certain types of person. In particular, the Criminal Justice Act 1967 disqualified for life those sentenced to more than five years in prison, whilst borstal training or a prison sentence of three months to five years carried disqualification for 10 years from jury service.

At the Committee stage of the Administration of Justice Bill 1982, the Government tabled amendments which would have extended the 10 years disqualification to all those convicted of an offence for which a prison sentence might be awarded. These amendments attracted a strong adverse parliamentary reaction and were not pursued. In an article published subsequently, Kelly (1982) estimated that between 5 and 10 million voters in England and Wales might be affected, out of around 36 million currently liable for jury service. The article suggested that the proposals had arisen as a result of continuing opposition in police and government circles to the widened basis for jury service, increased jury acquittal rates being used to justify restrictions on jury eligibility. Arguments in favour of a more selective approach include the need to protect the principle of a jury composed of sound and true persons, the increased complexity of some types of case, and the risk of intimidation or subversion of a jury which includes convicted persons. This chapter reviews available statistical and research information and the general background.

Statistics related to acquittal rates

Although regular statistical data are not available prior to 1973, analysis of a sample of 1956 higher court cases indicated an acquittal rate for contested cases of 38 per cent (Gibson, 1960). In the late 1960s it was generally considered that the acquittal rate varied betweeen 46 per cent and 50 per cent. The acquittal rates in the Crown Court for those pleading not guilty to at least one count rose from 42 per cent in 1973/74 to 50 per cent in 1980, dropping back to 48 per cent in 1981. The main rise occurred between 1973 and 1976, with a further significant rise in 1980. The increases in 1979 and 1980 may owe something to the implementation (in July 1978) of the Criminal Law Act 1977, which altered the range of cases which could reach the Crown Court. The rise in 1980, as discussed later, may have been associated with changes in guilty plea rates, and has not been maintained in 1981.

Acquittal rates in the magistrates' courts for contested cases are thought to be significantly lower. Reliable statistics are not available. The acquittal rates in magistrates' courts for those pleading not guilty, published in *Criminal Statistics* for 1976 to 1978, proved unreliable, and subsequent efforts to improve the standard of police reporting of plea data have had only limited success. Softley (1976) has reported Home Office research results indicating that acquittal rates in magistrates' courts, for contested cases and comparable offences, were uniformly lower than those in the Crown Court. More recently, a study in four magistrates' courts (Vennard, 1980) confirmed that acquittal rates in magistrates' courts were lower than the published statistics. For these magistrates' courts, an average acquittal rate of 25 per cent applied for contested charges; there is no particular reason why this figure should be unrepresentative of magistrates' courts as a whole in 1979 (see also Vennard, 1981). No information on changes of acquittal rates with time in magistrates' courts is available.

Reliable acquittal rates for contested cases are not available for the Crown Court by offence group. However, statistics are available for both the Crown Court and magistrates' courts for the period 1970 to 1981 on persons acquitted for different offence groups, irrespective of plea. These show that, in magistrates' courts, the proportions acquitted have remained fairly stable for most offence groups. In the Crown Court, the acquittal rates for criminal damage and violence against the person showed an increase by 1976 and there were slight overall increases for 1979 and 1980, associated with increases for several offence groups. These changes again may partly have resulted from implementation of the Criminal Law Act 1977. Between 1970 and 1980 the acquittal rate in the Crown Court for all cases rose from 14 per cent to 18 per cent, falling back to 17 per cent in 1981.

Table 13:1 shows the acquittal rates in the Crown Court for defendants in contested cases, broken down in terms of those decided by the judge (either by order prior to empanelling the jury or by directing the jury to acquit) and those decided by the jury.

Table 13:1 *Percentages of defendants, pleading not guilty to at least one count in the Crown Court, who were acquitted on all contested counts by order or direction of the judge; and by the jury (England and Wales)*

Year	Acquitted by order or direction of the judge	Acquitted by the jury	Total
1976	21	26	47
1977	19	26	45
1978	20	26	46
1979	20	27	47
1980	21	29	50
1981	21	27	48

The proportion of contested cases failing because they failed to reach the standard of proof required by the judge has remained at about 20 per cent for the period 1976 to 1980. Excluding these cases and considering only those cases which were determined by the jury (Table 13:2), the jury acquittal rate remained steady at 32–33 per cent between 1976 and 1979, increased to 36 per cent in 1980 and reverted to 34 per cent in 1981. There is then some basis for the assertion that juries have tended to acquit a slightly higher proportion of contested cases in the immediate past.

Table 13:2 *Percentage of defendants in the Crown Court (excluding those acquitted by order or direction of the judge), pleading not guilty to at least one count, who were acquitted by the jury on all contested counts (England and Wales)*

1976	1977	1978	1979	1980	1981
33	32	32	33	36	34

Source: *Judicial Statistics*

Acquittal trends for contested cases for the different Crown Court circuits vary greatly, however. The average acquittal rates by order or direction of the judge vary from about 17 per cent in the South Eastern circuit to about 27 per cent in the Northern and North-Eastern circuits. Generally, the inter-circuit judge acquittal rate differences have persisted for the period for which data are available. Omitting those cases settled by the judge, the average jury acquittal rates show rather less inter-circuit variation, from about 30 per cent (Midland and Oxford) to about 38 per cent (Northern). The jury acquittal rate increased noticeably in five of the seven circuits between 1976 and 1980, but fell back again in three of these in 1981. Only the Northern and the Wales and Chester circuits show a consistent upward trend for the whole six years.

The Gibson study (1960) indicated that about 25 per cent of higher court cases in 1956 were associated with a not guilty plea. In recent years, the not guilty plea rate in the Crown Court has been much higher, fluctuating between 37 per cent and 40 per cent for the period 1972 to 1981. However, the largest change occurred between 1979 (40 per cent) and 1980 (37 per cent); this could be largely responsible for the sudden rise in the Crown Court jury acquittal rate between 1979 and 1980 for contested cases already noted, as it would tend to remove from jury consideration mainly cases where a guilty finding would be expected. This hypothesis is consistent with the 1981 jury acquittal and not guilty plea rates each falling back towards the pre-1980 values. Substantial differences, however, have persisted during the decade beween circuits in the not guilty plea rate. Since 1976 the proportions of defendants pleading not guilty have varied from about 23 per cent for the North-Eastern circuit to about 56 per cent for London.

During the decade, the pressures on the Crown Court circuits have grown at different rates. There exist major inter-circuit differences in waiting times for cases. Waiting times increased generally until 1979, but the trend was reversed in 1980 for several circuits, with further improvement in 1981 for those circuits with particularly long waiting times. The average waiting time for committals for trial in the Crown Court increased from 11 to 17 weeks between 1976 and 1979/80 with correspondingly higher average waiting times for contested cases. A possible connection between such increases and acquittal rates is discussed later. Overall, a reduction of 10 per cent was achieved between 1980 and 1981 in Crown Court waiting times.

In the Scottish equivalent of the Crown Court, the Courts of Solemn Jurisdiction (High Court of Judiciary and the Sheriff Court), proceedings are taken on indictment and the judge sits with a jury. Recently, the proportion of not guilty pleas has reached 51 per cent, much higher than that applying generally in the Crown Court, although comparable with that for the SE (London) circuit. The overall acquittal rate (including non-proven verdicts) of about 33 per cent for contested cases in the higher courts in Scotland is substantially lower than the rate of about 50 per cent now applying in England and Wales. Indeed, between 1977 and 1980 the acquittal rate for Scottish Courts of Solemn Jurisdiction has remained below that for each of the Crown Court circuits. In view of the substantially higher rate of not guilty pleas for the Scottish courts, it may be preferable to make the comparison on the basis of the acquittal rate for all cases. In 1980 the Scottish higher court acquittal rate for all cases was about 10 per cent less than that for the Crown Court. Separate statistics for jury acquittal rates are not available for Scotland.

Factors contributing to changes in acquittal rates

A number of factors could affect Crown Court acquittal rates. In the first place, the availability of legal aid in the magistrates' court has increased in the past decade. Most defendants in triable either way cases should now receive legal advice on the question of plea, and on the choice between summary trial by magistrates and jury trial under a judge in the Crown Court. It would not seem possible to examine empirically the associated effects on judge and jury acquittal rates.

Secondly, acquittal rates could be affected by changes in the general standard of prosecution cases committed to the Crown Court. The continuing high level of ordered and directed acquittals in the Crown Court in part reflects inadequacies in the prosecution and committal system. Although the minimum criterion for prosecution is generally considered the existence of a *prima facie* case, on which magistrates or a jury reasonably could convict, police policy considerations governing the initial decision to prosecute may sometimes set aside this criterion. McCabe and Purves (1972) comment that wider social and peace-keeping objectives, pursued reasonably by the police, are often the reason for perseverance with prosecution of a relatively weak case. According to Weatheritt (1980), chief prosecuting solicitors may advise on the existence of a *prima facie* case and on the probability of acquittal, but police views on the desirability of persevering with a prosecution tend to prevail. In their study of ordered and directed acquittals Baldwin and McConville (1979) observed that ordered acquittals often were anticipated by both police and prosecution counsel, and only a small proportion (13 per cent) of directed acquittals were unexpected by the police. Half of these acquittals were associated with cases assessed by the researchers as so weak as possibly to raise doubts about the wisdom of proceeding in the first instance. Complementary research on pre-trial identification of very weak cases indicated that, for about 10 per cent of contested Crown Court cases, severe deficiencies in the prosecution case could be identified in advance and the probability of acquittal appeared so high that it could be argued that prosecution was difficult to justify (McConville and Baldwin, 1981). The effectiveness of existing procedures for identifying weak cases through the committals procedures were discussed in Chapter 8.

Thirdly, prevailing pressures on the Crown Court and prosecution, for which waiting time statistics represent a useful indicator, could affect the acquittal rate in a number of ways. For instance, in a proportion of contested cases, increased waiting time and number of remands could result eventually in a plea of guilty by the defendant (whether for personal reasons or on legal advice). Again, a high mean waiting time in a Crown Court circuit could indicate not only a high prosecution caseload but also a high average level of complexity in the prosecution case and increased probability of the construction of a successful defence. More directly, increased waiting times for contested Crown Court cases are thought to affect adversely both the availability and the credibility of prosecution witnesses. Recent research by McConville and Baldwin (1981) indicates that the availability and credibility of prosecution witnesses are two of the major factors which determine the probability of an acquittal.

There is substantial quantitative evidence that inter-circuit acquittal rate variations in recent years are partly associated with variations in average case waiting times. Three circuits (Western, Midlands and Oxford, North-Eastern) have exhibited consistently lower waiting times for contested cases and lower jury acquittal rates. Over the period 1976 to 1980, the rankings of the seven Crown Court circuits (treating the South Eastern circuit as two circuits) in respect of waiting times and acquittal rates are related in a statistically significant manner. Further analysis by the Home Office Statistical Department confirmed that such inter-circuit differences persist when principal offence categories are considered separately. The application of regression analysis to the data for 1976 to 1980 demonstrated that a longer average waiting time was associated in a statistically significant manner with a higher acquittal rate, whether variations between circuits or from year to year in a particular circuit are concerned. This analysis suggests further detailed studies of persisting differences between Crown Court circuits could lead to a better understanding of the interactions between court pressure, waiting times and case outcome and assist development of future policy and practice.

A fourth factor affecting jury acquittal rates could be changes in the attitudes of juries. The 1980/81 jury acquittal rate of about 35 per cent for contested Crown Court cases decided by the jury is higher than either the overall acquittal rate in the equivalent Scottish courts or the overall acquittal rate for summary trial in magistrates' courts of contested cases. The jury only decides cases where the judge considers the prosecution case sound enough that conviction would be a reasonable outcome. An increased jury acquittal rate could be associated with:

a. a higher proportion of prosecution cases which, though sound enough in law to go to the jury, nevertheless do not convince it, possibly because modern juries demand a higher standard of proof or are more critical of prosecution evidence;

b. a higher proportion of cases where the defence case provides an adequate answer in the view of the jury, possibly associated with a change in guilty-plea practice;

c. a decline in the average competence of prosecutors and/or an improvement in the defence;

d. an increased proportion of jury verdicts against the balance of evidence.

The study by Julie Vennard, described in Chapter 12, throws some light on variations between jury and magistrates' verdicts in triable either way cases. The sample, however, excludes those cases where the judge ordered acquittal; and no information has been collected to the extent to which non-availability of key prosecution witnesses may occur as a result of lengthy delays between committal and trial in the Crown Court.

Recent criticisms of the widening of jury service to voters in general appear to take two forms:

a. that some juries now bring 'perverse' acquittals, because of inability to make a rational assessment of the evidence, or because the wider range of juror attitudes leads to jury disagreement, or because more jurors are open to criminal pressures;

b. that juries tend to be more critical of the prosecution case and, in particular, may refuse to convict on uncorroborated police evidence, their distrust being reflected in rising jury acquittal rates.

There is, in fact, little evidence of frequent inter-juror disagreements. In 1981 there were some 570 re-trials in the Crown Court (about 2 per cent of the 25,000 contested cases), about 370 the result of jury disagreement (ie more than two dissenting jurors). Empirical studies by McCabe and Purves (1972) and Zander (1974) found a very low rate of 'perverse' verdicts. However, more recently, Baldwin and McConville (1979) reported that just over a third of the jury acquittals (36 per cent) in their sample of contested cases were considered questionable by the judge and at least one other respondent. Nevertheless, the majority of jury acquittals were not criticised by respondents.

As pointed out by Vennard in Chapter 12, there is no clear evidence to support the contention that juries are inherently distrustful of police evidence. Most jury acquittals still appear to occur as a result of the case not being proved beyond reasonable doubt in the view of the jury. Consistent application of a higher standard for prosecution cases might be expected to reduce the jury acquittal rate, as well as reducing the proportion of cases stopped by the judge. In this connection, the Attorney-General's guidelines to the police and others who prosecute on behalf of the public will, among other things, commend as a minimum test the DPP criterion that there should be a reasonable prospect of conviction (and not just a *prima facie* case); this may help to bring about a higher standard for prosecution cases. The establishment of an independent Crown Prosecution Service may reduce the number of weak cases which are pursued. A more demanding prosecution standard would alleviate court workloads, reduce waiting times, reduce the remand population and might lower the acquittal rate. Too high a standard, however, if only applicable to cases committed to the Crown Court, could encourage an increase in the proportion of triable either way cases in which the defendant elects for trial and places further pressure on the Crown Court.

Conclusions

Between 1973/74 and 1976, the Crown Court acquittal rate for contested cases rose from 42 per cent to 47 per cent. A period of stability was followed by a further rise from 47 per cent in 1979 to 50 per cent in 1980; this rise seems probably associated with a reduction in the not guilty plea rate from 40 per cent in 1979 to 37 per cent in 1980. The Crown Court acquittal rate and the not guilty plea rate for 1981 each have tended to revert to the 1979 levels. The Crown Court acquittal rates in the second half of this period are comparable with those reputed to apply towards the end of the previous decade. However, the general level is appreciably higher than in the equivalent Scottish high courts (and in the magistrates' courts). There is considerable variation in acquittal rates between the circuits of the Crown Court, which appears to be associated in recent years in a statistically significant manner with the differences in the caseload pressures and waiting times between circuits.

There is little evidence to show whether or not broadening of eligibility for jury service introduced in 1972 has led to an increased propensity for the jury to acquit. The persisting high level of Crown Court acquittals by order or direction of the judge emphasises the continuing importance of applying uniformly stricter standards to triable either way cases sent to the Crown Court.

14 Sentencing of adults and juveniles in magistrates' courts

ROGER TARLING, DAVID MOXON and PETER JONES

In dealing with offenders, sentencers have a number of objectives. They may seek to deter the individual offender from further offending; to deter potential offenders from being drawn into crime; and, through incarceration, to prevent people from committing further offences and thereby to protect the public from those who are a particular nuisance or a particular danger. Research into the effectiveness of different sentences in achieving these objectives is not clear-cut – there is only very limited evidence that particular sentencing strategies are better than others at deterring or reforming offenders. So there is no clear path for sentencers to follow – no definitive tariff – and a great deal of discretion in dealing with each case. This has the strength of enabling sentencers to match disposals closely to individual circumstances; to take account of a great variety of aggravating and mitigating circumstances relating to the offence and the offender. There is, however, a price to be paid. The consequence of wide discretion in dealing with each type of case is that different courts are free to deal with similar cases in very different ways.

Sharp variation – for example if a certain type of case is dealt with by way of a fine in one court but by custody in another – is liable to undermine public confidence in the concept of equality before the law. It is therefore not surprising that apparent inconsistencies and anomalies in the sentences awarded at magistrates' courts are frequently the subject of press comment, and lead to criticisms by members of the public, offenders (and organisations representing them) and on occasion by magistrates themselves, of the quality of justice meted out. This chapter describes two complementary studies of sentencing practice in magistrates' courts. Both studies examine and compare sentencing practices in magistrates' courts, but one focuses on adults, the other on juveniles. The latter study also examined whether courts appeared to operate a tariff in sentencing juveniles.

Adult sentencing

The penalties available to magistrates when dealing with male indictable offenders aged 21 or over range from an absolute discharge to sentences of imprisonment of up to six months or, in the case of some offences, of up to one year. At the time of this study, magistrates' courts also had the power to fine up to a maximum of £400 (by 1984 this had been raised to £2,000 for comparable offences), to make a hospital order, to make a community service order, to make a probation order, to order a conditional discharge and to suspend a prison sentence. They could also, in circumstances where they felt their powers to deal with an offender were not sufficient, commit him to the Crown Court to be sentenced. There are some detailed restrictions on the way these sentences may be used, but they are fairly minimal in terms of day-to-day sentencing decisions.

Although the independence enjoyed by magistrates permits variation between different benches it also has the positive effect of allowing them to take into account the particular circumstances of each case and thus encourages a unique system of 'individualised justice'.

These two aspects need not, of course, be seen as alternative views of the system, as public statements by those involved in what goes on in magistrates' courts show. Commenting on what it felt to be 'wide variation' in sentences awarded for motoring offences between different magistrates' courts, the Magistrates' Association has said: 'The conclusion that each case ought to be judged on its merits does not exclude the establishment of a greater measure of consistency'. In a similar vein, the Lord Chancellor's Office urges in its handbook for newly-appointed justices that 'it is obviously desirable that there should be no great divergence of general policy between members of the same bench. Similarly, it is desirable that the sentencing policies of adjacent benches, and even of benches in different parts of the country, should not differ too widely one from the other'. The wider purpose of this study was to present some evidence against which proposals to promote greater consistency in sentencing could be more critically appraised.

It was necessary first to estimate the size of sentencing discrepancies and the extent to which courts differed in their use of different disposals. The study was restricted to male indictable offenders aged 21 and over and only the main disposals then available are considered: discharge; probation; fine; imprisonment (immediate and suspended); and committal to the Crown Court for sentence. (At the time of the study community service was only just starting, on an experimental basis.) Differences between courts together with results from further investigation of their sentencing practice are discussed.

Obviously, not all differences between courts can be attributed simply to the arbitrariness of magistrates' decisions: differences in 'intake' – that is, in the types of offences and the characteristics of the offenders appearing before each court – are likely to account for a part of them. The research sought to determine how far intake can be said to account for differences between courts' sentencing patterns, and to look for other factors – such as the resources available to the courts, local prosecution policy, the economic and social conditions prevailing in different catchment areas and so on – which might also contribute. Accordingly a random sample of 30 of the larger magistrates' courts from all parts of the country was selected for detailed study.

In addition to this purely statistical study, courts' sentencing practice was discussed with clerks to the justices and with chairmen of benches of magistrates at 28 of the 30 courts in the sample. The aim here was to see whether, and in what ways, courts structure their own sentencing policy and sentencing decisions and the extent to which they attempted to achieve consistency with their neighbours as well as internally. The study was confined to larger magistrates' courts as the proposed statistical analysis could not be carried out on small courts.

Difference between courts in their use of disposals

Table 14:1 shows the extent to which the 30 courts in the sample varied in their use of each disposal. The figures relate to 1975. The average for all courts (taken from *Criminal Statistics*) is shown for comparison, and to set the figures for the selected courts in a national context.

Table 14:1 *Difference between extreme courts in their use of disposals (figures in percentages) and the average for all courts in 1975*

Disposal	Minimum use by any court	Maximum use by any court	Difference-range	Average all courts
Discharge	2	31	29	10
Probation	1	12	11	5
Fine	46	76	30	63
Immediate imprisonment	3	19	16	6
Committal to Crown Court	1	11	10	3
Custodial sentence (imprisonment and committal to Crown Court)	5	23	18	10
Suspended sentence	4	16	12	9

It can be seen that the 30 courts differed considerably in their use of each disposal. The greatest variation occurred in the use of fines. One court fined 46 per cent of offenders appearing before it, whereas at the other extreme another court fined 76 per cent, a difference of 30 per cent. But differences were also large for other disposals: probation varied from 1 per cent to 12 per cent; imprisonment from 3 per cent to 19 per cent; committals to the Crown Court from 1 per cent to 10 per cent; custodial sentences from 5 per cent to 23 per cent; and suspended sentences from 4 per cent to 16 per cent. However the difference between courts in their use of discharge was exaggerated by one exceptional court which discharged 31 per cent of offenders. If this court is omitted the range for the remaining 29 was from 2 to 18 per cent, a difference of 16 per cent. This was the only case of a single court distorting the difference between extremes.

Court sentencing traditions

Is each court consistent in its use of disposals from year to year and does it have its own traditional way of dealing with offenders? For example, if a court fined a high proportion of offenders in one year did it also fine a high proportion in all other years, or did its use of fines vary from year to year? To answer this question an analysis of variance was carried out. Although it was not possible to test directly the consistency of courts' sentencing patterns over the five years, there was strong evidence that any variation was small, and each court did appear to have its own sentencing tradition – in other words, a court which made frequent use of a disposal in one year tended to make frequent use of that disposal in other years.

Relationship between disposals

The correlation between a court's use of each disposal and its use of other disposals was analysed for the period 1971 to 1975. The use of fines was inversely correlated with discharges and custodial and suspended sentences; that is, courts which fined a high proportion of offenders tended to order fewer discharges and to award fewer custodial and suspended sentences, while courts which fined relatively few offenders made more use of these other disposals. This result was perhaps not unexpected. Fines are numerically the most important disposal, and therefore courts which fine a high proportion of offenders are unable to use the other disposals to any great extent.

Courts' use of probation was not related to their use of any other disposals. This may be due to magistrates' views of probation as a form of 'treatment', whereas other disposals are likely to reflect a range of other sentencing aims. It could mean that the decision to place an offender on probation is taken to meet his individual needs, and is not considered merely as a more or less severe alternative to discharge, fine, custodial and suspended sentences. Custodial sentences were positively correlated with suspended sentences: courts which favoured custodial sentences also favoured suspended sentences.

Offence and offender

Potentially the most important factors affecting sentencing practice are differences in the types of offences and characteristics of the offenders with which individual courts deal. If, for example, a particular court deals with a higher-than-average proportion of serious offences, it would be reasonable to expect it to award relatively more severe penalties. Three variables were readily accessible and the analysis had to be restricted to them. These were type of offence, age of the offender, and whether or not he had any previous convictions. Although further details about the offender and his offence were not available for investigation, previous research suggests that this may not be a serious omission. Green (1961) and Wilkins (1976) have shown type of offence and previous criminal history to be the most important factors in determining sentence. But both these studies were of American courts and thus their relevance to decisions taken by English magistrates may be limited; and both were principally concerned with the alternatives of being sent to prison or being dealt with by a non-custodial measure. Other studies conducted in this country have not found that additional factors explain differences between courts. Grunhut (1956) and Mannheim *et al*. (1957) looked at a number of indices relating to the family background and character of the boys appearing before their juvenile courts, and Hood (1962) included the employment record of the offenders before his adult magistrates' courts. But none of these factors could account for the different sentencing practices in their studies.

This part of the study was confined to offenders found guilty at the 30 magistrates' courts during 1975, a total of over 30,000 offenders. Type of offence undoubtedly affected the type of disposal awarded and this was most pronounced for offences of burglary. Only 37 per cent of offenders found guilty of burglary were fined, compared with 61 per cent of all offenders. More burglars (39 per cent) were sentenced to custody (imprisonment or committed to the Crown Court for sentence) or awarded a suspended sentence. Men convicted of violence and criminal damage had slightly better chances of being discharged than other types of offenders (the association between violence and discharge may be thought surprising but more serious cases of violence are dealt with by the Crown Court). Conversely, offenders convicted of theft or of unauthorised taking of a motor vehicle had the poorest chance of being discharged and stood a greater chance of receiving a custodial sentence. Fraud and forgery was also associated with custodial sentences, but convictions for sexual offences, damage or violence reduced the chance of custodial sentence. Suspended sentences of imprisonment showed a similar relationship to offence type as did custodial sentences. Probation was awarded most frequently in the case of sexual offences, burglary and fraud. These last two offences were least likely to attract a fine; sexual offences, causing criminal damage, and shoplifting most so.

The analysis of the relationship between age and disposal showed that use of discharges increased as age rose. This was most noticeable for the group aged 40 and over. The increase in the use of discharge had the effect of slightly reducing the use of probation, fine and suspended sentence. Otherwise, age had little effect on the disposal awarded.

Finally, the analysis showed that first offenders were more likely to be discharged or to receive a monetary penalty while those with a previous conviction were more likely to be placed on probation or given a custodial or a suspended sentence of imprisonment. Further analysis of the relationship between various combinations of the factors and the disposal awarded showed that the joint effect of type of offence and previous criminal history, in particular, was associated with disposal.

Effect of intake on sentencing practice

In common with other studies, it was found that differences in intake accounted for only some of the differences in courts' sentencing practice. For example, although a conviction for burglary was more likely to result in a custodial sentence and less likely to result in a fine, one court awarded a custodial sentence to only 7 per cent of burglars appearing before it whereas another court disposed of 47 per cent of burglars in this way and, similarly, the proportion of burglars fined ranged from 19 per cent at one court to 62 per cent at another. As previously mentioned, a larger proportion of offenders aged 40 or over were discharged than offenders in other age groups; but courts ranged from 4 per cent to 36 per cent in their use of discharge for this age group. Similar results were obtained for offenders with and without previous convictions. Offenders with no previous convictions were more likely to be fined and less likely to be given a custodial sentence, but one court fined 53 per cent of first offenders whereas another awarded fines to 11 per cent of first offenders, and custodial sentences were awarded to 0.3 per cent of first offenders at one court but to 11 per cent at another. Combinations of the factors did not account for differences between courts. For example, one court fined 48 per cent of first offenders convicted of shoplifting whereas another fined 86 per cent. Similarly, courts' use of custodial sentences for first offenders convicted of offences within the category 'other theft' ranged from 0 to 9 per cent.

Separate correlations were undertaken between the use of disposals for different types of offence, different age groups, and for offenders with and without previous convictions. It was found that the same pattern persisted after controlling for these three factors. This suggests, therefore, that courts have a preference for different disposals even after allowing for differences in intake. In particular, some courts fine offenders where others would discharge them or award a custodial or suspended sentence, and courts which imposed a custodial sentence on a high proportion of offenders seem also more likely to impose suspended sentences.

Further explanations of sentencing disparities

Various other possible explanations for sentencing discrepancies were investigated, including the crime rate in the area, the local police cautioning rate, probation resources, and local economic factors. In this study there was no evidence to support the notion that, for reasons of deterrence, more severe sentences were passed in response to a crime problem. Several studies, for example Ditchfield (1976), have shown an inverse relationship between the cautioning rate (that is those cautioned as a proportion of all those found guilty and cautioned) and the proportion discharged. The correlation between the cautioning rate and the proportion given custodial sentences was found to be .28 in both years and together they show a statistically significant relationship ($p < .05$). The cautioning rate was not found to be related to courts' use of probation, fine or suspended sentences. But as police cautioning affects the type of offender appearing before the court, much of this effect has already been accounted for in the offender and offence analysis presented earlier. Although it was not possible to estimate its exact value, it seems likely that some additional variation in courts' use of discharges and custodial sentences was attributable to local police prosecution policies.

Differences in resources are another possible reason for variation, and this applies particularly to probation. If courts are to place offenders on probation then resources must be available to supervise them during their probationary period. The amount of probation resources available to the court, therefore, may influence its use of probation. Barr and O'Leary (1966) first drew attention to regional inequalities in the size of the probation service. They noticed wide discrepancies in the probation resources available and those regions with the fewest resources made least use of probation. This finding was reinforced by the present study, in which a significant relationship was found to exist between the use of probation and the amount of probation resources available to the court. Where resources were greater, more social inquiry reports were prepared and more offenders were placed on probation. However the interpretation of these results is not straightforward. Resources could affect the use of probation. For example, probation officers may exert some influence on the numbers receiving probation by the number they recommend for it. If the probation service feels fully committed and unable to deal with many more probationers it could reduce the numbers recommended for probation. Obviously magistrates are not bound to follow probation officers' recommendations, and in many cases do not, but results from other studies (see Thorpe, 1979 for details) suggest that magistrates are not likely to place on probation offenders who have not been recommended for it. On the other hand the willingness to use probation may have determined the level of resources available. In his study Hood (1962) suggested that courts tended to use probation where the magistrates were favourably disposed to it, and where good relations existed between magistrates and probation officers.

Amount of fine

The average fine imposed by each of the 30 courts during 1975 varied between £18 and £47, a difference of almost £30 between extremes. Courts which fined a high proportion of offenders did not, on average, impose higher or lower fines than courts which made relatively little use of fines. Amount of fine did not appear to be influenced by the age of the offender or his previous criminal history, but was related to the type of offence: on average, higher fines were imposed on offenders convicted of sexual offences, offences of violence, burglary and theft or unauthorised taking of a motor vehicle, whereas lower fines were imposed for offences of criminal damage.

Court organisation and personnel

Although it appears that there is a reduction in the extent of the apparent discrepancies between different courts when differences in the types of offenders they deal with are taken into account, and that some of the remaining inconsistencies can be explained by reference to local circumstances, it is inevitable that individual members of a court will also contribute to its particular sentencing policy. It is the possibility of some sort of subjective element entering into sentencing decisions which seems to arouse most of the criticism directed against the present system.

The clerk to the justices and the chairman of the bench of magistrates at each court were invited to talk about their sentencing policy, what it owed to the co-ordinating efforts of the clerk, and how it was maintained. The topics for discussion were fairly matter-of-fact: whether clerks and magistrates were actually aware of sentencing inconsistencies or not, both within their own and between other courts; what steps were taken to minimise these inconsistencies; how sentencing policy was formulated; the extent to which clerks advised the bench on sentencing decisions; and the opportunities clerks took to bring matters of sentencing policy to the attention of magistrates. The information was obtained by informal interviews. What very soon became apparent – and this was perhaps the most interesting and useful result of the inquiry – was that the courts were really only interested in maintaining consistency within their own practice. With the exception of trying to even out the levels of fines for motoring offences within a locality, no court spokesman claimed that any attempt was made to achieve consistency with his neighbours or with courts over a wider area or with what was thought to be national practice. None of the courts knew much about the sentencing practice of any others, even about those next to them, and they regarded such knowledge as irrelevant to their own decisions or problems. Rightly or wrongly, local conditions and patterns of crime were seen as peculiar to that locality, and sentencing policy as thus to be uniquely adapted accordingly. This conviction on the part of influential figures in the courts, together with a strong and general tendency towards the preservation of autonomy, seems to ensure that very little emphasis is placed on action to achieve anything like a more uniform approach to sentencing even within a fairly small geographical area.

In contrast, definite steps are taken to maintain internal consistency. In the first place, the present study confirmed that the habits and traditions of a court act as an important constraint on the initiative of individual magistrates, presumably over-riding many of the personal prejudices or attitudes that they might otherwise reflect in their decisions (assuming, of course, that magistrates as a group do not hold more or less similar views). Clerks may act as mediators of these traditions, or they may exert a more direct influence. Thirdly, individual discretion may also be constrained more formally and more overtly by the use of 'basic penalties', that is, agreed penalties that are regarded as appropriate for any ordinary offence committed by an ordinary or average person and which can then be modified in accordance with whatever aggravating or mitigating circumstances hold in any particular case. Most of the courts studied here used a scheme like this as an aid to sentencing motoring offenders, and some extended it to a variety of other offences. Finally, some courts had adopted sentencing presumptions, or unwritten rules of thumb about how to approach certain types of cases. These either took the form of presumptions in favour of imprisonment for offences of particular kinds, or more often existed as rough agreements about what sorts of fines should be exacted from certain common classes of offenders.

Court traditions

Clerks spoke of the steadying influence of senior justices and court clerks in ensuring consistent sentencing practice within the bench, and of the effects of magistrates' long experience, their frequent discussions of common problems, their common training, and so on. More concretely, it is intended that blatant irregularities which might arise should magistrates become isolated from their colleagues and thus become able – or be forced – to develop a sentencing policy peculiar to themselves will be minimised by a rota system. The fact that – at least at the larger courts covered by the study – magistrates did not regularly form the same benches meant that the risk of benches developing individualistic sentencing policies were minimised.

The justices' clerk is a key figure in the magistrates' court. He, unlike a magistrate, occupies a full-time salaried position, and his expertise and experience allows him to advise magistrates about the range and purpose of sentencing options, notify them of guidance given by higher courts, suggest whether specialist reports are needed for particular offenders and so on. He has, indeed, a certain duty to ensure that courts' work *is* consistent. The clerk is also responsible for scheduling court business and drawing up the rota. In addition he is often involved in training courses for magistrates. By co-ordinating the affairs of the court the clerk is, to some extent, a mediator of court traditions. All sentencing involves questions of law, practice and procedure, and so falls within the range of matters on which magistrates may consult their clerks. The only thing magistrates must not ask is what sentence they ought to impose in a particular case. The potential influence of the clerk is therefore considerable. How much influence he exerts in practice depends on how he sees his role. All but seven clerks interviewed regarded advising on sentencing as of major importance in their job. The clerk's influence also depends on the relationship he has with his magistrates. It is interesting to note that many of the clerks who were satisfied with the way their role was defined stressed that they had good working relationships with the justices at their court and that clarification of their position was unnecessary.

Guidance for sentencers

As long ago as 1964 the Magistrates' Association issued a public statement expressing concern over the 'wide variation' throughout the country in the sentences imposed for motoring offences. Greater uniformity of approach was seen as desirable, and to be achieved 'only by the various benches following a common policy'. This common policy is set out as a list of recommended penalties, which is periodically updated. The recommendations are certainly not intended to be followed slavishly. The Association accepts that local benches may want to vary their recommendations from the national ones to take account of such local circumstances as, for example, economic conditions in their area. And in sentencing individual offenders, magistrates are urged not to treat the recommendations as a rigid tariff, but to vary them according to the gravity of the offence, its prevalence, the past record of the offender, his present means, and the impact of disqualification on different offenders. At the time of the study, recommended penalties had only recently been introduced, and it is clear that they had had only a limited impact in reducing disparities. More recent, but less detailed, evidence suggests that considerable differences between areas persist.

If traditions of local bench independence and autonomy can impede progress towards greater national uniformity in the sentencing of motoring offenders, the problem is even greater in the sentencing of crime generally. Here the use of a basic penalty scheme as an aid to sentencing is much more controversial and there are no nationally agreed recommendations to guide courts in setting the type or level of penalties. Nevertheless, six courts in the sample said they used recommended penalty lists for sentencing offenders convicted of indictable crimes. A further nine courts had unwritten sentencing norms, that is, they were able to specify the level of financial penalty that would normally be imposed for an indictable offence. Like written basic penalties, unwritten ones varied between different courts, the fine for shoplifting, for example, ranging from £10 to £50. All lists were fairly rudimentary, and all were aimed at internal consistency rather than consistency with other courts.

The question of how wider consistency between courts might be encouraged is discussed later. But first, it is interesting to compare sentencing practice in juvenile courts where there are many parallels with adult sentencing, but also some important distinctions.

Juvenile sentencing

The study of juvenile sentencing sought to establish whether courts appeared to apply a tariff in sentencing juveniles, and if so to describe it. The concept of a sentencing 'tariff' essentially means two things: first, the more serious the case the more severe will be the penalty, and second, this relationship will operate in a fairly consistent and predictable way. It is a concept which has come to be widely accepted in relation to the sentencing of adults and has been well described by Thomas (1979). But for juveniles, where sentencers have the added complication that they must have regard to the welfare of the child and the sentencing options accordingly include welfare measures, the concept of a tariff is less obviously applicable.

While a tariff is based on averaging out the practices of a number of disparate courts there is, as already noted, much evidence to suggest that sentencing practice varies between courts. Any examination of the tariff which juvenile courts apply would therefore be incomplete without some consideration of the nature of the variation between courts.

The year chosen for the study was 1978. The attractions of using 1978 data were threefold: firstly it seemed best to explore the extent to which the notion of a tariff could describe juvenile sentencing practice in a period when sentencing was not changing under the impact of new powers; secondly a pre-1982 study could later serve as a useful benchmark against which to assess changes in sentencing practice after the Criminal Justice Act 1982 was fully implemented; and thirdly it was the mid-point of the period for which data were available.

The Home Office Statistical Department provided data showing the number of each type of sentence made by individual juvenile courts in England and Wales over the five year period 1976–80. Nine courts were selected on the basis of their proportionate use of custodial sentences – three courts used custodial sentences more than the average, three were close to the average and three used custody less than average. The data showed that, as in adult courts, the sentencing pattern within each court was consistent over a five year period.

The sample of offenders used in the study consisted of all male juveniles appearing before the selected nine courts in 1978 (almost 7,000 cases). Female offenders were not included as their numbers were very small – in 1978 they constituted less than 13 per cent of all offenders aged between 10 and 16. The Home Office Statistical Department also provided information from their Offenders' Index covering type of offence, criminal record, the most serious previous disposal and the age of the offender.

Is there a tariff?

The law makes a distinction between children (10 to 13-year-olds) and young persons (14 to 16-year-olds) in terms of sentencing options. For children, courts must choose between a discharge, a fine, a supervision order, an attendance centre order and a care order. From the age of 14, an offender can in addition be given a custodial sentence – to detention from the age of 14 and (until 1982) to borstal from the age of 15[1].

The findings indicated that the concept of a tariff applied only in a very limited way to the younger (10 to 13) age group. Discharges were the most common disposal for all types of offence and, for the rest, disposals were almost evenly divided between 'welfare' (care orders and supervision orders) and 'punishment' (fines and attendance centre orders). With one exception there was no clear association between offence seriousness and the severity of the response. The exception was care orders, which were used most for the more serious offences, and progressively more as the number of previous convictions rose. It seems likely that for the less serious offences any effect of offence on sentence is subordinate to the influence of individual social factors which is likely to be particularly strong for this youngest age group.

Just over half the 14 to 16-year-olds had previous convictions, and 17 per cent

1. Figures for borstal relate to cases referred to the Crown Court with a recommendation for borstal training: not all such cases will have resulted in a borstal sentence.

– compared with 7 per cent of the younger group – had at least three. A series of analyses were conducted to evaluate the effect of age, offence and previous convictions on disposal. Each of these factors had a significant influence, with type of offence and number of previous convictions being the most important. A full tariff, showing the effect of offence and criminal record on disposal, is set out in Moxon, Jones and Tarling (1985).

Courts would often give a discharge to a first offender, but were much less inclined to use this, the least severe disposal, for those with previous convictions. For the rest, courts generally chose between a fine, supervision and an attendance centre for those with two or fewer previous convictions. The choice between them did not suggest that courts ranked these three disposals in a particular way but rather that the choice depended on individual circumstances, including the preferences of individual courts. As with the younger group there was a steady increase in the use of care orders as the number of previous convictions rose, though they were used for only 5 per cent of 14 to 16-year-olds compared with 13 per cent of the younger age group. As a rule custodial sentences, and particularly borstal, were only used in a substantial proportion of cases for those offenders with three or more previous convictions. However, for offences of burglary and robbery the pattern was somewhat different, with courts being less willing to persevere with non-custodial disposals beyond the second offence. In consequence there was a sharp jump in the use of custodial disposals for burglary and robbery offenders with two previous convictions, with detention the most common disposal. For those with three or more previous convictions borstal replaced detention as the most common disposal.

The effect of age on sentence was quite marked. Amongst 16-year-olds, as opposed to 14-year-olds, there was considerably less use of discharges, supervision orders and attendance centre orders. Conversely, the use of fines increased sharply – from 19 to 47 per cent. Among the more severe disposals the combined use of detention centres, borstal and care orders did not change greatly with age (it varied between 15 and 17 per cent). However, there were complementary trends within this group of disposals, with care orders declining from 8.5 per cent for 14-year-olds to 2.4 per cent for 16-year-olds, whilst borstal, not available for 14-year-olds, was used for 6.8 per cent of 16-year-olds. Interestingly, there was virtually no change in the use of detention across the age range.

Variation between courts

The range of use of each disposal across the nine courts is shown in the following table.

Table 14:2 *Range of nine courts' use of disposals for 14 to 16-year-olds*

Disposal	Min. use by any court %	Max. use by any court %	Mean %
Discharge	14	36	20
Supervision	11	22	16
Fine	23	48	32
Attendance	0	19	15
Care order	1	8	5
Detention	3	11	7
Borstal	1	8	4

It can be seen that there was very wide variation in the use of each type of sentence. The marked variation between the courts in the use of each sentence may reflect several factors. Firstly, there is the contrast in the intake of different courts, notably offence and previous convictions. For example, for the 14 to 16 age group the proportion of burglary and robbery cases ranged from 13 to 43 per cent; and the proportion of offenders with previous convictions ranged from 38 to 69 per cent. Secondly, there are differences in the options available to courts (one court did not have access to a local attendance centre). Thirdly, there may be differences in the resources and attitudes of local probation and social service departments – the decision to use supervision or care orders is often influenced by their recommendations (Harris and Webb, 1983). And fourthly, different courts may have different sentencing traditions.

One reason why some courts have a larger proportion of serious cases than others is the difference in cautioning practices between police forces – a Home Office Working Group has reviewed these wider issues (Home Office, 1984). The high use of discharges – by far the most common disposal for the younger age group – suggests that there may be scope for diverting more cases from the courts, at least in some areas, through an increase either in formal cautions or informal warnings.

Whilst the analysis showed that differences in the kinds of cases dealt with by different courts were clearly important, there was still substantial variation which appeared to result from the different approaches to sentencing of the courts studied. Examination of sentences for one offence category (burglary and robbery), controlling for number of previous convictions, revealed that even for offenders with no previous convictions, the three high custody courts gave proportionately twice as many custodial sentences as the three low custody courts; for those with three or more previous convictions, the high custody courts used custody in some 72 per cent of cases compared with 41 per cent in the case of the low custody courts. (A similar comparison for theft and fraud revealed comparable differences.) Whereas the low custody courts were content to persevere with non-custodial options for first, second and third offenders, in the high custody courts the use of custody rose sharply after a second conviction. These results clearly point to substantial differences in the sentencing traditions of courts.

In sum, the study showed that, for both the 10 to 13 and 14 to 16 age groups there is a clear link between sentences imposed by juvenile courts and the criminal record of offenders. However, the influence of offence is much less clear-cut for 10 to 13-year-olds than for those aged 14 to 16. The findings therefore point, as expected, to the conclusion that the balance between welfare and justice considerations alters as age rises.

The study reinforced earlier findings that there is a lack of consensus as to the circumstances which demand a custodial sentence. A key point to emerge from the analysis is that although only a small proportion (6 per cent) of those with two or fewer previous convictions received a custodial sentence, the numbers were substantial (253) because the great majority of offenders – 83 per cent – fell into this category. Proportionately six times as many (36 per cent) of those with three or more previous convictions were given custodial sentences, but this amounted to only 23 per cent more offenders (312). The point is underlined by *Prison Statistics* for 1978 (Home Office, 1979) which show that less than half of the 14 to 16-year-olds received into detention centres and borstals in that year had more than two previous convictions.

Discussion

In considering sentencing disparities, there are really two questions to be answered. First, is it desirable to achieve greater uniformity? And secondly, if so, how can this best be achieved? On the first point, greater consistency is not automatically desirable – it is possible to be consistently wrong. It is therefore necessary to give some thought to what practices can best achieve the objectives of sentencers, rather than simply encourage courts to converge on some arbitrary norm. As noted earlier, evidence as to the relative effectiveness of different sentences in reforming or deterring offenders is for the most part inconclusive. However, a comprehensive comparison of all sentences, both custodial and non-custodial, was carried out for the 1964 edition of *The Sentence of the Court*. In comparing the effectiveness of fines, discharges, probation and imprisonment, the results suggested that fines and discharges were more effective than probation and imprisonment. The study took account of the age and previous criminal history of the offender, but it was not possible to include the full range of factors which might have affected sentencing decisions. And it is probable that the courts will have selected the less severe options for those whom they were persuaded were least likely to reoffend. A more recent, and in some respects more detailed study (Walker, Farrington and Tucker, 1981), suggested that the only measures which were consistently more effective than others were financial (usually fines, but sometimes compensation orders).

In the case of juveniles there is the particular risk that a custodial sentence may harm an offender's educational, training or employment opportunities and may impede development towards a law-abiding way of life. The negative effects of custody have been fully recognised, and much effort has gone into extending the range of non-custodial options to ensure that custody is not used where some alternative would suffice. That custody ought to be used as sparingly as possible for juveniles was emphasised by the then Home Secretary, William Whitelaw, who said in the course of the second reading debate on the Criminal Justice Bill in 1982: 'No court may impose any custodial sentence on a young offender unless it is satisfied that no other method of dealing with him is appropriate. By broadening and strengthening existing non-custodial provisions [the Act] will assist the courts to avoid a custodial sentence except where absolutely necessary.'

What the studies of both adult and juvenile sentencing have shown is that courts have, at any rate in the past, tended to act very much in isolation, achieving internal consistency but with little regard to practice elsewhere. There are signs that this is gradually changing: since these studies were completed, information as to the sentencing patterns in different areas has become more widely available – for example, the Home Office Statistical Department now produces annual sentencing statistics by Commission of the Peace area, partly in response to the research findings. And the growing interest which courts are displaying in monitoring their own sentencing practice, both locally and by comparison with national data, reflects a growing awareness that consistency is a worthwhile objective for sentencers. It is nevertheless no easy matter for courts to adjust their practices to bring them more into line with norms which are not clearly defined and which are themselves formed of a wide range of disparate practices. Ideas for promoting greater uniformity have been considered in the past – for example, mandatory sentences, sentencing panels or replacing lay justices by stipendiaries – but for various reasons these would be impractical or unlikely to achieve the intended results. (For a fuller discussion of these issues see Tarling, 1979.) Policies directed at giving greater guidance to magistrates on the type of sentence to be imposed are potentially more useful. For example, the Magistrates' Association's list of recommended penalties might be extended to a much wider range of offences with clear guidance as to the principles to be applied and the criteria to be used in doing so.

To achieve a more general agreement and acceptance of these recommendations consideration needs to be given to ways of improving communication between courts on sentencing matters. Magistrates' courts committees, by bringing together representatives from different courts, and through their responsibility for training magistrates could help by initiating a greater discussion on this topic. The Magistrates' Association (1979–80) has made efforts to reduce disparities by promoting consistency in the approach to sentencing, though this has in general stopped short of suggesting particular sentences other than for motoring offences (TV licence evasion is an exception). They could have a part to play in the formulation of recommended sentences for other offences. It could also be advantageous to review the appeal procedures for cases tried summarily. An appeal procedure more in line with that of the Court of Appeal would perhaps help to clarify the principles which magistrates are to follow.

Improved communications could help to break down court traditions. Perhaps the most significant finding of the studies is the degree of importance attached by court officials to establishing and maintaining a consistent policy within their own individual courts and their relative disregard for the policies of their neighbours. If one is considering modifications to court practices it is probably this feature which is the most important one. Indeed, one could, if one wished, see the insularity and durability of court traditions as major obstacles to attaining greater consistency between courts. Any attempts to change existing procedures cannot afford to underestimate the strengths and weaknesses of these traditions.

15 Fines and their enforcement

DAVID MOXON

The fine is central to the criminal justice system. In 1983 nearly 1.8 million offenders were fined – more than 84 per cent of all those sentenced. Any change in the proportionate use of fines therefore has major implications throughout the criminal justice system, both because changes in the use of fines affects the burden on all the agencies which deal with offenders; and because fine enforcement can involve other agencies directly. In most cases enforcement begins and ends with the court. But where simple measures fail or are not used, as often happens, the police may be employed to execute warrants; the probation service may be called upon to supervise payment through the money payment supervision order; and, as a last resort, defaulters may be imprisoned. Unfortunately, this last resort is often reached: in recent years fine defaulters have accounted for about a quarter of all receptions of sentenced prisoners.

Successive Home Office studies over the past 15 years or so have focused on different aspects of enforcement to provide a composite picture of the enforcement process. This chapter draws together some of the threads, though the main emphasis is on the more recent studies.

Fine enforcement – the first survey

Research into fine enforcement began with a study which looked at the effect of the Criminal Justice Act 1967 on enforcement (Softley, 1972). This Act introduced new methods of payment, but also placed new restrictions on courts' powers to impose imprisonment in default of payment. In particular, the circumstances in which a term of imprisonment could be fixed at the time the fine was imposed as an alternative to payment were narrowed. In consequence the proportion of cases in which an alternative of imprisonment was fixed when the fine was imposed fell by two thirds, and the number of fine defaulters received into prison fell by one third.

There were predictions from those at the sharp end of enforcement that the curbs on the powers to imprison would make enforcement more difficult. The restrictions imposed by the 1967 Act on the use of committal warrants did indeed appear to add to the workload of the courts: in 1968 courts proceeded against more defaulters than in the previous years, more means warrants were issued, and more defendants appeared at means inquiries. However, courts were no less successful in recovering the sums due, so it seems that the overall effectiveness of enforcement changed little as a result of the Act. This early study therefore gave the first indications that the extent to which courts resort to imprisonment as an enforcement measure may have little bearing on their success in securing payment of fines.

Interviews with fine and maintenance defaulters in prison

Doubts as to whether imprisonment was used as sparingly as it might be were reinforced by a small-scale (unpublished) study undertaken by Vennard in 1975. For this study fine and maintenance defaulters were interviewed in prison, and were asked detailed questions both about their means and about their attitudes to payment of the fines. Only one of the fine defaulters had refused to pay on principle – the majority claimed that they simply did not have the money. The answers given to questions about means seemed to bear this out, if only by suggesting that the financial affairs of most of those interviewed were in disarray. Occasionally it seemed that the court had only imposed a fine as a formality, never expecting that it would actually be paid: for example two men had been given till 2 pm on the day of the hearing to come up with the money and were then locked in a police cell until 2 pm, with no access to a telephone.

An important qualification to this study was that people who paid themselves out quickly – and for whom the tactic of imprisonment was therefore successful in terms of enforcement – were under-represented. Nevertheless, the study gave rise to some concern that a substantial number of defaulters might be ending up in prison simply because they were unable to pay – either because they lacked the money or because such money as they had was poorly managed.

Indictable offences and the use of fines

The first study had confirmed the common-sense expectation that the ranks of defaulters would be drawn mainly from those convicted of indictable property offences, drunks, and TV and vehicle licence evaders. The next study, by Softley (1978), looked at those convicted of indictable offences who were tried summarily, but this time the sample was not restricted to those who were fined. The aims of this study included:

- an investigation of the use of fines in relation to particular categories of offence and offender;
- a comparison of reconviction rates for people fined with those for offenders given other sentences;
- an assessment of the financial effects of fines and other sums on those who had to pay them.

A comparison of the effectiveness of different measures was also a major feature of the study. However, a later study (discussed below) provided a more up-to-date and more comprehensive comparison of enforcement methods, and so this aspect of the study is not discussed further here.

The study gave a fuller profile of the typical defaulter than had been available hitherto. It was found that offenders with previous convictions were twice as likely to default as those with none; 63 per cent of those fined over £25 defaulted compared with 40 per cent of those fined smaller sums; 60 per cent of the unemployed defaulted, compared with 48 per cent of those in work; and 57 per cent of those under 30 defaulted compared with 41 per cent of offenders aged 31 or over. Given these findings, it is perhaps not surprising that courts used fines less for those with previous convictions – particularly those who had several – whilst custodial penalties were used more. That courts do take account of the financial circumstances of the offender was shown by the fact that fines were used for three-quarters of all employed offenders but only half of those who were unemployed – discharges, probation and custodial sentences were all used more for the unemployed. The rise in unemployment is therefore the most likely explanation for the fall in the proportionate use of fines for indictable offenders in recent years, from a peak of around 50 per cent in the mid to late 1970s to 43 per cent in 1983.

After allowing for two of the most important factors bearing on re-offending – the number of previous convictions and age – it was found that the re-conviction rate was a little lower for those fined. This finding, which is consistent with other studies of the effectiveness of sentencing (see for example Brody, 1976, and Phillpotts and Lancucki, 1979) does suggest that the fine is at least as effective as other sentences in terms of deterring the individual offender from further crime.

A questionnaire was sent to those who had been fined, in an attempt to discover what the financial impact of the fine had been on them. The results suggested that a substantial number of those fined had had to cut back on basic necessities such as food and clothing. Even in this sample, which dates from a time (1974) when overall unemployment was less than 3 per cent, 40 per cent of defaulters were unemployed. This underlines both the need for care in fixing the amount of fines to keep them within the offender's capacity to pay, and the difficulties of making wider use of heavy fines as an alternative to imprisonment in cases where the decision between a custodial and a non-custodial sentence is borderline.

Comparison of courts' enforcement methods

It had long been recognised by auditors that courts vary widely in their success at collecting the fines they impose, and a study by Softley and Moxon (1982), based on fines imposed in 1979, compared the practices of a sample of 34 courts, to ascertain the reasons for this variation with the aim of identifying the ingredients of successful enforcement. The main way in which the performance of courts was assessed was by looking at the proportion of offenders who paid, and the proportion of sums imposed that were recovered, within

12 months. Performance was found to vary widely. For example, the proportion of fines unpaid after 12 months ranged from 1 to 39 per cent. It was thought that some of the variation might be explained by factors which had nothing to do with enforcement practices, such as local income levels, unemployment rates and the size of fines, which could affect offenders' ability to pay. No strong relationship was found between local economic factors and successful enforcement but, not surprisingly, large fines proved more difficult to collect; and courts which had a particularly high proportion of motoring offenders had proportionately fewer defaulters and recovered fines more quickly.

The study looked both at the resources employed on enforcement and at the actions taken to enforce payment. Workloads, as measured by the ratio of offenders fined to man-hours devoted to enforcement ranged from 0.5 to 8.6 offenders fined per man-hour spent on enforcement. Despite this startling variation the workload had no discernible bearing on enforcement performance. What mattered seemed to be the organisation and quality of staff rather than numbers.

The study looked at the actions taken in each case and how quickly courts responded in the event of default. At 13 of the courts the issue of a means warrant was the most common first action, and for most others it was the second; 11 courts usually sent a reminder letter in the first instance, and 10 typically issued a means summons. The extent to which an alternative of imprisonment was fixed within 12 months ranged from 2 per cent of those against whom action was taken at one court, to 40 per cent at another. Other methods of enforcement – attachment of earnings orders, money payment supervision orders and distress warrants – were not in general widely used, although two courts did make substantial use of distress warrants.

The only clear relationship that emerged between methods and enforcement was that, overall, courts which relied most on means warrants performed relatively badly. The most likely explanation is delay in the execution of warrants: at the majority of courts, it was claimed that execution of warrants generally took more than six weeks – and in some cases it took many months. The good results of some courts where warrants were executed promptly showed that heavy reliance on warrants did not in itself undermine performance.

The main finding was that the key to successful enforcement lay not in particular measures but in a prompt response by court staff in the event of default, and in swift follow-up action where initial measures failed.

Means inquiries

As noted earlier, the Criminal Justice Act 1967 sought to curb magistrates' powers to order imprisonment in default of a fine. The Act was effective in reducing receptions into prison in default of payment of a fine by approximately one third, from nearly 12,000 in 1967 to less than 8,000 in 1968.

However, thereafter there was a steady rise in the number of defaulters received into prison. In 1977 a further restriction on courts' powers to imprison defaulters was introduced in an amendment to the 1967 Act which required that after the occasion of sentence a warrant of commitment should not be issued in default of payment of a fine unless the court was satisfied that the default was due to wilful refusal or culpable neglect. Apart from this attempt to ensure that imprisonment did not occur because the defaulter lacked the means to pay, further restriction on the power to imprison for non-payment has been resisted. Among those involved in the collection of fines it is widely held that the threat of imprisonment is an essential sanction.

The number of defaulters imprisoned rose from around 10,000 in 1973 to a peak of 24,500 in 1982, after which the number fell back slightly, to 23,000, in 1983. This trend caused growing unease that some defaulters might be ending up in prison because they could not, rather than because they would not, pay their fines. An observational study of means inquiries was therefore undertaken at eight magistrates' courts in 1982 (Softley, 1983). This involved an examination of the amounts of fines and the terms of payment imposed on fined offenders in relation to their means.

Courts usually obtained at least some information as to defaulters' income and outgoings, though this was not done in every case. However, in most cases where details of income were not obtained the explanation was that there was swift agreement between the court and the defaulter as to terms of payment. Inquiries into outgoings were much less consistent: information about the main items of essential expenditure seemed complete in only 31 of the 228 cases observed, and in 77 cases there were no inquiries into defaulters' outgoings and no details were given to the court.

The main reason for cutting short an inquiry was that the defaulter made an offer. Occasionally this was increased or decreased, according to the court's appreciation of the circumstances. In some courts there appeared to be a 'going rate', which for unemployed defaulters ranged from £1 to £5 per week. Inquiries were seldom made about defaulters' savings or other assets. This may have been because experience showed that such inquiries were seldom fruitful: in six of the cases observed, magistrates asked whether the defaulter had a car – only two admitted to owning a car and both insisted it was worthless.

A further reason why inquiries into outgoings were so limited may have been that they were not necessarily very helpful. For example, if one family of four spends £30 per week on food and another spends £50, this tells the court nothing about what each family *needs* to spend on food. Again, if someone includes cigarettes in their list of outgoings, should courts regard this as an immutable part of their weekly expenditure (which in practice may well be the case) or a sum which should find its way to the fines office in preference to the tobacconist? In the face of such difficulties, the supplementary benefit scales were taken as a guide to necessary expenditure. The scale does not, of course, represent an absolute minimum. This is implicit in the fact that the DHSS has a claw-back rate, which is applied in the case of overpayment of benefit, which was up to £3.60 a week at the time of the study. This figure was therefore added to the figure which the court had as to the defaulter's income, and outgoings were calculated according to the supplementary benefit rates. On this basis, around one third of the fine defaulters would not be able to afford the terms of payment fixed at the means inquiry. A third of this group received a prison sentence to be served if a payment was missed. As in the earlier comparison of courts' enforcement practices there was great variation between courts in the proportion of cases resulting in a suspended committal, which ranged from 4 to 60 per cent of the cases dealt with.

Another particularly striking feature of the study was the high proportion of those appearing at means inquiries – two thirds – who were living on state benefits, mainly unemployment benefit. The average amount outstanding for these offenders was about £190 – a very substantial sum for an unemployed offender to have to find. If a suspended committal is ordered on terms that the defaulter really cannot afford and no friend or relative happens to pay the fine, he will go to prison. Unlike the procedure in cases of maintenance arrears there is no clear procedure for a court to review its decision once a term of imprisonment has been imposed[1]. This prompted a more detailed examination of the relationship between fines, unemployment, and enforcement.

Fines and unemployment

The correlation which earlier research found between unemployment and default led to a study which focused on the links between unemployment, default and the imprisonment of defaulters (Moxon, 1983).

The relationship between unemployment rates and committal rates was explored for 138 towns for which individual unemployment statistics are published by the Department of Employment. After allowing for size of court (which was found to be related to enforcement performance, with larger courts being less successful than smaller ones) there remained a strong and statistically significant correlation between committal rates and local unemployment levels. It is to be expected that areas of high unemployment will contain a higher proportion of offenders who will have difficulty in paying their fines, and the correlation between unemployment rates and committal rates suggests that the means of fined offenders has a bearing on the likelihood that they will be imprisoned for default. However, it cannot be assumed that the relationship between unemployment and committals arises solely because unemployed defaulters cannot afford to pay. It may be that the unemployed offender has less to lose by imprisonment (since he has no job) and more to

1. In the case of *R* v *Colchester Justices* it was decided, contrary to earlier judgments, that justices can take account of default brought about by misfortune, such as redundancy or illness, to vary the conditions upon which they had previously postponed the issue of a committal warrant. It is too early to say what the practical consequences of this judgment will be.

lose by paying (since tight finances mean that payment hurts more). Thus the incentive to pay may be weaker for the unemployed, making eventual imprisonment more likely.

The relationship between default, unemployment and size of fine inevitably raises the question of whether a fine for an offence for which a court feels obliged to impose a substantial penalty is appropriate for the unemployed offender. That this view is shared by the courts may be inferred from the fact that the unemployed are less likely to be fined, and from the decline in the overall use of the fine as unemployment has risen. But if a fine is often judged unsuitable at the sentencing stage because the offender's means are considered to be inadequate to pay an appropriate fine, then the same criterion might logically be applied at a means inquiry when circumstances have changed since sentence was passed. The law recognises this to the extent of providing for remission of all or part of a fine in such cases.

Whilst official advice (Home Office, 1978) specifically cites loss of employment as ground for remission magistrates are understandably reluctant to let a defendant escape punishment altogether, or to reduce a penalty which their colleagues have deemed appropriate at the time of trial. There is, in particular, a very real problem where current circumstances might justify remission, but where the defaulter made little or no effort to pay the fine in different circumstances, when payment could have been made. To reduce the penalty in this situation would be to place the conscientious offender at a disadvantage compared with the neglectful offender. The power to impose an alternative penalty where there is little prospect of securing payment of a fine might therefore be welcomed by the courts.

Committal rates and enforcement performance

The argument for the use of some alternative to imprisonment in order to enforce fine collection is strengthened when the effectiveness of imprisonment as an aid to fine collection is examined. In order to do this, accounting ratios – the ratios of fines recovered to the amounts imposed plus the arrears brought forward – were used as the measure of performance. Accounting ratios have been shown to provide a useful guide to courts' effectiveness at securing payment of fines (Softley and Moxon, 1982). After allowing for variations in size of court it was found that courts which had relatively high committal rates performed neither better nor worse than courts which imprisoned relatively few defaulters.

The analysis showed that committals are concentrated – in both relative and absolute terms – in the larger courts. No less than half of all fines were accounted for by just 35 out of 650 courts. At one end of the scale, nine large courts accounted for a tenth of all fines, but a quarter of all committals; at the other extreme there were 166 courts with no recorded committals for default, but these accounted for only 6 per cent of all fines. The fact that committals to prison are used more by large courts than by small ones probably owes much to the sheer pressure of business in large courts – and perhaps also to a hardening of attitudes when a constant stream of defaulters passes through a court. It may in addition reflect differences of intake between urban and rural courts. For the hard-pressed court, struggling to keep abreast of its workload, a measure which often secures payment, and which transfers the burden to other agencies if it does not, has obvious attractions. It may also be that courts sometimes see a short term of imprisonment as providing a simple means of writing off an unrecoverable fine. However, the fact that the extent to which courts resorted to imprisonment had no significant bearing on enforcement performance suggests that the level of imprisonment at many courts has no justification in terms of its overt objectives – which are to secure payment from defaulters who could not be persuaded to pay by other means, and to encourage potential defaulters to pay.

Distress warrants and money payment supervision orders

Section 82 of the Magistrates' Courts Act 1980 lays down that a court may not issue a warrant of commitment for default unless it 'has considered or tried all other methods of enforcing payment of the sum and it appears to the court that they are inappropriate or unsuccessful'. A key question is therefore: could courts reduce reliance on imprisonment in part by making greater use of measures which are not at present widely used, but which might be expected to serve as effective alternatives to committals? Available information on two measures – distress warrants and money payment supervision orders – was analysed to see whether there was evidence that above-average use of these measures was associated with lower-than-average committal rates.

A distress warrant entitles bailiffs to seize property to cover the value of the unpaid fine. Seven courts which use distress warrants as a routine element in their enforcement process were identified. Two of these courts had below-average committal rates, two were close to the average, and three were above average. Clearly, there was no simple substitution of distress warrants for committal warrants, and more frequent use of distress warrants does not guarantee a lower level of imprisonment. The experience of individual courts using distress warrants is very variable: in three areas for which some data were available one court had reported successful execution of warrants in only 20 per cent of cases, another in 37 per cent of cases, whereas at the third court the success rate was a remarkable 77 per cent. The variation appeared to reflect differences in the criteria used in deciding where distress warrants should be used; it may also have reflected different problems between areas – for example, problems in executing warrants of any sort are greater in areas where there is a highly mobile population. It was notable that in very few cases – less than 1 per cent – were goods actually removed and auctioned. This is in marked contrast to defaulters' response to suspended committals of imprisonment: it would seem that people find the threat of the permanent loss of their belongings far more persuasive than a temporary threat to their liberty.

The potential for using distress warrants as a substitute for imprisonment may be considerable. But in practice the very mixed results achieved by different courts suggest that the rewards are elusive – that whilst distress warrants can be a substantial aid to enforcement if the circumstances are right, their effect on committal rates would not necessarily be very great.

With money payment supervision orders a court official or, more usually a probation officer, is assigned to supervise payment. The supervisor acts as a link between the court and the offender. He fixes terms of payment in consultation with the offender and should maintain regular contact to ensure that the terms are adhered to. Payment is made direct to the court which will notify the supervisor if payment is not made. These orders are not used very widely – between different probation areas their use ranged in 1981 from 0.01 to 1.25 per cent of fines imposed, with an average of 0.35 per cent – but they have attracted some attention (eg NACRO 1981) as expansion in their use is seen as providing a means of effective enforcement without recourse to imprisonment for certain types of offender, especially young offenders and others whose default appears to be due to particular problems in managing their finances.

Discussion and conclusions

Research has served to underline the importance of swift and persistent action in the event of default. So courts should do first what they can do quickest. The corollary to this is that the weightier, more expensive actions should not be used until simpler measures have been exhausted. A problem of enforcement arrangements is that decisions as to the actions to be taken must inevitably lie with the court, whilst the costs often lie elsewhere. In difficult cases it is easier for the court to impose a suspended committal than to persevere with less coercive measures. There is also a widespread feeling among justices' clerks that the threat of imprisonment is very persuasive. Often, of course, it is: but the fact remains that in well over 20,000 cases a year the threat fails. There is substantial evidence that a considerable proportion of these failures occur because the defaulter is unable to pay, either because of insufficient funds or because of poor organisation of such funds as he has.

The recent drop in the use of fines for indictable offenders perhaps reflects courts' acknowledgement of the difficulties of enforcing fines in particular types of case. Sentencers are faced with very real problems. The more serious (indictable) offences are more likely to be committed by those who have the least money. This leads to a situation in which those who deserve the heaviest fines can afford the least. Yet the fine is an attractive option, both because it brings in revenue, whereas all other disposals are costly in varying degrees; and because the fine seems to be associated with a lower rate of recidivism than any other disposal. It is therefore cause for some concern that the proportionate use of the fine for indictable offences has fallen. It is worth looking at the way the problems of imposition and enforcement of fines have been tackled in other countries, as they suggest possible ways of resolving some of the difficulties that have been identified here.

Although information in respect of other countries is limited, some comparisons have been made by Hillsman *et al.* (1984), who looked at practices in Sweden and West Germany, as well as England and Wales. West Germany and, in particular, Sweden, make very much more use of distress than do most courts in England and Wales. Imprisonment is retained as a last resort in all these countries, though Sweden has come close to eliminating imprisonment for default (in 1979 only 17 defaulters were imprisoned). There, distress is the primary enforcement tool, and one that is apparently very effective. Fines are treated like civil debts and means inquiries are used to identify wilful defaulters whose property is then vigorously pursued. Both the Swedish experience and that of courts which have used distress successfully in this country suggest that this is an option which could be more widely used, but with a high proportion of defaulters being young and unemployed the scope may be less than in more affluent countries.

To the extent that the problem lies with imposition of fines which are beyond the means of the offender, measures which match the amount of the fine more closely to the offender's income would ease the problem. A solution which has been adopted in some countries is the day-fine. The day-fine originated in Finland in 1921, and has since been adopted by a number of other countries including Sweden and, most recently, France. With this system the fine is expressed in units based on the offender's income after allowing for essential outgoings. It is the *number* of units which reflect the severity of the offence, so for a given offence the impoverished and the well-off offender would be fined the same number of units. But the *amount* of each unit, being determined by means, would be very different. An unemployed offender would therefore automatically be fined much less than one who is well paid whilst the *number* of units would be the same, and would mark the severity of the offence. The day-fine thus resolves the dilemma of matching the severity of the fine to the seriousness of the offence whilst keeping it within the offender's means. However, it is a system which would present considerable administrative problems in the British context. The present system in which magistrates are required to take account of means, but in a way which does not rely on quite such precise information as is needed in a day-fines system, could provide a sufficient basis for matching fines more closely to offenders' means.

Whatever system may be used for determining the amounts of fines, problems of enforcement will remain. The links between unemployment, default and eventual imprisonment for default are clear and strong. The fact that a very substantial proportion of offenders appearing at means inquiries and (to an even greater degree) being received into prison for default are unemployed reinforces the view that persistent default may often be due to something other than 'wilful refusal' or 'culpable neglect'. Two measures, in particular, have been suggested as likely to make a contribution to the enforcement of fines imposed on offenders who are particularly hard-up.

An idea which was floated by a NACRO working party (NACRO, 1981) was that the principle of attachment of earnings should be extended to all forms of income. It is anomalous that people in steady employment who find difficulty in paying their fines are given the option of paying by deduction from wages whilst those who have no job, and so may be in most need of this option, have no such choice. This contrasts not only with the situation facing employed offenders but also with the situation facing those who have been overpaid by DHSS, where money is withheld to enable any overpayment to be recovered. Bearing in mind that at least two thirds of those appearing in means inquiries (and in all probability an even higher proportion of those received into prison) are in receipt of state benefits, the problem of recovering fines from these offenders could clearly be greatly reduced if the practical difficulties could be overcome.

It was suggested earlier that courts might welcome the opportunity to impose a different sentence in cases where the offender's circumstances change after the occasion of sentence. Community service is a possible candidate, and the Criminal Justice Act 1972 provided for the substitution of community service for a fine in appropriate cases. Implementation of this provision would raise very considerable practical difficulties, and to date it has been felt that it would create too many problems for it to be worth pursuing. However, it is a possibility which is being re-examined at the time of writing.

The fine is sure to remain by far the most common penalty for offenders. But if the decline in the proportionate use of fines for the more serious offences is to be reversed new approaches to the imposition and enforcement of fines may be needed. The studies discussed here have identified the problems which arise in relation to fines, and point to some possible solutions. The complex network of agencies involved in enforcement underlines the need for the court, which takes the key decisions, to have regard to the full implications of its actions on other agencies such as the police and prisons.

16 Working together? The 'system' in action

GEORGE MAIR

Introduction

During the second half of the 1970s and the beginning of the 1980s the size of the prison population and the resulting overcrowding was seen as a major problem by the criminal justice system, and at one point the Home Secretary himself (William Whitelaw, in 1981) went so far as to call it the most serious problem facing him. A number of reports from a variety of sources (the House of Commons Expenditure Committee, 1978; the May Inquiry, 1979; the Parliamentary All-Party Penal Affairs Group, 1980) had investigated the problem of prison overcrowding and had, in general, pointed towards two possible methods of resolving the problem. One of these was to cut sentence lengths and thus send people to prison for shorter periods, and the other (not incompatible with the first) was to utilise to a much greater extent than hitherto the various so-called alternatives to custody which were available. The second of these two approaches is much more amenable to research than the first, and during 1981–82 a team of researchers from the Home Office Research and Planning Unit carried out a major empirical study in the county of Hampshire with the purpose of exploring ways of reducing the prison population and focusing upon the alternatives approach (reported in full in Smith, Sheppard, Mair and Williams, 1984).

The detailed aims of the project were as follows: to ascertain how far alternatives to custody were available; how far they were used and how, if at all, they could be made more useful to sentencers; to consider with participants in the criminal justice system in Hampshire how information about the relevant services might be improved and to what effect; and to explore how far, if at all, there might be other courses available for reducing the extent to which imprisonment was used. The research concentrated on the sentencing of adults and young adults, that is all those aged 17 and over.

Given the nature of the project it was vital to have the full and active co-operation of all those organisations and bodies which would be involved, and approaches were made first at the national and then the local level to find out whether the research would be acceptable. In Hampshire a Consultative Committee was set up which brought together the various agencies and helped to advise the researchers; the members of the Committee included representatives from the local probation service and police force, a local Resettlement of Offenders Co-ordinating Committee, the Magistrates' Association, the Justices' Clerks Society, the Central Council of Probation and After-Care Committees, the National Association of Probation Officers, the National Association for the Care and Resettlement of Offenders, and the Home Office.

The fieldwork for the project was envisaged as falling into two stages: first, ascertaining the views of sentencers, justices' clerks and probation officers on the use and availability of both custodial and non-custodial disposals; and second, conducting, with the co-operation of those directly affected, a series of studies arising from the work in stage one which would investigate non-custodial measures which had been perceived as being likely to reduce the use made of imprisonment.

Fieldwork

A series of informal, loosely-structured interviews and discussions were conducted with judges, chairmen of benches, justices' clerks and a sample of probation officers. The discussions helped to identify the range of views which existed on such matters as the scope for shorter sentences, the diversionary potential of existing non-custodial sentences and so on, and thus contributed to the formulation of a questionnaire which was sent to all probation officers (excluding those working in hostels and penal establishments, and community service organisers) and to a one in five sample of magistrates in the county. The response rate for probation officers was 78 per cent and for magistrates 79 per cent.

On the whole, the sentencers consulted thought that the scope for reducing the prison population was limited. In contrast, most probation officers saw either a fair or large degree of scope for reduction. Sentencers claimed that when incarceration was imposed, justice usually afforded no alternative course of action. For them, a sizeable reduction in the numbers in custody could not precede a fall in the crime rate, and while they did seem to recognise that difficulties existed in the prison system, this did not seem to play a very important role in individual sentencing decisions. Both sentencers and probation officers recognised that certain types of offender were sometimes imprisoned simply because no adequate facilities existed for them in the community, or else because access to appropriate facilities was limited. But the great majority of probation officers saw a variety of offenders falling into this category – those with drink and drug problems, fine and maintenance defaulters, petty persistent offenders, minor sexual offenders and mentally disturbed but not dangerous offenders – while the majority of magistrates saw only those with drink, drug and psychiatric problems as being capable of being dealt with to a greater degree within the community.

The length of custodial sentences given was seen as appropriate by sentencers, although judges intimated that some of their colleagues could perhaps occasionally reduce slightly the terms they imposed. For their part, the magistrates and justices' clerks had some sympathy for the proposal that scope existed for shortening custodial sentences, particularly if institutional regimes could be made stricter as in the case of 'short, sharp shock' detention centres. This raised the possibility that any reduction of the prison population brought about in this way might be offset by a more frequent use of custody arising from the perceived attractiveness of 'tougher' regimes. Most probation officers, on the other hand, considered the length of custodial sentences to be excessive.

The majority of both magistrates and probation officers thought that probation, community service, hostels, attendance centres and hospital orders were, at the least, useful in diverting significant numbers of offenders from custody. Given that the justices identified only limited scope for reducing the prison population, it can be concluded that they considered that they were already using these disposals as alternatives to custody – at least in the sense that the disposals were routinely imposed before imprisonment became 'unavoidable'. It seemed that they believed that major improvements in the diversionary contribution of disposals were held back by lack of resources, most of them agreeing with the probation officers that it was desirable to reduce the prison population through enhanced provision for community service, hostels, day centres, senior attendance centres and 'drying out' facilities.

The pivotal role of the probation service in the non-custodial field was affirmed. Social inquiry reports were generally received favourably by the magistrates (less so by the judges), but apparently more because of the factual material they contained than the sentencing recommendations they put forward. In addition, community service schemes and various residential and community facilities, which the service is responsible for running, were seen as attractive alternatives to custody. Over half the magistrates and probation officers thought it desirable to reduce the prison population through the stricter supervision of offenders. That probation officers had this opinion is perhaps somewhat surprising given what is perceived as their customary emphasis on the importance of their social work role, but it appeared that they were willing to consider acting in a more controlling way if they believed that this would serve to divert more people from prison.

Findings such as these demonstrated some diversity in the views of sentencing held by those participating in the criminal justice system. Indeed, whatever the relevance of the notion of 'system' to describe the collective working of the various institutions and agencies concerned with the detection, prosecution, sentencing and treatment of offenders, the differences found between the attitudes of judges, justices' clerks, magistrates and probation officers seemed to show that the interdependence of these bodies did not necessarily result in a similarity of outlook. But having said this, perhaps it was to be expected that persons who performed different roles – albeit to some extent with a common purpose – would have different views. Sentencers see themselves as obliged to protect the public, a duty which sometimes necessitates decisions that seem harsh when measured by the perspective of probation officers who are expected to advise, assist and befriend their charges. It is likely that if other groups – drawn from the police, the prison service and the public – had been studied, other distinctive viewpoints would have emerged.

Having ascertained the views of those most involved with sentencing in Hampshire, the researchers set up a series of studies to investigate those areas which respondents had agreed were of most relevance to diversion from custody and therefore most likely to have an impact on the size of the prison population. These sub-projects will be described below. They involved investigating the operation of a revised form of probation, hostels, community service and a senior attendance centre and looking at the problem of dealing with mentally disordered offenders.

The new approach to the supervision of probationers was implemented by two probation teams in the county throughout 1981. It entailed the local magistrates' courts stipulating as part of the probation order, the frequency with which probationers should report to a probation office; any other activity was purely voluntary. Since the scheme involved reporting conditions which were possibly more demanding than usual and breach proceedings which were certainly stricter, the researchers hypothesised that it might be used more often as an alternative to custody than the normal form of probation order.

Overall, it seemed that the scheme resulted in improved attendance rates, but without any increase in the incidence of breach. More orders were made during the experimental year. The probationers who received the new orders seemed to be content to conform to their orders, although those with considerable distances to travel were more dissatisfied than others. The kinds of people given orders were little different from those placed on probation previously and this suggests that the scheme was not being used any more often as an alternative to custody than normal probation orders. Nor did magistrates appear to view the scheme as a more viable alternative than the traditional probation order.

Inquiries into community service and hostels in the county revealed that there was considerable scope for further use of both these facilities as alternatives. In the case of hostels, residents tended to be young rootless offenders who were troublesome rather than dangerous. In voluntary sector hostels there was a willingness to accept offenders who would otherwise be sent to prison, but there was some doubt that courts were willing to use the voluntary hostels in this way and some problems were perceived over the element of coercion. Further, these hostels were used in a variety of ways and further resources would be needed to expand any use as a custodial alternative. On the whole, hostels seemed to act as social welfare provision, which tended to weaken the part they might have played in diverting offenders from custody. Investigation of the community service scheme tended to confirm the work of Pease *et al.* (1977), which suggested that while at times it was used for fairly criminally sophisticated offenders, in many instances it was used for offenders who did not appear to be at risk of an immediate sentence of custody.

The senior attendance centre was the only new disposal set up in the county as part of the research, and thus if any impact was to be made in diverting offenders from custody it might have been expected to have been here. But while the centre worked well and did not have any serious operational problems – and, incidentally, impressed the magistrates who visited it – research indicated that it was not used in place of custodial sentences. If anything, it was used in place of fines; magistrates argued that it was a waste of time to fine an unemployed 17 to 20-year-old (the vast majority of those ordered to attend the centre did not have a job) and saw the attendance centre as the most appropriate alternative (Mair, 1984).

It is often claimed that certain groups, such as mentally disordered offenders, petty persistent offenders and alcoholics, should not be in custody. But while keeping such groups out of prison may be desirable, endeavouring to do so cannot be justified on the grounds that such action will substantially reduce the prison population. The study of mentally disordered offenders which was carried out illustrated that definitional problems emerged in practice; exactly who should be classified as mentally disordered tended to be very much a matter of opinion, and groups were found to overlap. In addition, the mentally disordered offenders who were seen as a problem by magistrates did not appear to be the same type who bothered prison administrators: for the former, it was those such as vagrants who were borderline subnormal or borderline schizophrenic and who kept reappearing before the courts charged with minor offences who tended to be seen as a problem; for the latter, it was serious offenders who were mentally ill and in prison because placement in a psychiatric hospital could not be arranged who caused concern.

None of the sub-projects just described found evidence of considerable diversion from custody and this would suggest that there is some potential for enhancing the diversionary role of current non-custodial measures. But it is vital to note that there was some difference of views as to how measures should be used between magistrates and those who ran the measures, and, in addition, magistrates appeared to have a tendency to hold one view of a non-custodial disposal in theory, but to use the disposal in a different way in practice. Sentencers have a wide degree of latitude as to which disposals they use in a particular case. They are likely to use community service orders, hostels, attendance centres, probation and so on whenever they deem it appropriate to do so; and when they decide that such disposals are suitable, their reasons may have little to do with the putative desirability of diverting offenders from custody. When it is argued that in order to divert cases from custody more resources should be ploughed into the non-custodial sector, it must be remembered that if new and extra community facilities are provided these will probably be used mainly for cases where there is no immediate risk of incarceration. Thus any new alternatives to custody may simply act as alternatives to already existing disposals which aim to divert from custody. Further, it should be realised that compared to many other countries. England and Wales already have a wide range of non-custodial disposals at hand. More effective use of existing facilities (in the sense of maximising their potential to divert from custody) rather than more facilities would seem to be the way forward.

Sentencing patterns

Although the individual projects uncovered little evidence of diversion from custody, it seemed possible that such activities coupled with the work on attitudes might have some influence on sentencing patterns in Hampshire – if only because they had drawn attention to the case for reducing the prison population. This issue was investigated by comparing data on court disposals made before and after the project was under way. It was reasoned that any before/after changes identified in this manner and that occurred in Hampshire but not in most other police force areas in England and Wales (or that occurred elsewhere but not in Hampshire) might indicate that the project had had some effect on local sentencing practice. Apart from the introduction of the project, there appeared to be no grounds for expecting to find sentencing patterns for Hampshire different from those for other parts of England and Wales.

In the Hampshire magistrates' courts more adults and young adults were found guilty of indictable offences in 1981 than in 1980, but as shown in Table 16:1 the extent to which the various disposals were used varied little Although there was a slight increase in 1981 in the proportion of offenders sent to detention centre and prison, this was also true of magistrates' courts in England and Wales generally. Examining the average (mean) lengths of sentences of immediate imprisonment imposed on young adult and adult males for indictable offences also did not uncover any notable divergence of local from national practice. For the Hampshire magistrates' courts the average lengths for 1979, 1980 and 1981 were 3.8, 3.6 and 3.0 months respectively; the corresponding figures for England and Wales as a whole were scarcely different, being 3.8, 3.5 and 3.2.

The number of adults and young adults found guilty in the Hampshire Crown Court centres (that is, excluding those sentenced at the Crown Court after having been found guilty at magistrates' courts) changed little between 1980 and 1981, but as is shown in Table 16:2 the percentages of such persons sentenced to the various forms of immediate custody – particularly imprisonment – dropped. Grouping together figures for detention centre orders, borstal training and imprisonment, the persons awarded immediate custodial disposals accounted for 48.1 per cent of the total found guilty in 1980, but only 41.6 per cent in 1981. For England and Wales as a whole the comparable percentages were 46.2 and 47.2. Looking in this way at all the

Table 16:1 *Persons aged 17 and over found guilty of indictable offences at magistrates' courts, by sentence or order (percentages)*

	Total	Absolute/ conditional discharge	Probation order	Fine	Community service order	Detention centre order	Suspended sentence	Partly suspended sentence	Immediate imprison- ment	Committed to Crown Court	Otherwise dealt with
Hampshire police force area											
1980	100(N = 8,874)	11.3	11.1	57.8	2.2	1.4	6.8	—	5.2	3.3	0.9
1981	100(N = 9,719)	11.0	11.7	55.4	3.2	2.0	6.7	—	6.1	3.4	0.5
1982	100(N = 9,292)	10.7	12.1	51.8	3.6	1.8	6.9	0.1	7.2	4.2	1.6
Change 1980–1981		-0.3	+0.6	-2.4	+1.0	+0.6	-0.1	—	+0.9	+0.1	-0.4
Change 1981–1982		-0.3	+0.4	-3.6	+0.4	-0.2	+0.2	+0.1	+1.1	+0.8	+1.1
England and Wales											
1980	100(N = 306,183)	9.7	7.9	59.2	4.8	1.3	6.5	—	5.7	3.6	1.3
1981	100(N = 315,119)	10.5	8.4	55.5	6.0	1.5	6.9	—	6.4	3.5	1.3
1982	100(N = 325,959)	11.1	8.4	54.3	6.4	1.4	7.0	—	6.6	3.1	1.6
Change 1980–1981		+0.8	+0.5	-3.7	+1.2	+0.2	+0.4	—	+0.7	-0.1	0.0
Change 1981–1982		+0.6	0.0	-1.2	+0.4	-0.1	+0.1	—	+0.2	-0.4	+0.3

Table 16:2 *Persons aged 17 and over found guilty at the Crown Court, by sentence or order (percentages)*

	Total	Absolute/ conditional discharge on re-cognisance	Hospital or restriction order	Probation order	Fine	Community service order	Detention centre	Borstal training	Suspended sentence	Partly suspended sentence	Immediate imprison-ment	Other-wise dealt with
Hampshire police force area												
1980	100(N = 1,443)	4.0	0.5	7.6	14.5	3.6	2.6	6.5	21.3	—	39.0	0.4
1981	100(N = 1,461)	4.2	1.0	9.2	17.9	4.4	2.3	6.2	21.1	—	33.1	0.6
1982	100(N = 1,485)	3.8	0.4	9.9	12.3	4.8	2.4	7.2	21.2	1.2	36.1	0.7
Change 1980–1981		+0.2	+0.5	+1.6	+3.4	+0.8	–0.3	–0.3	–0.2	—	–5.9	+0.2
Change 1981–1982		–0.4	–0.6	+0.7	–5.6	+0.4	+0.1	+1.0	+0.1	+1.2	+3.0	+0.1
England and Wales												
1980	100(N – 57,867)	5.5	0.4	6.3	14.8	6.4	2.5	6.6	19.0	—	37.1	1.4
1981	100(N = 61,653	5.6	0.3	6.4	12.9	7.9	3.0	6.7	18.6	—	37.5	1.1
1982	100(N = 66,091)	4.9	0.4	6.7	11.0	9.1	3.1	6.6	17.6	1.6	37.2	1.8
Change 1980–1981		+0.1	–0.1	+0.1	–1.9	+1.5	+0.5	+0.1	–0.4	—	+0.4	–0.3
Change 1981–1982		–0.7	+0.1	+0.3	–1.9	+1.2	+0.1	–0.1	–1.0	+1.6	–0.3	+0.7

individual police force areas in England and Wales, only Surrey showed a larger percentage decrease than Hampshire; and there the numbers of offenders involved were smaller, so greater chance fluctuation from year to year in the percentage distribution of disposals would normally be expected. It can also be seen from Table 16:2 that the Crown Court centres in Hampshire made greater use of fines and probation orders in 1981 than in 1980, which virtually matched their lesser use of custody: the percentage fined rose from 14.5 to 17.9, and the percentage placed on probation rose from 7.6 to 9.2. The increased proportionate use of fines was particularly significant, since it contrasted with a decrease for England and Wales as a whole from 14.8 per cent in 1980 to 12.9 per cent in 1981.

Since relatively few females are sent to prison, the proportionate use of immediate imprisonment for males aged 17 and over is displayed in Figure 16:1. Between 1980 and 1981, this measure fell considerably for Hampshire but stayed much the same for England and Wales as a whole. Before 1981, the year-to-year variation of the measure was fairly similar for Hampshire and England and Wales, with an upward trend between 1975 and 1979 and a slight fall in 1980.

Average lengths of sentences of immediate imprisonment imposed on young adult and adult males found guilty at the Crown Court were examined for the three years 1979–1981. For Hampshire there was a drop in average length of just over five months between 1979 and 1981, compared to a drop of just over two months for England and Wales. Further, the bulk of the reduction for Hampshire – unlike that for England and Wales generally – occurred some time after the Upton and Bibi judgments (which might have been expected to have an impact upon the length of Crown Court sentences), and after the project had been mounted.

Similar though less pronounced findings emerged when those sentenced at the Crown Court for indictable offences after being convicted at magistrates' courts were considered.

There is little evidence, then, to suggest that the project may have affected the way in which the Hampshire magistrates used custodial disposals. On the other hand, it seems likely that the project contributed to changes in sentencing practice that occurred in the Hampshire Crown Court. But these changes were not permanent; nor was there any sign of their filtering through to the magistrates' courts in the following year. The 1982 figures in Table 16:2 show that custodial sentences in the Hampshire Crown Court all increased compared to 1981 although the number of those aged 17 and over found guilty showed little change: immediate custodial disposals (including partly suspended sentences of imprisonment) accounted for 46.9 per cent of those found guilty in 1982 – an increase of 5.3 per cent from 1981. For England and

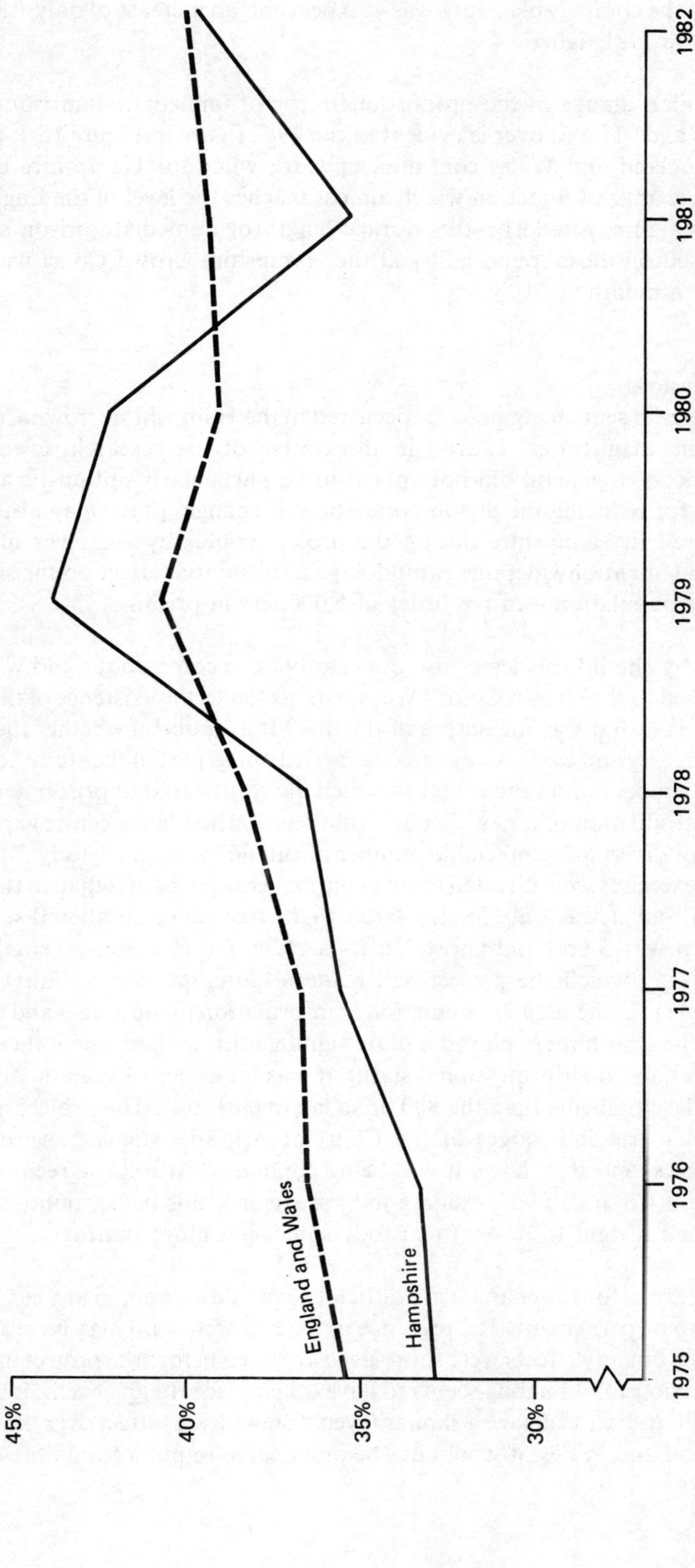

Figure 16:1 *Percentage use of immediate imprisonment for males aged 17 or over found guilty at the Crown Court*

Wales the comparable figure was 48.5 per cent, an increase of only 1.3 per cent over the 1981 figure.

A similar change in the proportionate use of immediate imprisonment for males aged 17 and over is evident in the 1982 figure in Figure 16:1: the trend for England and Wales continues upward, while for Hampshire there is a sharp change of direction which almost reaches the level of the England and Wales figure. Similarly, the average length of immediate prison sentences imposed on those found guilty at the Hampshire Crown Court went up by about a month.

Conclusions

Changes in sentencing practice occurred in the Hampshire Crown Court (but not the magistrates' courts) in the course of the research, even though sentencers in general did not appear to be particularly optimistic about the scope for reducing the prison population. If changes of the magnitude which occurred in Hampshire during the project could, by whatever means, be replicated nationwide, they would have a substantial effect on the size of the prison population – of the order of 5,000 less in prison.

But why should this lesser use of custody have come about and why was it confined to the Crown Court? Was it connected to the existence of the project and if so, what was the nature of the link? It is doubtful whether the various exploratory and evaluative exercises carried out as part of the study had much, if any, impact upon the extent to which the courts used imprisonment – even the introduction of a new disposal (the senior attendance centre) apparently did not divert an appreciable number of offenders from custody. Moreover, these exercises were directed more at the magistrates' courts than at the Crown Court, but it was only for the latter that evidence of an altered sentencing pattern was found and part of this – a reduction in sentence lengths – was something which the project had made no attempt to study directly. It is possible that the regular circulation of information to the judges and the interviews held with them played a more significant role. Because of their limited number and their professional status, it was far easier to keep them in touch with developments than the 800 or so lay magistrates. The project may have served to remind judges of the Court of Appeal's stance towards prison sentences, and they knew it was being conducted with the agreement of the Western Circuit's two presiding judges. Against this background, they may have felt it right to resort to custody somewhat more sparingly.

The reasons for the changes are difficult to pin down and, in any case, did not seem to be permanent. The presence of the research team may have acted as a catalyst but any effects were short-lived and even before the project had ended a reversion to old habits seems to have taken place. In any event, it would be difficult to try to achieve a similar (even if short-lived) effect over the whole of England and Wales; it would not be practicable to put a team of researchers into each area, and there would be no guarantee that a similar effect would ensue.

The project as a whole provided a good deal of evidence of divergence of views and action on the part, not only of individuals, but amongst the various organisations and bodies involved. The most direct sign of this emerged from the interviews where the views of probation officers and sentencers tended to be different. Similar signs also came through from the various sub-projects. Probation officers probably saw the revised form of the probation order as providing a more appealing alternative to custody for sentencers than the normal order, but sentencers did not seem to use it any more often in such a role (which might lead one to conclude that the traditional order may be quite adequate as an alternative to custody). In Hampshire, probation service policy was to use community service as a direct alternative to custody, but it was clear that this policy was not always followed by the courts. In the case of hostels, their possible role as an alternative was considerably greater than their use by the courts might suggest, and, especially in the case of those hostels run by the voluntary sector, there were serious organisational and financial problems in using them more often in a diversionary role. Whatever magistrates might say in theory about the use of senior attendance centres they did not seem to apply in practice. And finally, in practice, the problem of mentally disordered offenders meant different things to sentencers on the one hand and to prison administrators on the other.

The fact of such divergence in the criminal justice system should come as no real surprise (and has been argued previously by Bottomley, 1977). In fact, it is perhaps only by using the term 'system' that we have come to expect uniformity; a 'system' implies notions of smooth-running, interdependence, feedback and structured interaction. Such factors are not conspicuous amongst the various bodies which have a role in the criminal justice enterprise – and why should they be? The judiciary are professionally trained lawyers, magistrates are amateurs drawn from the general public, probation officers are professionals with a strong social work tradition; and sentencers and probation officers have different immediate objectives. The other main components of the 'system' – the police and the prison service – which did not feature in the research reported on here, have very different backgrounds, objectives and thus professional ideologies too. All of these parts were never designed specifically to work together (and the term 'designed' of course has implications in itself) and it is perhaps a credit to the power of the ideology of working together to help reduce crime that the 'system' works as well as it does. One method of achieving greater efficiency might be to develop stronger, more formal lines of communication between the various components. Perhaps the simplest change would be to refer to the criminal justice *process*, which might help to counter the impersonal and mechanical overtones inherent in the term 'system' and eventually lead to a more realistic sense of the limits of professional intervention in crime.

References

Ackoff, R. L. (1974a). *Redesigning the Future – A Systems Approach to Societal Problems*. New York: John Wiley.

Ackoff, R. L. (1974b). 'The systems revolution'. *Long Range Planning*, 7, 2–20.

Ashby, W. R. (1956). *An Introduction to Cybernetics*. London: Chapman and Hall.

Ashworth, A. (1985). *The English Criminal Process: A Review of Empirical Research*. Occasional Paper No. 11. Oxford: Centre for Criminological Research.

Babington, A. (1969). *A House in Bow Street. Crime and magistracy 1740–1881*. London: Macdonald.

Baker, R. J. and Nelder, J. A. (1978). *The GLIM System: Release 3. Generalised linear interactive modelling manual*. Oxford: NAG.

Baldwin, J. (1985). *Pre-trial Justice*. Oxford: Basil Blackwell.

Baldwin, J. and McConville, M. (1977). *Negotiated Justice*. London: Martin Robertson.

Baldwin, J. and McConville, M. (1979). *Jury Trials*. Oxford: Clarendon Press.

Baldwin, J. and McConville, M. (1981). *Courts, Prosecution and Conviction*. Oxford: Clarendon Press.

Barnatt, G. M. (1983). 'Section 48 – A Viable Alternative?'. *Justice of the Peace*, 147, 117.

Barr, H. and O'Leary, E. (1966). *Trends and Regional Comparisons in Probation (England and Wales)*. Home Office Studies in the Causes of Delinquency and the Treatment of Offenders No. 8. London: HMSO.

Barton, A. (1984). *The Criminal Justice System Model: Police Sub-Model*. Home Office Scientific Research and Development Branch Publication 39/84.

Beer, S. (1972). *Brain of the Firm*. London: Allen Lane.

Beer, S. (1979). *The Heart of Enterprise*. London: John Wiley.

Bennett, T. (1979). 'The Social Distribution of Criminal Labels'. *British Journal of Criminology*, 19, 134–145.

Bennett, W. L. and Feldman, M. S. (1981). *Reconstructing Reality in the Courtroom*. London: Tavistock.

Bishop, Y. M. M., Fienberg, S. E. and Holland, F. W. (1975). *Discrete Multivariate Analysis*. MIT Press.

Bittner, E. (1969). 'The police in skid row: a study of peace-keeping'. In: Chambliss, W. J. (Ed.) *Crime and the legal process*. New York: McGraw-Hill.

Blumstein, A. and Larson, R. (1969). 'Models of a Total Criminal Justice System', *Operations Research*, 17, 199–232.

Bottomley, A. K. (1970). *Prison Before Trial*. London: Bell & Sons.

Bottomley, A. K. (1977). 'Conflict and Communication in Criminal Justice', *Howard Journal of Penology and Crime Prevention*, XV (3) 1977, 3–11.

Bottoms, A. E. and McClean, J. D. (1976). *Defendants in the Criminal Process*. London: Routledge & Kegan Paul.

Bowden, J. and Stevens, M. (1980). *Delays in Dealing with Juvenile Offenders in Northampton*. (Unpublished).

Bridges, G. S. (1982). 'The Speedy Trial Act of 1974: Effects on Delays of Federal Criminal Litigation', *Journal of Criminal Law and Criminology*, 73/1.

Bright, J. A. (1969). *The Beat Patrol Experiment*. Home Office Police Research and Development Branch. (Unpublished).

Brody, S. R. (1976). *The Effectiveness of Sentencing*. Home Office Research Study No. 35. London: HMSO.

Brogden, M. (1982). *The Police – Autonomy and Consent*. London: Academic Press.

Burney, E. (1979). *JP: Magistrate, Court and Community*. London: Hutchinson.

Burrows, J. and Tarling, R. (1982). *Clearing Up Crime*. Home Office Research Study No. 73. London: HMSO.

Chatterton, M. (1975). *Organisational Relationships and Processes in Police Work*. Ph.D thesis, University of Manchester. (Unpublished).

Chatterton, M. (1976). 'Police in social control'. In: King, J. F. S. and Young, W. (Eds.) *Control without custody?* Papers presented to the Cropwood Round Table Conference. Cambridge: Institute of Criminology.

Checkland, P. B. (1981). *Systems Thinking, Systems Practice*. London: John Wiley.

Church, T. Jr. and others. (1978). *Justice Delayed: the pace of litigation in urban trial courts*. Williamsburg National Center for State Courts.

Church, T. Jr. (1982). *Examining Local Legal Culture*. US Department of Justice: National Institute of Justice.

Cross, R. (1979). *Evidence, 5th Edition*. London: Butterworths.

Crust, P. E. (1975). *Criminal Investigation Project*. Home Office Police Research Services Unit. (Unpublished).

Derbyshire, P. (1984). *The Magistrates' Clerk*. Chichester: Barry Rose.

Desbruslais, A. (1982). 'Pre-trial Disclosure in Magistrates' Courts: Why Wait?' *Justice of the Peace*, 146, 384.

Ditchfield, J. A. (1976). *Police Cautioning in England and Wales*. Home Office Research Study No. 37. London: HMSO.

Edwards, L. J. (1984). *The Attorney-General, Politics, and the Public Interest*. London: Sweet and Maxwell.

Eggleston, R. *Evidence, Proof and Probability, 2nd Edition*. London: Weidenfeld & Nicolson.

Emery, F. E. (Ed.) (1981). *Systems Thinking*. London: Penguin.

Expenditure Committee (1978). *The Reduction of Pressure on the Prison System*. Fifteenth Report from the Expenditure Committee, Volume 1. London: HMSO.

Farrington, D. P. and Bennett, T. (1981). 'Police Cautioning of Juveniles in London'. *British Journal of Criminology*, 21, 123–135.

Feeley, M. (1983). *Court Reform on Trial: why simple solutions fail*. New York: Basic Books.

Fisher, C. J. and Mawby, R. I. (1982). 'Juvenile Delinquency and Police Discretion in an Inner City Area'. *British Journal of Criminology*, 22, 63–75.

Forrester, J. W. (1961). *Industrial Dynamics*. MIT Press.

Forrester, J. W. (1969). *Urban Dynamics*. MIT Press.

Forrester, J. W. (1971). *World Dynamics*. MIT Press.

Frankenburg, C. and Tarling, R. (1983). *Time Taken to Deal with Juveniles Under Criminal Proceedings*. Home Office Research and Planning Unit Paper No. 18. London: Home Office.

Frase, R. S. (1976). 'The Speedy Trial Act of 1974'. *University of Chicago Law Review*. 43/4, 667–723.

Gemmill, R. and Morgan-Giles, R. F. (1980). *Arrest Charge and Summons*. Royal Commission on Criminal Procedure, Research Study No. 9. London: HMSO.

Gibson, E. (1960). *Time Spent Awaiting Trial*. Home Office Research Report No. 2. London: HMSO.

Goldman, H. (1984). 'Prisons and Performance Measurement'. *Research Bulletin* No. 18, 36–38. London: Home Office Research and Planning Unit.

Green, E. (1961). *Judicial Attitudes in Sentencing*. London: Macmillan.

Gregory, J. (1976). *Crown Court or Magistrates' Court?* Office of Population Censuses and Surveys. London: HMSO.

Grunhut, M. (1956). *Juvenile Offenders Before the Courts*. Oxford: The Clarendon Press.

Halyk, S. (1967/8). 'The Preliminary Inquiry in Canada'. *Criminal Law Quarterly*, 10, 181.

Hansard, Session 1981–82, Vol. 16, Col. 294 *et seq*.

Harris, B. (1982). 'Committal Proceedings and Selecting the Mode of Trial'.

Harris, R. and Webb, D. (1983). 'Social work and the supervision order'. *Research Bulletin* No. 16, 35–37. London: Home Office Research and Planning Unit.

Heal, K. H., Tarling, R. and Burrows, J. N. (1985). *Policing Today*. London: HMSO.

Hillsman, S. T., Sichel, J. L. and Mahoney, B. (1984). *Fines in Sentencing: A Study of the Use of the Fine as a Criminal Sanction*. Washington: US Department of Justice.

Home Office Scientific Research and Development Branch (1984). *Report on a Method for Evaluating Policing Experiments and its Application to the Experiment at Chelmsley Wood a Sub-division of West Midlands Police*. London: Home Office.

Home Office (annually). *Criminal Statistics England and Wales*. London: HMSO.

Home Office (annually). *Prison Statistics England and Wales*. London: HMSO.

Home Office Working Party (1974). *Bail Procedures in Magistrates' Courts*. London: HMSO.

Home Office (1978). *The Sentence of the Court*. London: HMSO.

Home Office (1979). *Prison Statistics England and Wales*. London: HMSO.

Home Office (1982). *Report of the Working Group on Magistrates' Courts*. London: Home Office.

Home Office (1983). *An Independent Prosecution Service for England and Wales*. Cmnd. 6323. London: HMSO.

Home Office (1984a). *Home Office Research and Planning Unit Research Programme 1984–85*. London: Home Office.

Home Office (1984b). *Cautioning by the Police: a consultative document*. London: Home Office.

Hood, R. (1962). *Sentencing in Magistrates' Courts*. London: Stevens.

Jackson, M. X. and Keys, P. (1984). 'Towards a System of Systems Methodologies'. *Journal of the Operational Research Society*, 35/6, 473–486.

Jackson, R. M. (1979). *The Machinery of Justice, 7th Edition*. Cambridge University Press.

James Committee (1975). *The Distribution of Criminal Business Between the Crown Court and Magistrates' Courts*. London: HMSO.

Jefferson, A. and Grimshaw, R. (1984). *Controlling the constable*. London: F. Muller in association with the Cobden Trust.

Jenkins, G. M. (1969). 'The systems approach'. In: Beishon, J. and Peters, G. (Eds.). *Systems Behaviour*. London: HMSO.

Justice (1966). *Availability of Prosecution Evidence for the Defence*. London: Justice.

Kelly, P. (1982). 'Deemed unfit to serve'. *New Statesman*, 104/2675, 9–10.

King, M. (1971). *Bail or Custody*. London: Cobden Trust.

King, M. (1981). *The Framework of Criminal Justice*. London: Croom Helm.

Landau, S. F. (1981). 'Juveniles and the Police: Who is Charged Immediately and Who is Referred to the Juvenile Bureau?' *British Journal of Criminology*, 23, 128–149.

Law Society's Gazette (1983). 'Pre-trial reviews in the Magistrates' Court: Guidance for defence solicitors', 80/35 2330.

Law Society (1983). *Advance Disclosure in the Magistrates' Court*. (Unpublished).

Leigh, L. H. and Hall-Williams, J. E. (1982). *The Management of the Prosecution Process in Denmark, Sweden, the Netherlands*. Leamington Spa: James Hall.

Lidstone, K. W. (1983). *Magisterial review of the pre-trial process*. Report by the Centre of Criminological and Socio-Legal Studies, University of Sheffield. (Unpublished).

Lidstone, K. W., Hogg, R. and Sutcliffe, F. in collaboration with Bottoms, A. E. and Walker, M. A. (1980). *Prosecutions by Private Individuals and Non-Police Agencies*. Royal Commission on Criminal Procedure. Research Study No. 10. London: HMSO.

Lord Chancellor's Department (annually). *Judicial Statistics*. London: HMSO.

Lupton, C. and Roberts, G. (1982). *On Record . . . Young people appearing before a juvenile court*. Portsmouth, Hampshire: Social Services Research and Intelligence Unit.

McCabe, S. (1975). 'Discussions in the Jury Room: Are they like this?' In: Walker, N. D. (Ed.). *The British Jury System*, Papers presented to the Cropwood Round Table Conference. Cambridge: Institute of Criminology.

McCabe, S. and Purves, R. (1972a). *By-passing the Jury*. Oxford University Penal Research Unit, Occasional Paper No. 3. Oxford: Blackwell.

McCabe, S. and Purves, R. (1972b). *The Jury at Work*. Oxford University Penal Research Unit, Occasional Paper No. 4. Oxford: Blackwell.

McCabe, S. and Purves, R. (1974). *The Shadow Jury at Work*. Oxford University Penal Research Unit, Occasional Paper No. 8. Oxford: Blackwell.

McConville, M. and Baldwin, J. (1981). *Courts, Prosecution and Conviction*. Oxford: Clarendon Press.

McBarnet, D. J. (1983). *Conviction: Law, the State and the Construction of Justice*. London: Macmillan.

Magistrates' Association (1979–80). 'A realistic approach to sentencing in magistrates' courts; and 'Consistency in sentencing'. *Sixtieth Annual Report*.

Mair, G. (1984). 'The senior attendance centre as an alternative to custody'. *Research Bulletin* No. 18, 28–30. London: Home Office Research and Planning Unit.

Mannheim, H., Spencer, J. C. and Lynch, G. (1957). 'Magisterial policy in the London juvenile courts'. *British Journal of Delinquency*, 8, 13–33 and 119–138.

Marshall, G. (1965). *Police and Government: the status and accountability of the English constable*. London: Methuen.

Marshall, G. (1975). 'The judgement of one's peers: some aims and ideals of jury trial'. In: Walker, N. D. (Ed.). *The British Jury System*, Papers presented to the Cropwood Round Table Conference. Cambridge: Institute of Criminology.

Melvin, M. and Didcott, P. J. (1976). *Pre-trial Bail and Custody in the Scottish Sheriffs' Courts*. Edinburgh: HMSO.

Miller, N. (1983). *Monitoring Norfolk's Juvenile Justice System: Report No. 2*. Norwich: Norfolk Social Services Department.

Moody, S. R. and Tombs, J. (1982). *Prosecution in the Public Interest*. Edinburgh: Scottish Academic Press.

Morgan, G. (1982). 'Cybernetics and organisation theory: epistemology or technique'. *Human Relations*, 35, 521–537.

Morgan, P. M. (1984). 'The Remand Population'. *Research Bulletin* No. 16, 28–31. London: Home Office Research and Planning Unit.

Mott, J. (1983). 'Police Decisions for Dealing with Juvenile Offenders'. *British Journal of Criminology*, 23, 249–262.

Moxon, A. D. (1983). 'Fine default: unemployment and the use of imprisonment'. *Research Bulletin* No. 16, 38–41. London: Home Office Research and Planning Unit.

Moxon, A. D., Jones, P. R. and Tarling, R. *Juvenile sentencing: is there a tariff?* Research and Planning Unit Paper No. 32 London: Home Office.

Mungham, G. and Thomas, P. (1979). 'Advocacy and the Solicitor Advocate in magistrates' courts in England and Wales'. International Journal of the Sociology of Law. May.

Napley, D. (1966). 'The Case for Preliminary Inquiries'. *Criminal Law Review*, September, 490–498.

National Association for the Care and Resettlement of Offenders (1981). *Fine Default: report of a NACRO Working Party*. London: NACRO.

Nightingale, G. M. (1979). 'The Scandal of the Delays in the Juvenile Court'. *Justice of the Peace*, 143/13, 169–170.

Parliamentary All-Party Penal Affairs Group. (1981). *Young Offenders – A Strategy for the Future*. Chichester: Barry Rose.

Pease, K., Billingham, S. and Earnshaw, I. (1977). *Community Service Assessed in 1976*. Home Office Research Study No. 39. London: HMSO.

Phillpotts, G. J. O. and Lancucki, B. (1979). *Previous convictions, sentence and reconviction: a statistical study of a sample of 5,000 convicted in January 1971*. Home Office Research Study No. 53. London HMSO.

Prosecuting Solicitors' Society of England and Wales (1979). *Evidence to the Royal Commission on Criminal Procedure*. (Unpublished).

Redmond-Pyle, D. and Stevens, M. (1983). *Report on the Northampton Juvenile Criminal Justice System – 2nd Edition*. University of Lancaster: Centre of Youth, Crime and Community.

Reeson, D. and Vicary, M. (1982). *Analysis of Offence Generation Rates*. Local Government Operational Research Unit. (Unpublished).

Rice, S. E. (1984). *The Criminal Justice System Model: Magistrates' Courts Sub-model*. Research and Planning Unit Paper No. 24. London: Home Office.

Royal Commission on Criminal Procedure (1981a). *Report.* Cmnd 8092. London: HMSO.

Royal Commission on Criminal Procedure (1981b). *The Investigation and Prosecution of Criminal Offences in England and Wales: The Law and Procedure.* Cmnd 8092–1. London: HMSO.

Sanders, A. (1985a). 'Prosecution Decisions and The Attorney-General's Guidelines'. *Criminal Law Review*, January, 4–.

Sanders, A. (1985b). 'Class Bias in Prosecutions'. *Howard Journal*, 24, 176.

Sanders, A. (1985c). 'The Uncertain Powers of Crown Prosecutors'. *New Law Journal*, 29 March, 313–314, 5 April, 352.

Simon, F. and Weatheritt, M. (1974). *The Use of Bail and Custody by London Magistrates' Courts Before and After the Criminal Justice Act 1967*. London: HMSO.

Smith, D., Sheppard, B., Mair, G. and Williams, K. (1984). *Reducing the Prison Population*. Research and Planning Unit Paper No. 23. London: Home Office.

Softley, P. (1972). *A Study of Fine Enforcement*. Home Office Research Unit Report No. 16. London: HMSO.

Softley P. (1976). 'A comparison of acquittal rates in magistrates' courts and the Crown Court'. *Justice of the Peace*, 140/34, 455–456.

Softley, P. (1978). *Fines in Magistrates' Courts*. Home Office Research Study No. 46. London: HMSO.

Softley, P. (1984a). 'The Imprisonment of Fine Defaulters'. *Justice of the Peace*, 147/30, 470–472.

Softley, P. (1984b). 'TV licence evasion'. *Research Bulletin*. No. 18. London: Home Office Research and Planning Unit.

Softley, P. and Moxon, D. (1982). *Fine enforcement: an evaluation of the practices of individual courts*. Research and Planning Unit Paper No. 12. London: Home Office.

Steer, D. (1970). *Police cautions – a study of the exercise of police discretion*. Oxford University Penal Research Unit, Occasional Paper No. 2. Oxford: Blackwell.

Steer, D. (1980). *Uncovering Crime: the role of the police*. Royal Commission on Criminal Procedure Research Study No. 7. London: HMSO.

Stewart Committee (1983). *Keeping Offenders Out of Court: further alternatives to prosecution*. London: HMSO.

Stephen, Sir J. F. (1883). *A History of Criminal Law in England.* London: Macmillan.

Streatfeild Committee (1961). *The Business of the Criminal Courts*. London: HMSO.

Sunderland, E. (1933). 'Scope and Method of Discovery Before Trial', *Yale Law Journal*, 42, 863.

Tarling, R. (1979). *Sentencing Practice in Magistrates' Courts*. Home Office Research Study No. 56. London: HMSO.

Thomas, D. A. (1979). *Principles of Sentencing*. London: Heinemann.

Thorpe, J. (1979). *Social Inquiry Reports: A Survey*. Home Office Research Study No. 48. London: HMSO.

Vennard, J. (1975). *Imprisonment for non payment of fines or maintenance*. Home Office Research Unit. (Unpublished).

Vennard, J. (1981). 'Acquittal rates in magistrates' courts'. *Research Bulletin* No. 11, 21–23. London: Home Office Research and Planning Unit.

Vennard, J. (1984). 'Disputes within trials over the Admissibility and Accuracy of Incriminating Statements'. *Criminal Law Review*, January, 15–24.

Vennard, J. with the assistance of Williams, K. (1980). *Contested Trials in Magistrates' Courts: the case for the prosecution*. Royal Commission on Criminal Procedure, Research Study No. 6. London: HMSO.

Vera Institute of Justice (1979). *Waiting Times in Magistrates' Courts – an exploratory study*. London: Vera Institute of Justice.

Walker, N., Farrington, D. P. and Tucker, G. (1981). 'Reconviction Rates of Adult Males After Different Sentences'. *British Journal of Criminology*, 21, 357–360.

Weatheritt, M. (1980). *The Prosecution System: survey of prosecuting solicitors' departments.* Royal Commission on Criminal Procedure, Research Study No. 11. London: HMSO.

Wiener, N. (1948). *Cybernetics*. London: John Wiley.

Wilkins, L. T., Kress, J. M., Gottfredson, D. M., Calpin, J. C. and Gelman, A. M. (1976). *Sentencing Guidelines: Structuring Judicial Discretion*. United States Department of Justice.

Williams, G. (1979). 'The mathematics of proof'. *Criminal Law Review*, May 279–308.

Wootton, B. (1978). *Crime and Penal Policy*. London: Allen and Unwin.

Zander, M. (1971). 'A study of bail/custody decisions in London magistrates' courts'. *Criminal Law Review*, April, 197–211.

Zander, M. (1974). 'Are too many professional criminals avoiding conviction? A study in Britain's two busiest courts'. *The Modern Law Review*, 37, 28–61.

SUBJECT INDEX

AUTHOR INDEX

Publications

Titles already published for the Home Office

Studies in the Causes of Delinquency and the Treatment of Offenders (SCDTO)

1. Prediction methods in relation to borstal training. Hermann Mannheim and Leslie T. Wilkins. 1955 viii + 276pp. (11 340051 9).
2. *Time spent awaiting trial. Evelyn Gibson. 1960. v + 45pp. (34-368-2).
3. *Delinquent generations. Leslie T. Wilkins. 1960. vi. + 20pp. (11 340053 5).
4. *Murder. Evelyn Gibson and S. Klein. 1961. iv + 44pp. (11 340054 3).
5. Persistent criminals. A study of all offenders liable to preventive detention in 1956. W. H. Hammond and Edna Chayen. 1963. ix + 237pp. (34-368-5).
6. *Some statistical and other numerical techniques for classifying individuals. P. McNaughton-Smith. 1965. v + 33pp. (34-368-6).
7. Probation research: a preliminary report. Part I. General outline of research. Part II. Study of Middlesex probation area (SOMPA). Steven Folkard, Kate Lyon, Margaret M. Carver and Erica O'Leary. 1966. vi + 58pp. (11 340374 7).
8. *Probation research: national study of probation. Trends and regional comparisons in probation (England and Wales). Hugh Barr and Erica O'Leary. 1966. vii + 51pp. (34-368-8).
9. *Probation research. A survey of group work in the probation service. Hugh Barr. 1966. vii + 94pp. (34-368-9).
10. *Types of delinquency and home background. A validation study of Hewitt and Jenkins' hypothesis. Elizabeth Field. 1967. vi + 21pp. (34-368-10).
11. *Studies of female offenders. No. 1—Girls of 16-20 years sentenced to borstal or detention centre training in 1963. No. 2—Women offenders in the Metropolitan Police District in March and April 1957. No. 3—A description of women in prison on January 1, 1965 Nancy Goodman and Jean Price. 1967. v + 78pp. (34-368-11).
12. *The use of the Jesness Inventory on a sample of British probationers. Martin Davis. 1967 iv + 20pp. (34-368-12).
13. *The Jesness Inventory: application to approved school boys. Joy Mott. 1969. iv + 27pp. (11 340063 2).

Home Office Research Studies (HORS)

1. *Workloads in children's departments. Eleanor Grey. 1969. vi + 75pp. (11 340101 9).
2. *Probationers in their social environment. A study of male probationers aged 17-20, together with an analysis of those reconvicted within twelve months. Martin Davies. 1969. vii + 204pp. (11 340102 7).
3. *Murder 1957 to 1968. A Home Office Statistical Division report on murder in England and Wales. Evelyn Gibson and S. Klein (with annex by the Scottish Home and Health Department on murder in Scotland). 1969. vi + 94pp. (11 340103 5).
4. Firearms in crime. A Home Office Statistical Division report on indicatable offences involving firearms in England and Wales. A. D. Weatherhead and B. M. Robinson. 1970. viii + 39pp. (11 340104 3).
5. *Financial penalties and probation. Martin Davis. 1970. vii + 39pp. (11 340105 1).

*Out of print.

6. *Hostels for probationers. A study of the aims, working and variations in effectiveness of male probation hostels with special reference to the influence of the environment on delinquency. Ian Sinclair. 1971. ix + 200pp. (11 340106 X).

7. *Prediction methods in criminology—including a prediction study of young men on probation. Frances H. Simon. 1971. xi + 234pp. (11 340107 8).

8. *Study of the juvenile liaison scheme in West Ham 1961-65. Marilyn Taylor. 1971. vi + 46pp. (11 340108 6).

9. *Exploration in after-care. I—After-care units in London, Liverpool and Manchester. Martin Silberman (Royal London Prisoners' Aid Society) and Brenda Chapman. II—After-care hostels receiving a Home Office grant. Ian Sinclair and David Snow (HORU). III—St. Martin of Tours House, Ayreh Leissner (National Bureau for Co-operation in Child Care). 1971. xi + 140pp. (11 340109 4).

10. A survey of adoption in Great Britain. Eleanor Grey in collaboration with Ronald M. Blunden. 1971. ix + 168pp. (11 340110 8).

11. *Thirteen-year-old approved school boys in 1962. Elizabeth Field, W. H. Hammond and J. Tizard. 1971. ix + 46pp. (11 34011 6).

12. Absconding from approved schools. R. V. G. Clarke and D. N. Martin. 1971. vi + 146pp. (11 340112 4).

13. An experiment in personality assessment of young men remanded in custody. H. Sylvia Anthony. 1972. viii + 79pp. (11 340113 2).

14. *Girl offenders aged 17-20 years. I—Statistics relating to girl offenders aged 17-20 years from 1960 to 1970. II—Re-offending by girls released from borstal or detention centre training. III—The Problems of girls released from borstal training during their period on after-care. Jean Davies and Nancy Goodman. 1972. v + 77p. (11 340114 0).

15. *The controlled trial in insitutional research—paradigm or pitfall for penal evaluators? R. V. G. Clarke and D. B. Cornish. 1972. v + 33pp. (11 340115 9).

16. *A survey of fine enforcement. Paul Softley. 1973. v + 65pp. (11 340116 7).

17. *An index of social environment—designed for use in social work research. Martin Davies. 1973. vi + 63pp. (11 340117 5).

18. *Social enquiry reports and the probation service. Martin Davies and Andrea Knopf. 1973. v + 49pp. (11 340118 3).

19. *Depression, psychopathic personality and attempted suicide in a borstal sample. H. Sylvia Anthony. 1973. viii + 44pp. (0 11 340119 1).

20. *The use of bail and custody by London magistrates' courts before and after the Criminal Justice Act 1967. Frances Simon and Mollie Weatheritt. 1974. vi + 78pp. (0 11 340120 5).

21. *Social work in the environment. A study of one aspect of probation practice. Martin Davies, with Margaret Rayfield, Alaster Calder and Tony Fowles. 1974. ix + 151pp. (0 11 340121 3).

22. Social work in prison. An experiment in the use of extended contact with offenders. Margaret Shaw. 1974. vii + 154pp. (0 11 340122 1).

23. Delinquency amongst opiate users. Joy Mott and Marilyn Taylor. vi + 31pp. (0 11 340663 0).

24. IMPACT. Intensive matched probation and after-care treatment. Vol. I—The design of the probation experiment and an interim evaluation. M. S. Folkard, A. J. Fowles, B. C. McWilliams, W. McWilliams, D. D. Smith, D. E. Smith and G. R. Walmsley. 1974. v + 54pp. (0 11 340664 9).

25. The approved school experience. An account of boys' experiences of training under differing regimes of approved schools, with an attempt to evaluate the effectiveness of that training. Anne B. Dunlop. 1974. vii + 124pp. (0 11 340665 7).

26. *Absconding from open prisons. Charlotte Banks, Patricia Mayhew and R. J. Sapsford. 1975. viii + 89pp. (0 11 340666 5).

27. Driving while disqualified. Sue Kriefman. 1975. vi + 136pp. (0 11 340667 3).

28. Some male offenders' problems. I—Homeless offenders in Liverpool. W. McWilliams. II—Casework with short-term prisoners. Julie Holborn. 1975. x + 147pp. (0 11 340668 1).

*Out of print.

29. *Community service orders. K. Pease, P. Durkin, I. Earnshaw, D. Payne and J. Thorpe, 1975. viii + 80pp. (0 11 340669 X).
30. Field Wing Bail Hostel: the first nine months. Frances Simon and Sheena Wilson. 1975. viii + 55pp. (0 11 340670 3).
31. Homicide in England and Wales 1967–1971. Evelyn Gibson. 1975. iv + 59pp. (0 11 340753 X).
32. Residential treatment and its effects on deliquency. D. B. Cornish and R. V. G. Clarke. 1975. vi + 74pp. (0 11 340672 X).
33. Further studies of female offenders. Part A: Borstal girls eight years after release. Nancy Goodman, Elizabeth Maloney and Jean Davies. Part B: The sentencing of women at the London Higher Courts. Nancy Goodman. Paul Durkin and Janet Halton. Part C: Girls appearing before a juvenile court. Jean Davies. 1976 vi + 114pp. (0 11 340673 8).
34. *Crime as opportunity. P. Mayhew, R. V. G. Clarke, A. Sturman and J. M. Hough. 1976. vii + 36pp. (0 11 340674 6).
35. The effectiveness of sentencing a review of the literature. S. R. Brody. 1976. v + 89pp. (0 11 340675 4).
36. IMPACT. Intensive matched probation and after-care treatment. Vol II—The results of the experiment. M. S. Folkard, D. E. Smith and D. D. 1976 xi + 400pp. (0 11 340676 2).
37. Police cautioning in England and Wales. J. A. Ditchfield. 1976. v + 31pp. (0 11 340677 2).
38. Parole in England and Wales. C. P. Nuttall, with E. E. Barnard, A. J. Fowles, A. Frost, W. H. Hammond, P. Mayhew, K. Pease, R. Tarling and M. J. Weatheritt. 1977. vi + 90pp. (0 11 340678 9).
39. Community service assessed in 1976. K. Pease, S. Billingham and I. Earnshaw. 1977. vi + 29pp. (0 11 340679 7).
40. Screen violence and film censorship: a review of research. Stephen Brody. 1977. vii + 179pp. (0 11 340680 0).
41. Absconding from borstals. Gloria K. Laycock. 1977. v + 82pp. (0 11 340681 9).
42. Gambling: a review of the literature and its implications for policy and research. D. B. Cornish. 1978. xii + 284pp. (0 11 340682 7).
43. Compensation orders in magistrates' courts. Paul Softley. 1978. v + 41pp. (0 11 340683 5).
44. Research in criminal justice. John Croft. 1978. iv + 16pp. (0 11 340684 3).
45. Prison welfare: an account of an experiment at Liverpool. A. J. Fowles. 1978. v + 34pp. (0 11 340685 1).
46. Fines in magistrates' courts. Paul Softley. 1978. v + 42pp. (0 11 340686 X).
47. Tackling vandalism. R. V. G. Clarke (editor), F. J. Gladstone, A. Sturman and Sheena Wilson (contributors). 1978. vi + 91pp. (0 11 340687 8).
48. Social inquiry reports: a surey. Jennifer Thorpe. 1979. vi − 55pp. (0 11 340688 6).
49. Crime in public view. P. Mayhew, R. V. G. Clarke, J. N. Burrows, J. M. Hough and S. W. C. Winchester. 1979. v + 36pp. (0 11 340689 4).
50. *Crime and the community. John Croft. 1979. v + 16pp. (0 11 340690 8).
51. Life-sentence prisoners. David Smith (editor), Christopher Brown, Joan Worth, Roger Sapsford and Charlotte Banks (contributors). 1979. iv + 51pp. (0 11 340691 6).
52. Hostels for offenders. Jane E. Andrews, with an appendix by Bill Sheppard, 1979. v + 30pp. (0 11 340692 4).
53. Previous convictions, sentence and reconviction: a statistical study of a sample of 5,000 offenders convicted in January 1971. G. J. O. Phillpotts and L. B. Lancucki. 1979. v + 55pp. (0 11 340693 2).
54. Sexual offences, consent and sentencing. Roy Walmsley and Karen White. 1979. vi + 77p. (0 11 340694 0).
55. Crime prevention and the police. John Burrows, Paul Ekblom and Kevin Heal. 1979. v + 37pp. (0 11 340695 9).

---

*Out of print.

56. Sentencing practice in magistrates' courts. Roger Tarling, with the assistance of Mollie Weatheritt. 1979. vii + 54pp. (0 11 340696).
57. Crime and comparative research. John Croft. 1979. iv + 16pp. (0 11 340697 5).
58. Race, crime and arrests. Philip Stevens and Carole F. Willis. 1979. v + 69pp. (0 11 340698 3).
59. Research and criminal policy. John Croft. 1980. iv + 14pp. (0 11 340699 1).
60. Junior attendance centres. Anne B. Dunlop. 1980. v + 47pp. (0 11 340700 9).
61. Police interrogation: an observational study in four police stations. Paul Softley, with the assistance of David Brown, Bob Forde, George Mair and David Moxon. 1980. vii + 67pp. (0 11 340701 7).
62. Co-ordinating crime prevention efforts. F. J. Gladstone, 1980. v + 74pp. (0 11 340702 5).
63. Crime prevention publicity: an assessment. D. Riley and P. Mayhew. 1980. v + 47pp. (0 11 340703 3).
64. Taking offenders out of circulation. Stephen Brody and Roger Tarling. 1980. v + 46pp. (0 11 340704 1).
65. *Alcoholism and social policy: are we on the right lines? Mary Tuck. 1980. v + 30pp. (0 11 340705 X).
66. Persistent petty offenders. Suzan Fairhead. 1981. vi + 78pp. (0 11 340706 8).
67. Crime control and the police. Pauline Morris and Kevin Heal. 1981. v + 71pp. (0 11 340707 6).
68. Ethnic minorities in Britain: a study of trends in their positions since 1961. Simon Field, George Mair, Tom Rees and Philip Stevens. 1981. v + 48pp. (0 11 340708 4).
69. Managing criminological research. John Croft. 1981. iv + 17pp. (0 11 340709 2).
70. Ethnic minorities, crime and policing: a survey of the experiences of West Indians and whites. Mary Tuck and Peter Southgate. iv + 54pp. (0 11 340765 3).
71. Contested trials in magistrates' courts. Julie Vennard. 1982. v + 32pp. (0 11 340766 1).
72. Public disorder: a review of research and a study in one inner city area. Simon Field and Peter Southgate. 1982. v + 77pp. (0 11 340767 X).
73. Clearing up crime. John Burrows and Roger Tarling. 1982. vii + 31pp. (0 11 340768 8).
74. Residential burglary: the limits of prevention. Stuart Winchester and Hilary Jackson. 1982. v + 47pp. (0 11 340769 6).
75. Concerning crime. John Croft. 1982. iv + 16pp. (0 11 340770 X).
76. The British Crime Survey: first report. Mike Hough and Pat Mayhew. 1983. v + 62pp. (0 11 340789 6).
77. Contacts between police and public: findings from the British Crime Survey. Peter Southgate and Paul Ekblom. 1984. v + 42pp. (0 11 340771 8).
78. Fear of crime in England and Wales. Michael Maxfield. 1984. v + 51pp. (0 11 340772 6).
79. Crime and police effectiveness. Ronald V. Clarke and Mike Hough. 1984. iv + 33p. (0 11 340773 4).
80. The attitudes of ethnic minorities. Simon Field. 1984. v + 50pp. (0 11 340774 2).
81. Victims of crime: the dimensions of risk. Michael Gottfredson. 1984. v + 54pp. (0 11 340775 0).
82. The tape recording of police interviews with suspects: an interim report. Carole Willis. 1984. v + 45pp. (0 11 340776 9).
83. Parental supervision and juvenile delinquency. David Riley and Margaret Shaw. 1985. v + 90pp. (0 11 340799 8).
84. Adult prisons and prisoners in England and Wales 1970–82: a review of the findings of social research. Joy Mott. 1985. vi + 73pp. (0 11 340801 3).
85. Taking account of crime: key findings from the 1984 British Crime Survey. Mike Hough and Pat Mayhew. 1985. vi + 115pp. (0 11 340810 2).
86. **Implementing Crime Prevention Measures. Tim Hope 1985 vi + 82 pp (0 11 340812 9).**

---

*Out of print

ALSO

Designing out crime. R. V. G. Clarke and P. Mayhew (editors). 1980. vii + 186pp. (0 11 340732 7).
(This book collects, with an introduction, studies that were originally published in HORS 34, 47, 49, 55, 62 and 63 and which are illustrative of the 'situational' approach to crime prevention.)

Policing today. Kevin Heal, Roger Tarling and John Burrows (editors). 1985. v + 181pp. (0 11 340800 5).
(This book brings together twelve separate studies on police matters produced during the last few years by the Unit. The collection records some relatively little known contributions to the debate on policing.)

The above HMSO publications can be purchased from Government Bookshops or through booksellers.

The following Home Office research publications are available on request from the Home Office Research and Planning Unit, 50 Queen Anne's Gate, London, SW1H 9AT.

Research Unit Papers (RUP)

1. Uniformed police work and management technology. J. M. Hough, 1980.
2. Supplementary information on sexual offences and sentencing. Roy Walmsley and Karen White. 1980.
3. Board of visitor adjudications. David Smith, Claire Austin and John Ditchfield, 1981.
4. Day centres and probations. Suzan Fairhead, with the assistance of J. Wilkinson-Grey. 1981.

Research and Planning Unit Papers (RPUP)

5. Ethnic minorities and complaints against the police. Philip Stevens and Carole Willis. 1982.
6. *Crime and public housing. Mike Hough and Pat Mayhew (editors). 1982.
7. *Abstracts of race relations research. George Mair and Philip Stevens (editors). 1982.
8. Police probationer training in race relations. Peter Southgate. 1982.
9. *The police response to calls from the public. Paul Ekblom and Kevin Heal. 1982.
10. City centre crime: a situational approach to prevention. Malcolm Ramsay 1982.
11. Burglary in schools: the prospects for prevention. Tim Hope. 1982.
12. *Fine enforcement. Paul Softley and David Moxon. 1982.
13. Vietnamese refugees. Peter Jones. 1982.
14. Community resources for victims of crime. Karen Williams. 1983.
15. The use, effectiveness and impact of police stop and search powers. Carole Willis, 1983.
16. Acquittal rates. Sid Butler. 1983.
17. Criminal justice comparisons: the case of Scotland and England and Wales. Lorna J. F. Smith. 1983.
18. Time taken to deal with juveniles under criminal proceedings. Catherine Frankenburg and Roger Tarling. 1983.
19. Civilian review of complaints against the police: a survey of the United States literature. David C. Brown. 1983.
20. Police action on motoring offences. David Riley. 1983.
21. *Diverting drunks from the criminal justice system. Sue Kingsley and George Mair. 1983.
23. Reducing the prison population: an exploratory study in Hampshire. David Smith, Bill Sheppard, George Mair and Karen Williams. 1984.
24. Criminal justice system model: magistrates' courts' sub-model. Susan Rice. 1984.
25. Measures of police effectiveness and efficiency. Ian Sinclair and Clive Miller. 1984.

*Out of print

26. Punishment practice by prison Boards of Visitors. Susan Iles, Adrienne Connors, Chris May, Joy Mott. 1984.
27. Reparation, conciliation and mediation. Tony Marshall. 1984.
28. Magistrates domestic courts: new perspectives. Tony Marshall (editor). 1984.
29. Racism awareness training for the police. Peter Southgate. 1984.
30. Community constables: a study of policing initiative. David Brown and Susan Iles. 1985.
31. Recruiting volunteers. Hilary Jackson. 1985.
32. Juvenile sentencing is there a tariff? David Moxon, Peter Jones and Roger Tarling. 1985.

Research Bulletin

The Research Bulletin is published twice a year and consists mainly of short articles relating to projects which are part of the Home Office Research and Planning Unit's research programme.

Printed for Her Majesty's Stationery Office
by Robendene Ltd, Amersham, Bucks
Dd 738771 C25 8/85